The Politics of
Special Educational Needs

Disability, Handicap and Life Chances Series

Series Editor: Len Barton

1 The Politics of Caring
   Susan Bannerman Foster

2 Schooling the Different
   Adrian Bennet

3 Disabling Policies? A Comparative Approach to Education Policy and
   Disability
   Gillian Fulcher

4 The Politics of Special Educational Needs
   Edited by Len Barton

5 An Uneasy Alliance
   Deborah Bart

Disability, Handicap and Life Chances Series

The Politics of Special Educational Needs

Edited by
Len Barton
Bristol Polytechnic

 The Falmer Press

(A member of the Taylor & Francis Group)
London . New York . Philadelphia

UK   The Falmer Press, Falmer House, Barcombe, Lewes,
          East Sussex, BN8 5DL

USA   The Falmer Press, Taylor & Francis Inc., 242 Cherry Street,
          Philadelphia, PA 19106-1906

First published in 1988

British Library Cataloguing in Publication Data

The Politics of special educational needs—(Disability handicap and
life chances series).
    1. Special education. Sociopolitical aspects.
    I. Barton, Len.   II. Series
    371.9

ISBN 1-85000-370-X
ISBN 1-85000-371-8 (Pbk.)

Library of Congress Cataloging-in-Publication Data

The Politics of special educational needs.
    (Disability, handicap and life chances series).
    Bibliography: p.
    Includes index.
    1. Special education—Political aspects.   2. Education and state.
    I. Barton, Len.   II. Series.LC3969.P65   1988   371.9   88-3554
ISBN 1-85000-370-X
ISBN 1-85000-371-8 (Pbk.)

Typeset in 11/13 Bembo by
Alresford Typesetting & Design, New Farm Road, Alresford, Hants.

*Printed in Great Britain by
Redwood Burn Limited, Trowbridge, Wiltshire.*

to Jay, Rachel and Sarai

Contents

The Politics of Special Educational Needs: An Introduction   1
Len Barton

Part 1: Setting the Scene   11

1   The Social and Political Context of Educational Policy:
The Case of Special Needs   13
Mike Oliver

2   From the Other Side of the Wall   32
Marion Blythman

3   The Appearance and Reality of Change within Special
Educational Needs   58
Alvin Jeffs

4   Research and Practice: The Need for Alternative Perspectives   79
Len Barton

Part 2: Examining Key Issues   95

5   Challenging Conceptions of Integration   97
Tony Booth

6   Who's Moving the Goal Posts and What Games are We
Playing Anyway: Social Competence Examined   123
Andrea Freeman

7   Equality, Community and Individualism: The Development
and Implementation of the 'Whole School Approach' to
Special Educational Needs   145
Hazel Bines

8   The Curriculum: Some Issues for Debate   161
Bunty Davidson

9   Power in Disguise   175
    Rob Withers and John Lee

10 Parents: Whose Partners?   190
    Sue Wood

Notes on Contributors   208

Index   211

The Politics of Special Educational Needs: An Introduction

Len Barton

This book has been produced during a particular historical period, one characterized by crisis and change. Major changes are taking place in the industrial, housing, welfare and educational sectors of society. A series of radical policies are being implemented through a process of extensive centralized intervention. The Government's explicit intention behind these actions is to redefine responsibilities, relationships, practices and priorities of those people participating in these sectors. These policies, based on a particular monetarist perspective, have heralded in a commitment to competition, privatization and extensive legislative powers. This has been legitimated by the use of a populist ideology in which 'parents' and 'the public at large' are depicted as supporting such policies and interventions. However, criticism is being expressed not only over the nature of some of these changes, but also the manner and speed with which they are being pursued. They are viewed as essentially divisive and will contribute to the widening of inequalities and serious social problems (Loney, 1986; MacInnes, 1987; Walker and Barton, 1986).

Despite the official rhetoric of increased prosperity for all and economic expansion, social deprivation and disadvantage are on the increase and as Stuart Hall (1987) so forcefully reminds us:

> . . . one must recognize the way in which the processes of de-industrialization in large sectors of society have undermined the following: the opportunities of the worst-off for material sustenance; their capacities to maintain an adequate standard of life; the hopes, especially of those who are young, for permanent and secure employment; and their chances of advancement, whether they are men or women, in the employment field (pp. 46–47).

What is particularly disturbing, Hall argues, is that where these conditions are experienced within our society, those who are black are doubly disadvantaged. Young black people are discriminated against in the job market (Miles, 1986; Solomos, 1986).

The future prospects for increasing numbers of young people particularly from lower-socio-economic backgrounds is very bleak. The realities of a world without work or of long periods of under-employment are very evident. Many of these young people are disenchanted and do not recognize the existence of a caring society or even a user-friendly bureaucracy. Instead, they are increasingly suspicious of officialdom and view government as instigating oppressive policies and measures that are concerned with controlling and containing the young (Willis, 1986). It is important not to view young people as a homogenous mass. Gender differences need to be recognized, for example, in terms of the ways in which young women deal with these experiences (Cockburn, 1987; Finn, 1987).

Government interventions in the form of the Manpower Services Commission and its Youth Training Scheme, developed to build a bridge between school and work, have been the subject of numerous critical analyses. Not only have questions of sexism been raised in relation to some aspects of these schemes, but also the specific difficulties that young people from ethnic minorities face have been highlighted in recent research. It is not only a question of discrimination through racism but also of the tensions within the family between parents and young people. This is exacerbated by the unfamiliarity and thus lack of experience that some parents may have with regard to the system of education and post-school provision. (De Sousa, 1987; Verma and Darby, 1987).

This brief overview of some aspects of the prevailing socio-economic and political conditions of contemporary society, provides the context against which this book needs to be understood. It is a society increasingly characterized by gross inequalities, discriminatory policies and practices. For many people this means real disadvantages including very restricted opportunities and lack of choice or decision-making powers. This is particularly applicable to people with disabilities. The cultural context in which they must live and learn to survive is fundamentally handicapping and oppressive, affecting all levels of their existence.

The Educational Context

Discussions concerning special education need to be set within the more general context of the educational system as a whole. The nature of schooling, the kind of education children ought to receive, as well as the responsibilities and roles of teachers in this process, are all topics of crucial significance in the prevailing climate of public opinion. Through the powerful mechanism of the mass media, a moral panic has been encouraged over such issues as the decline of standards in school, discipline, and the general irrelevance of a great deal of school experience in terms of equipping young people to take their place in the workforce and to become good citizens.

Questions such as what, how, and when children should learn, have become crucial issues within this climate. A series of Government interventions have taken place within the educational system that are concerned with both radically restructuring and more effectively controlling the content and outcome of schooling.

A major intention on the part of Government is to introduce a national curriculum in schools for 5 to 16 year olds. In a recently circulated 'Consultative Document' the reason for such a radical change is clearly spelt out. It is to raise standards:

> The challenge for the education service is to raise standards through the full and successful implementation of the national curriculum — to the point where every pupil is studying for, and being regularly assessed against, worthwhile attainment targets in all the essential foundation subjects . . . (DES, pp. 33 and 34).

Children and young people are to be tested, possibly at the ages of 7, 11, 14 and 16. This will involve the building up of a battery of tests.

Apart from the clear message that such proposals entail, i.e., a general criticism of the past performance of schools and teachers, from the point of view of the topics and issues this book seeks to cover, as the editorial in the Times Educational Supplement so aptly warns us:

> Changes are in hand which will transform the style as well as the content of English education: no single development threatens to do more damage than the latest obsession with national testing (1987, p. 2).

Reinforcing these concerns is the added intention to make public the results of these tests at both the level of the individual school and the Local Education Authority. Coupled with the emphasis on increased parental choice, this will provide the impetus for schools to compete for pupils, thereby increasing the influence of market forces within the school system.

There are several reasons why these developments must not be accepted uncritically. First, they will involve an intensification of competitiveness and legitimate a narrow definition of ability. This will necessitate a clearer establishment of hierarchical forms of curriculum knowledge within schools, which will inevitably lead to the marginalizing of particular low-status forms of knowledge. Secondly, by offering the opportunity for schools, particularly at the secondary levels, to opt out of the state system and to concentrate on being centres of academic excellence, the pursuit of a comprehensive form of integration becomes much more difficult. The increase of inferior (sink) schools, particularly for white and black working-class children within the inner cities, will be one of the divisive out-workings of this type of policy. Lastly, given the potentially huge costs involved in setting up a national testing system and that according to the Consultative Document the:

> ... Secretaries of State will expect the national curriculum and associated assessment to be developed and implemented broadly *within the planned levels of resources* (p. 30, my emphasis).

we can envisage a system in which more children will be defined as having particular needs as a result of not being able to reach the particular bench marks relating to their age. But they will be identified within a system that will have insufficient resources, both human and material, to satisfy their needs. Thus, we will have the legitimization of institutionalized failure on a rather alarming scale.

The issue here is not the idea of a national curriculum as such, but rather the one that is being presented to us and the manner in which it has been generated. Many important reservations have already been expressed by a wide range of individuals and associations. These include: the increase in teachers who will teach to tests, that rigid streaming will be viewed as essential if schools are to provide the sort of organization that produces the right results, and as Hargreaves (1987) also notes, there will be:

> ... a focus on content rather than processes and skills, on memor-ization of facts and propositional knowledge and on written forms of communication (p. 4).

However, in view of the issues which this book seeks to examine, the most disturbing outcome of the proposed radical changes will be that children and young people with special educational needs become more 'deviant' and there will be many more of them.

A Question of Needs

Since the publication of the Warnock Report in which the term 'special educational needs' is used, numerous critical analyses have been presented in which the value of specific categories has been questioned. Sociologists (Tomlinson, 1982; Ford *et al.*, 1982; Barton, 1986) and Educational Psy-chologists (Galloway, 1985; Booth, 1985; Dessent, 1987) have contributed to this appraisal.

The use of the term 'need' or 'special need' has often been derived from a belief in a '... set of objective characteristics that render people needy' (Stone, 1985, p. 172). Identifying children's needs has thus been understood as a task for empirical study by professionals. This also presupposes the existence of reliable and accurate testing procedures. However, it is these and other taken-for-granted assumptions that have been challenged. The criticisms have covered many issues, as can be seen from the following examples:

1. The concept 'special needs' is a mystifying one, in that it detracts attention away from the real needs that are being served by the process of expansion of special education. Also, the issues are viewed in individualistic terms (Tomlinson, 1982).
2. The concept 'need', with its connotations of bodily functions has been used in such a way as to marginalize questions of power, power-relations or conflict between professionals (Booth. 1985).
3. The concept 'special need' has been used as an administrative category, thereby supporting the interests of others, than of those it purports to serve (Ford *et al.*, 1982).
4. Needs are relative to available resources (Dessent, 1987; Galloway, 1985).
5. Within the constraints of the system in which it is used, 'special educational needs' has become a euphemism for failure (Barton, 1986).

It is also important to note the comparative links that can be drawn over those sorts of issues. (Fulcher, 1986; Stone, 1985; Sigmon, 1987; Franklin, 1987; and Lin, 1987).

These critiques have given some legitimation to the introduction of alternative perspectives, particularly to those which are concerned with widening the nature of the debate and challenging the individualistic or deficit models that are prevalent within the literature and which are evident in people's views to this question.

The Politics of Special Educational Needs

Despite the fact that we are now witnessing the most explicit political interference on the part of the Government in the field of education, there is an orthodoxy abroad which views any reference to the question of politics as being biased, irrelevant and counter-productive. This is particularly applicable to those who would seek to raise the question of politics in relation to special educational policy or practice. To do so is to raise doubts about the nature of your commitment and whether you have the *proper* interests of individuals with learning difficulties in view.

However, if we are to achieve an adequate understanding and explanation of developments surrounding special education, or to provide a basis from which change can be attempted, then the question of politics needs to be at the centre of consideration. A major motivation and justification for this contention is derived from the example of people with disabilities themselves. They are increasingly determined to control their own lives and are vociferously expressing their views, both as private persons and through their own associations. Criticisms are being expressed not only over the role of professionals in their lives, but also over the ways in which able-bodied people are constant sources of oppression and dehumanization (Sutherland, 1982).

An indication of the strength of their feelings can be seen in the following example:

> We desire a place *in society*, participating as equal members with something to say and a life to lead; we are demanding the right to take the same risks and seek the same rewards. Society disables us by taking away our right to take decisions on our own behalf, and therefore the equality we are demanding is rooted in the concept of control; it stems from our desire to be individuals who can choose for themselves. People with disabilities are increasingly beginning to fight against structures that deprive us of control of, and responsibility for, ourselves, and hence leave us with no real chance of participation in society. We are the victims of a vicious circle, for the control that is denied the disabled individual by the medical profession, social services, relatives, etc. conditions the individual to accept a dependent status in which their life only takes place by proxy, resulting in them being unable to visualize independent ways of living (Brisenden 1986, pp. 177 and 178).

A critical analysis of power, control, vested interests, choice and decision-making must be constantly called for and developed. Explanations or analyses that focus their consideration on individual factors will fail to understand the complex and wide-ranging nature of the issues involved.

The question of the 'politics of special educational needs' has to be defended and I wish to argue that it can be viewed in the following ways. First, there needs to be a relentless systematic effort on the part of all interested parties in attempts to influence governments in relation to enhancing the lives and opportunities of people who are labelled in this way, particularly as the vast majority of these children and young people are, or will increasingly be, from lower socio-economic backgrounds. Secondly, there is an essential revelationary role to be undertaken in highlighting the ways in which various policies and practices, including the assumptions and expectations underpinning daily interactions, contribute to the creation of handicaps and the resultant suffering which follows. Thirdly, in endeavouring to connect the personal with the political, it is crucial that the thoughts of those with disabilities are made public and that these become the basis for political alliances and endeavour. Lastly, part of the work will be that of redefining the issues and moving the concern from a question of needs to that of rights.

The task is both challenging and urgent. The issue of politics does not only raise questions about the nature of power and how it is manifested, but also to what extent people are able to exercise choice and control over their own lives.

Conclusion

The contributors to this volume do not share a unified perspective from which they approach the issues under consideration. They represent a range of traditions and differ in some of the interpretations and emphasis they would wish to offer. Thus, they can be seen as being engaged in a creative tension. However, they do share some common concerns, including:

1. A commitment to comprehensive education and a belief that the question of special educational needs must be set within the wider context of education for all.
2. The belief that critical analysis of existing policy and practice is an essential pre-condition for change. This will include a concern with issues of power and control.
3. A desire for more attention to be given to the social creation of categories of handicap, that includes both micro and macro factors.
4. A belief that unless some fundamental changes take place with regard to both existing definitions, policies and practices, then many more children and young people will be defined as having 'special educational needs'. This will lead to a more oppressive system of schooling.

The topics which are covered in this book are important for all teachers and for all those people who are interested in the nature and purpose of education. Much more discussion is needed and further research must be encouraged. This book is offered in the hope that it will contribute to the sort of debate, dialogue, research and knowledge that will lead to the demand for a more equitable and just system, one that is less divisive and more collectively enriching.

References

BARTON, L. (1986) 'The Politics of Special Educational Needs' in *Disability, Handicap and Society*. Vol. 1, No. 3, pp. 273–290.

BOOTH, T. (1985) 'Training and Progress in Special Education' in Sayer, J. and Jones, N. (Eds) *Teacher Training in Special Educational Needs*. London, Croom Helm.

BRISENDEN, S. (1986) 'Independent Living and the Medical Model of Disability' in *Disability, Handicap and Society*, Vol. 1, No. 2, pp. 173–178.

COCKBURN, C. (1987) *Two Track Training: Sex Inequalities and the YTS*. Basingstoke, Macmillan.

DEPARTMENT OF EDUCATION AND SCIENCE (1987) *The National Curriculum 5–16. A Consultation Document*. London: HMSO.

DESSENT, T. (1987) *Making the Ordinary School Special*. Lewes, Falmer Press.

DE SOUSA, E. (1987) 'Racism and the YTS' in *Critical Social Policy*. Issue 20, pp. 66–73.

FINN, D. (1987) *Training Without Jobs. New Deals and Broken Promises*. Basingstoke, Macmillan.

FORD, J., MONGON D. and WHELAN, M. (1982) *Special Education and Social Control*. London, Routledge & Kegan Paul.

FRANKLIN, B. (Ed.) (1987) *Learning Disability: Dissenting Essays*. Lewes, Falmer Press.

FULCHER, G. (1986) 'Australian Policies on Special Education: Towards a Sociological Account' in *Disability, Handicap and Society*. Vol. 1, No. 1, pp. 19–52.

GALLOWAY, D. (1985) *Schools, Pupils and Special Educational Needs*. Beckenham, Croom Helm.

HALL, S. (1987) 'Urban Unrest in Britain' in Benyon, J. and Solomos, J. (Eds) *The Roots of Urban Unrest*. London, Pergamon Press.

HARGREAVES, D. (1987) 'Getting the Mixture Right' in *The Times Educational Supplement*. 11.9.87, p. 4.

LONEY, M. (1986) *The Politics of Greed*. London, Pluto Press.

LIN, W.T. (1987) 'The Development of Special Education in Brazil' in *Disability, Handicap and Society*, Vol. 2, No. 3, pp. 259–273.

MacINNES, J. (1987) *Thatcherism at Work*. Milton Keynes, Open University Press.

MILES, S. (1986) 'Asian Girls and the Transition from School to . . .?' in Ball, S. (Ed.) *Comprehensive Schooling: A Reader*. Lewes, Falmer Press.

SIGMON, S. (1987) *Radical Analysis of Special Education*, Lewes, Falmer Press.

SOLOMOS, J. (1986) 'The Social and Political Context of Black Youth Unemployment: A Decade of Policy Developments and the Limits of Reform' in Walker, S. and Barton, L. (Eds) *op. cit.*

STONE, D. (1985) *The Disabled State*. Basingstoke, Macmillan.

SUTHERLAND A. (1982) *Disabled We Stand*. London, Souvenir Press.

TOMLINSON, S. (1982) *The Sociology of Special Education*. London, Routledge & Kegan Paul.

TIMES EDUCATIONAL SUPPLEMENT (1987) 'Testing to Destruction'. Editorial, 7.8.87, p. 2.

VERMA, G. and DARBY, A. (1987) *Race, Training and Employment*. Lewes, Falmer Press.

WALKER, S. and BARTON, L. (Eds) (1986) *Youth, Unemployment and Schooling*. Milton Keynes, Open University Press.

WILLIS, P. (1986) 'Unemployment: The final inequality' in *The British Journal of Sociology of Education*. Vol. 7, No. 2, pp. 155–169.

PART ONE
Setting the Scene

The Social and Political Context of Educational Policy: The Case of Special Needs

Mike Oliver

Introduction

Policy for special educational needs is part of social policy and the Welfare State in general. Educational policy has not developed separately from other initiatives in the area of health, housing, social security, family support and so on. Much can be learnt from studying the relationships between educational and social policy in this area.

In the next section of this chapter, I will consider four accounts of the way social policies have developed. These view social policy respectively as a humanitarian response, as social investment, as the outcome of conflict between competing groups, and as social control. All social policies contain implicit and sometimes explicit assumptions about the nature of the problems they are set up to tackle. I shall argue that, initially, disability was perceived as an individual problem; it then came to be seen as a social construction and, finally, it is beginning to be perceived as a social creation. In the third section, I will describe recent developments in education policy and special needs in the light of the four accounts of social policy development. I will then analyse the changing definitions of disability in relation to these accounts. In the fourth section I will consider the relationship between definitions of disability and definitions of special needs. The fifth section will suggest that, largely due to the growing power of disabled people, the definition of disability as a social creation is now gradually being accepted as the most appropriate one. I shall then discuss some of the specific implications of this view both for social policy and disability, and education policy and special needs.

Accounts of Social Policy and Disability

The dominant account of social policy developments, at least for the first twenty years after World War II, was a humanitarian one. This has been characterized as 'the social administration approach to social welfare'. There are two major elements to this account: it is argued that policy decisions are rationally based on the collection of facts and that these decisions are under-pinned by humanitarian values and the concern to do good and to resolve the problem once the facts are known. This account is rooted in the tradition of social investigation and reform which goes back into the last century and includes the work of Chadwick, Booth and Rowntree. It was encapsu-lated in the Beveridge Report, and Townsend's (1979) work on poverty is its present day counterpart. Gathering facts about the problems of disability has characterized the activities of research sponsored both by government (Harris, 1971) and by various disability organizations like the Disablement Income Group (Tomlinson, 1980) and the Disability Alliance (Durward, 1981).

While this account was dominant until the late 1960s, a number of factors have brought alternative explanations to the fore. The 're-discovery of poverty' only twenty years after the inception of the Welfare State provoked a crisis in confidence in the humanitarian account. The develop-ing economic crisis in the 1970s forced cut-backs in state spending on welfare and a disintegration of the previous political consensus over the Welfare State which became a battleground for competing political ideologies. The rise of the academic disciplines of economics and sociology provided a rich theoretical background against which to argue the pros and cons of welfare spending.

The account of social policy as social investment is related to a socio-logical theory known as functionalism. According to Mishra:

> State welfare institutions come under this category. Their main 'function' was to integrate — to co-ordinate and harmonize various institutions and groups within advanced industrial society in order that the social system worked smoothly (Mishra, 1984, p. 9).

Social investment on welfare therefore is not just about doing good; it also ensures social and political stability. This idea has been applied to social policy on disability by Topliss (1979), who argues:

> The history of provision for the disabled members of society may be seen primarily as the development of recognition that certain needs of certain groups of the disabled are compatible with promoting or safeguarding the wider interests of society. Sympathy for the handi-capped has been translated into effective legislation when, and in so

far as, it could be shown that the provisions would in some way bring an economic return to compensate for the economic cost of the resources so committed (p. 7).

This view is sometimes called the 'consensus paradigm'. However, this consensual view was beginning to break in the 1960s in the face of reality: workers against employers, students against authority, mods against rockers and conflict over values concerning sexual behaviour, family life, the place of minority groups and so on.

A competing conflict account developed, influenced by two political theories, pluralist and Marxist. Pluralists see the outcome of political decisions as deriving from the activities of a number of groups and loose federations of interest: voters, politicians, businessmen, tradesmen, farmers, professionals, consumers and specific pressure groups. None of these groups is homogeneous for all purposes and influence varies between groups and over particular issues. Welfare policy is thus determined by a variety of groups pushing their own particular interests and concerns (Hall, Land, Parker and Webb 1975). Marxists do not deny the reality of this conflict but they argue that it is reducible to conflict between classes: between labour and capital, and workers and employers. Thus, the nature and form of the Welfare State is determined by the interests of employers for a fit, healthy and stable workforce and the interests of workers for health-care, education, housing and income support during times of crisis.

The problem in using these conflict accounts to explain policy on disability is that there have been no specific analyses. The humanitarian and consensus views of social policy which were breaking down in the 1960s in discussions of welfare generally, did not begin to break down with regard to disability until after the 1979 General Election. It was not until then that a government of either persuasion admitted that disabled people would have to compete with and against other groups for scarce resources.

The final explanation of welfare policy argues that the aim of policy is to ensure order and stability through social control. Again there are two versions of this, the pluralist and the Marxist. Pluralists limit the scope and intentions of social control to disruptive and disaffected groups. Marxists on the other hand see the process of social control as much broader: 'gentling the masses', 'pacification of the working class' as well as ensuring social order and social reproduction (Taylor-Gooby and Dale 1981).

Again there have been few, if any, attempts to suggest that social policy towards disabled people is part of the process of social control, although some disabled people have suggested that segregative social practices like residential homes, special schools, day centres and sheltered workshops are about controlling disabled people by removing them from society (Finkelstein, 1980; Union of the Physically Impaired Against Segregation

(UPIAS), 1981; 1983). Recently, Stone (1984) has argued that the category 'disability' is used as a means of controlling the balance between the working and non-working population. People's needs are either met through the work system, in that they earn enough to meet their own needs, or through state welfare. Disability as a category serves to separate out those who cannot from those who will not work, and being admitted to the category sanctions the meeting of needs through state welfare.

Each of these accounts contains elements of truth. Social policy is shaped by humanitarian concerns, by economically rational social investment, by conflict between a variety of interests and by the need for social control.

Each account, when applied to disability, carries with it a basic definition and understanding of the nature of disability. The definitions underpinning policy initiatives are then clearly important for they shape the direction and nature of such initiatives. Initially disability was seen as an individual problem and therefore its meaning was non-problematic. This has been called 'the personal tragedy theory of disability'; it assumes that becoming disabled is a tragic event and that disabled individuals have to adapt themselves to society, physically and psychologically. This definition has proved particularly unsuccessful in resolving the problems of disability (Shearer, 1981). This failure has given rise to a view of disability which has attempted to add a social dimension to its definition (Harris, 1971 WHO, 1981). I shall call this view *social constructionist*. These attempts have been criticized by disabled people themselves (UPIAS, 1975; Sutherland, 1981) for failing to break with the individualization of the problem, which they argue is a *social creation*. Our current definitions of disability contain elements of individual, social constructionist and social creationist views. Let us expand on this:

(a) Disabilities are an individual problem

This definition underlies most approaches in the field of professional practice adopted by teachers, social workers, doctors, occupational therapists and psychologists. Stated simply, this position suggests that it is the individual with disability who has the problem and intervention aims to provide him or her with the appropriate skills to cope with it.

(b) Disabilities are socially constructed

This definition has been used by many academics and researchers who have taken an interest in special needs. It has also been relied upon heavily by policy makers who seek to solve problems through changing terminology as with the World Health Organization's definitions of impairment, disability and handicap (WHO, 1981). This position is that the solutions to the problem of disability have usually failed because the problem was wrongly defined in the first place, and once we identify it correctly, the solution will be forthcoming. According to this argument the problem lies in the fact that some human beings define other human beings as disabled, and therefore treat them differently. Change the way people think about disability, and you eliminate the problems of disabled people.

(c) Disabilities are socially created

This position is often articulated by disabled people and has involved intense disputes with able-bodied professionals and academics about what the problem actually is. This has an international dimension in the current debate between Disabled Peoples' International and the World Health Organization over the latter's classification of Illnesses, Diseases and Disabilities (Finkelstein, 1985). This position argues that society disables people with impairments by the way it responds to those impairments. The inaccessibility of buildings stems from decisions to design them in particular ways and not from the inability of some people to walk. The solution to this particular problem is to create a barrier-free environment, not to attempt to provide disabled people with the skills necessary to cope with steps.

These definitions do not apply solely to disability. They can be used as a means of analysing other social problems, for example, poverty. This can be seen as an individual problem: people are too idle, lazy or feckless to earn an adequate income. It can also be seen as a social construction: changing relative standards affect our definitions. What might have been regarded as a luxury a hundred years ago — an inside toilet, electricity, for example — are now regarded as necessities and their absence taken as indicators of poverty. Finally, poverty can also be socially created by an unequal, capitalist society, where one class exploits another.

Disability, Special Needs and Educational Policy

I shall now consider the way humanitarian forces, social investment, conflict and social control have shaped the development of special education.[1] The individual, social constructionist and social creationist definitions underpinning various policy initiatives can then be elaborated.

A humanitarian account of the development of special education can be detected in explanations in terms of the benefits that accrue to the disabled child: access to particular expertise, skills and resources and protection from the harsher realities of ordinary school life. Current demands and moves towards integration are not seen to contradict this but are a consequence of gradually acquired knowledge that special schools may not always be the best or most appropriate place to educate children with disabilities.

Explanations couched in terms of social investment suggest that the State never intervenes for purely humanitarian reasons. It always acts with underlying economic motives. Thus there were two main reasons for including children with disabilities in the universal state system of education from the beginning of the twentieth century onwards. During this period there was a moral panic about the 'burdens of pauperism' and the consequent high levels of taxation that were going to be necessary to meet such burdens, and secondly the demand for labour far outstripped the supply. Thus social investment in special education was both a means of reducing the burdens of pauperism through training children to be independent,[2] and was a means of enabling more and more children to become part of the industrial workforce. These two elements are also important today. Current curricular concerns about the teaching of life skills are underpinned by earlier ideas about reducing the burden of the state. The concept of 'significant living without work' is directly related to the turnaround in the economy and the current situation where the supply of labour far outstrips demand.

Notions of conflict and vested interests can also be used to explain the development of special education. The power of certain groups to advance their interest at the expense of others is a crucial part of this explanation. Thus the initial development of segregated special education was a consequence of the vested interest of the ordinary school sector who were concerned that their payment-by-results benefits would be adversely affected by the presence of a variety of demanding and disruptive pupils. Subsequent trends were shaped by the growing power of newly developing professions, notably school doctors, teachers, educational administrators and psychologists. The 1944 Education Act represents the dominance of the medical profession and subsequent developments culminating in the 1981 Education Act sprang from the gradual challenge to this dominance by educational administrators and educational psychologists.

The idea of special education as a form of social control has recently been developed, particularly in the area of behaviour problems, where the following question has been posed:

> To what extent, therefore, is the establishment of special educational provisions an expression of the wish to control a deviant

section of the school population? (Ford, Mongon and Whelan, 1982, p. 27).

While Ford and her colleagues show that the answer to this question is 'yes' in the context of the development of separate facilities for children with behaviour problems, a similar answer can be given in the case of children with disabilities. Such children are also regarded as deviant and their location in segregated establishments is thus part of the process of controlling deviant sections of the school population.

The sociologist, Louis Althusser (1971) drew a distinction between 'ideological' and 'repressive' forms of social control and the segregated special school fits this distinction very well in being both repressive and ideological in its forms of control:

> It is part of the repressive state apparatus in that it removes disruptive and potentially disturbing children from ordinary schools regardless of whether their disruption is based upon handicap, impairment, behaviour or performance. Further, it is part of the ideological state apparatus in that the very existence of these schools serves as a warning to all other children if they fail to conform to currently acceptable health or behavioural norms (Oliver, 1985 b, p. 83).

The degree to which the move back to integration can be seen as an expansion of social control rather than a reduction of it has not yet been explored,[3] but there is clear evidence in the field of juvenile justice that diversion away from punishment in segregated establishments is precisely this (Cohen, 1985).

Just as these explanations were not mutually exclusive in discussing social policy generally, nor are they in discussing special education policy. The development of special education has undoubtedly been shaped by humanitarian concerns to do the best for these children, by considerations of social investment, by conflict between various vested interests and by concerns about social control.

Definitions of Special Educational Needs

Definitions of disability and of special educational needs are not synonymous. The recommendation of the Warnock Report to dispense with the essentially medical classifications of the 1944 Education Act contributed to breaking any direct link between the two.

The definition of special educational need which still dominates today is one that sees it as an individual problem. This individualization pervades the teaching process, the categorization and assessment of children, and the practice of the professionals, notably teachers, doctors and educational psychologists.

A cursory glance at the history of special education shows clearly how it was underpinned by notions of special educational needs as an individual problem. Medical accounts of mental processes profoundly influenced the categorization used in the 1870, 1899 and 1921 Education Acts (Potts, 1983) and the rise of child guidance clinics and special schools was dominated by doctors. The perception of educational problems as individual reached its zenith with the categories introduced by the 1944 Education Act. Even those categories which were not strictly medical were given quasi-medical labels (maladjustment) or admittance to the category was through the operation of a diagnostic screening device as in the case of the ESN category.

In breaking the direct link between disability and educational problems, the Warnock Report, it can be argued, socially constructed the categories 'special educational needs' and 'children with learning difficulties'.

> To describe someone as handicapped conveys nothing of the type of educational help, and hence provision that is required. We wish to see a more positive approach, and we have adopted the concept of special educational needs, seen not in terms of a particular disability that a child may be deemed to have, but in relation to everything about him, his abilities as well as his disabilities — indeed all the factors which may impinge on his educational progress. (Warnock, 1978, p. 37).

There is also a sense in which the history of special education can be seen as a social construction, or rather, a social reconstruction of the problem. From the introduction of categories such as 'idiots and imbeciles' in early legislation, through the medical categories of 1944, to special educational needs in 1981, it could be argued that only the labels have changed; the underlying reality of an education system unable or unwilling to meet the needs of all children remains the same.[4]

The problem with such attempts to redefine and relabel children's educational problems is that they are limited to the level of attitudes, interests, values and beliefs. Just as disabled people found this an inadequate basis for an understanding of the problems that they faced, so too did other oppressed groups like women and blacks who insisted that issues of *institutionalized* sexism and racism be brought to the surface and confronted openly. Thus the problems of sexism, racism and disablism[5] were not just in the minds of people — a problem of attitudes, values and beliefs — but were real and socially created by a racist, sexist, disabilist society. Practices like institutionalized racism or sexism, or indeed disablism exist independently of the attitudes or values of individuals or groups. From this, it logically follows that interventions aimed at resolving the problem cannot be based on assumptions that the two are the same or that by changing attitudes, we can change practices. This issue will be discussed further in the context of anti-discrimination legislation in the next section.

The arguments of disabled people about how society creates their disabilities have also begun to have an influence on educational thinking. The recent review of special educational provision in the ILEA adopted the following definition:

> Disabilities and difficulties become more or less handicapping depending on the expectations of others and on social contexts. Handicaps arise from the mis-match between the intellectual, physical, emotional and social behaviour and aspirations of the individual and the expectations, appropriate or otherwise, of the community and society at large. Individuals with disabilities or significant difficulties may be handicapped by their own attitude to them and by the attitude of others. Of equal significance, the degree to which the individual is handicapped is determined by the educational, social, physical and emotional situations which he or she encounters. Handicapping effects will vary from situation to situation and may change over time (ILEA, 1985, p. 4).

This quote almost captures all three of the definitions that have been discussed: the individual, the social constructionist and the social creationist view of special educational needs.

The fundamental point to be made about the forces that shaped the development of educational policies towards children with special needs, and indeed the definitions that underpin them, is that they are broadly similar to the forces and definitions that have shaped the development of social policies towards disabled people. Any consideration of the future development of educational policies towards children with special needs should therefore also be considered in the wider context of forces shaping the development of social policies towards disabled people. This then will be the subject of the final section.

The Politics of Disability and Special Educational Needs

Since 1979 there has been a move away from the traditional bi-partisan approach to disability based upon humanitarian concerns underpinned by notions of disability as an individual problem and personal tragedy. This bi-partisan approach was based upon the implicit and sometimes explicit assumption that services for disabled people would gradually be improved regardless of the state of the economy or the claims of other groups (Oliver, 1984). There are two factors, one economic and the other political, which have brought about this change. Firstly there has been a massive structural decline in the economy which has resulted in severe cut-backs in public spending. Secondly, 1979 saw the coming of a government which admitted openly that disabled people would have to suffer their share of economic cut-backs and compete with other groups for available scarce resources. In response to these two factors, a new politics of disability has emerged, based upon three distinct elements: a critique of existing services, a re-definition of the problem and an attempt to create alternative service structures con-trolled by disabled people themselves.

There are a number of dimensions to the critique of existing services. Firstly, many local authorities fail to meet their obligations to disabled people under the Chronically Sick and Disabled Persons Act, 1970 by exploiting a legal loophole. The Act lays a statutory obligation on local authorities to provide appropriate services once a need has been acknowledged. The simple way out of this is not to acknowledge particular needs, for there is then no legal obligation to meet them. Financial cutbacks coupled with the weakness of the law have exacerbated this state of affairs. Secondly, much service provision and financial support remains contingent upon medical definitions of disability. Doctors are usually the gatekeepers to scarce resources. Unfortunately, they are often lacking in any detailed knowledge of the resources they are supposed to guard. For example, wheelchairs are supplied on the basis of a recommendation by a general practitioner or hospital doctor. The Association for Spina Bifida and Hydrocephalus in the recent submission to the Review of the Artificial Limb and Appliance Centre Services (DHSS, 1986) claimed that 'nine out of ten of all young people with Spina Bifida who attend their assessment weeks are in wheelchairs which are either unsuitable, need adjustment or require further accessories'.

A third criticism concerns the lack of uniformity in levels and standards of provision at both local and national level. Services like home help provi-sion, holidays, subsidized telephones and occupational therapy vary widely from one geographical area to another, and often from one neighbouring borough to another (Shearer, 1981). Nationally, access to financial benefits can vary widely as well: in the case of the Attendance Allowance, people with exactly the same clinical condition often will get different levels of benefit or no benefit at all. The structure of services is so complicated that it is difficult for individuals to know precisely what their entitlements are and no one, not even those who administer them, understand the services in their totality.

A fourth criticism concerns the professionalization of provision. The assumptions underlying such provision are that the professionals know best what disabled people need and that they, the professionals, define what is actually needed and hand it out once a decision has been made. This is at best patronizing and at worst it disables people further; they become passive recipients of the services other people think they ought to have. This can become a vicious circle into which both the professional and the disabled person become locked. Finkelstein discusses this in the context of what he calls the helper/helped relationship:

> The existence of helper/helped builds into this relationship norma-
> tive assumptions. 'If they had not lost something, they would not
> need help' goes the logic 'and since it is us', the representatives of
> society doing the help, it is society which sets the norms for the
> problem solutions (Finkelstein, 1980, p. 17).

A final telling criticism of the existing infrastructure of services is that rights to such services are difficult to obtain and disabled people have virtually no redress for discriminatory actions or practices. Influenced by the Civil Rights Movement in the United States, and the pursuit of equal opportunities policies in this country, the growing power of the disabled people's movement throughout the world has led to demands by disabled people in this country for anti-discrimination legislation.[6] This demand has not been universally accepted by all political parties, though the Labour Party has recently signalled its commitment to such an approach (Meacher, Beckett and Morris, 1986). The debate has centred around the issue of whether it is better to persuade people by changing their attitudes, not to discriminate against disabled people or to give disabled people legalized redress against such institutionalized practices. For example, at a recent meeting between architects and disabled people, architects were arguing that it was better to persuade their colleagues to design buildings fully accessible to disabled people rather than create resentment by forcing them to do so. Disabled people on the other hand were arguing that they would rather have resent-ful architects and accessible buildings than happy architects and inaccessible buildings.

Can this critique of existing services be applied to special education? Certainly the issue of financial cut-backs is of equal relevance. Despite the passage of the 1981 Education Act, the Government has made it clear that no extra resources will be made available to implement it. In fact it has been claimed that 'the Tory Government is planning to reduce expenditure on special education in real terms by 11.3 per cent over the three years from

1983/4. Over the same period the special school population is projected to fall by only 1.7 per cent' (Bennett, 1985, p. 5).

The dominance of medical conceptions has already been discussed and cannot be doubted. There is also a failure to provide uniform standards for children with the same or similar needs. The degree of integration, the level of support and the spending per capita on children with special needs may vary widely between one authority and another.

The issue of services being provided by professionals on the assumption that they know best and are in control of the process was certainly the way a visiting American scholar, David Kirp, recently viewed special education: 'The idea that handicapped children or their guardians might have legally recognizable rights', he remarked, 'scarcely figures'. While the 1981 Education Act grants parents certain rights to participate in the decision-making process, it does not go as far as the American legislation nor as far as many parents in this country would wish.

The disabling effects of professional interventions are also apparent in the sphere of special education and disabled people have recently begun to develop a critique in this area in response to a European Commission study on disabled youth:

> The special education system, then, is one of the main channels for disseminating the predominant able-bodied/minded perception of the world and ensuring that disabled school leavers are socially immature and isolated. This isolation results in passive acceptance of social discrimination, lack of skills in facing the tasks of adulthood and ignorance about the main social issues of our times. All this reinforces the 'eternal children' myth and ensures at the same time disabled school leavers lack the skills for overcoming the myth (John, 1986, p. 6).

Clearly then, the critique of provision for disability can be applied with equal force to the area of special educational needs.

Let me now consider the second element in a politics of disability; an attempt to redefine the problem. This process of re-definition has been described by Sutherland (1981) as follows:

> It is widely assumed that most disabilities impose considerable restrictions, such as lack of mobility, limitations in finding and holding employment, isolation and difficulty in integrating with able-bodied people. People with disabilities do have to face all these restrictions, and others, but such restrictions are not imposed by their disabilities. *They are imposed by a society which discriminates against people with disabilities, creating restrictions by denying people the means to exercise their capabilities* (Sutherland, 1981, p. 22, my emphasis).

Redefinition has been aided by a growing confidence of disabled people and their organizations:

> Disabled spokesmen and spokeswomen have become increasingly active in articulating their own perceptions of the situation. Since the Second World War there has been a rapid growth in the numbers and size of organizations of disabled people and increasingly, particularly in the last decade, a growing group identity (Finkelstein, 1980, p. 1).

This redefinition has been part of a wider political struggle by disabled people to control and create their own organizations. There has been in recent years the beginnings of a move away from organizations for disabled people based upon a partnership approach to statutory agencies, and a move towards organizations of disabled people based upon self-help and populist approaches (Oliver, 1984). Organizations like the Union of the Physically Impaired Against Segregation, the Spinal Injuries Association, Liberation of People with Disabilities and the Association of Disabled Professionals have sprung up alongside more traditional organizations for disabled people like the Spastics Society, Royal National Institute for the Blind, and the Multiple Sclerosis Society. While organizations *of* disabled people do not yet in any way rival organizations *for* disabled people in numbers, size or scope, their growing collective strength is gradually being tested with the formation of an umbrella national organization, the British Council of Organizations of Disabled People (BCODP) in 1981. As well as co-ordinating the activities of local and national organizations, BCODP sends representatives to Disabled Peoples' International (DPI) which has now become the international forum for expressing the views of disabled people, and been recognized by the United Nations.

The politics of re-definition has however not progressed very far in special education. Part of the reason for this lack of concern over re-definition is explained by Kirp (1983):

> Voluntary organizations concerned with particular handicapped groups, such as the Royal National Institute for the Deaf, and the Spastics Society, do exist; but these are not interest groups. For one thing, they are typically charitable enterprises, not membership organizations designed to serve a particular group and not represent it. They are primarily engaged in improving the lot of handicapped individuals and their families, by offering support, not calling for government action: indeed their legal status as charitable organizations formally precludes them from acting otherwise (p. 83).

Where self-help and populist organizations like the National Union of the Deaf and the Association of Blind and Partially Sighted Teachers and Students do exist, they have tended to focus on gaining access to the kinds of education their members want. More recently, organizations like the Parents Campaign for Integrated Education and the Centre for Studies on Integration in Education based at the Spastics Society have come into being to press for integrated education, and the British Council of Organizations of Disabled People through its Standing Committee on Education has adopted as its aim the reduction by half of the number of children attending special schools within ten years.

The third element in the development of a politics of disability is through the creation of alternative service structures which does not necessarily imply that they are completely separate from and independent of other agencies. The fundamental point about these alternative services is that they must be geared to meet the needs of disabled people as they themselves define them and not either to impose needs on disabled people or be organized in such a way as to meet the needs of the professionals running the services[7]. Thus, organizations like the Crossroads Care Attendants Scheme, the Independent Living Schemes run by Community Service Volunteers and the Care Attendant Agency run by the Spinal Injuries Association are all examples of services run to meet the needs of disabled people as they themselves perceive them. Even within some organizations for disabled people, groups are being set up and run by disabled people to provide a range of services like peer counselling, information and advice, social outings and so on.

Potentially the most exciting and far-reaching of all such developments is the establishment of a number of 'centres for integrated living' (CILS) throughout the country. The development of CILS in this country followed similar developments in the United States where from the 1980s onwards a number of 'centres for independent living' were established by disabled people in order to assist them to live in the community by providing services, information and advice, care attendants, equipment, repairs to wheelchairs, housing, employment and so on (Crewe and Zola, 1983). There are now over 150 CILS in the United States and, allowing for cultural and other differences, similar organizations are springing up in other parts of the world including Australia, Canada and Japan.

While there are similarities in the development of centres for independent living in the United States and centres for integrated living here, there are differences as well. The major difference is that in this country, through the Welfare State, an infrastructure of services already exists. In the United States the struggle by disabled people has been to establish and control their own support services. In this country, however, the struggle by disabled people has been to gain joint control of services that already exist, albeit in patchy and piecemeal form. Undoubtedly the Derbyshire Coalition of Disabled People has gone farthest down this road in establishing a centre for integrated living in cooperation with Derbyshire County Council. Similar projects are now being developed, notably in London and Hampshire.

'Centres for integrated living' neatly encapsulate the three elements of the new politics of disability discussed in this section; they contain criticisms, sometimes implicit, sometimes explicit, of existing services; they attempt to re-define the problem; and they provide an alternative service structure. K. Davis (1983) observes:

> CILs are thus nicely poised at the fulcrum of the contemporary struggle to tilt the balance of history in favour of a fairer and more equitable future for disabled people. The Derbyshire Coalition argues that the key to social change is the active participation of people who are themselves disabled and that CILS, properly re-oriented and adapted, can exert a beneficial influence on the existing service infrastructure in Britain (p. 16).

These developments are likely to gain in strength not just because of the growing power and confidence of disabled people but also due to current policies aimed at reducing the size, scope and expense of the Welfare State by privatising many services that are currently the responsibility of the statutory authorities[8].

In considering the restructuring of services to meet special educational needs, it seems unlikely that similar trends will emerge. The major reason for this is that the statutory obligations of education departments are different from those of social services or health authorities. They are required to provide education for all children, whereas health care, community support, accommodation and so on do not have to be provided for all disabled people. Thus, because of this comprehensive framework, alternative special schools are unlikely to emerge, although some ethnic minorities are beginning to develop part-time provision as an addition rather than an alternative to existing arrangements.

This does not mean that a politics of special educational needs is irrelevant for there are at least three key issues that need to be addressed over the next few years. Firstly, it must be recognized that the needs of parents and children are not necessarily the same and may sometimes be in conflict. It is gradually being recognized that the needs of disabled people and their carers may also be in conflict. The usual solution to such conflicts through professional definitions of who needs what and the subsequent provision of professionalized services, must be avoided if the mistakes of the past are not to be repeated. Secondly, disabled adults must participate much more actively in the education of disabled children for it is only these people with direct experience of the special education system who can know just how disabling it can be. Thirdly, and following on from the Warnock expansion of the categories of special educational needs, it must not be assumed that parents of and indeed children with moderate learning difficulties and emotional or behavioural problems cannot be actively involved in making decisions about their own or their children's education. These and other issues can only be tackled by building upon existing critiques and by following through the implications of defining special educational need as a social creation.

Conclusion

This chapter has suggested that services for disabled people generally and education services for children with special educational needs in particular have been shaped by a variety of social forces other than the purely humanitarian desire to help individuals defined and perceived as unfortunate. Underpinning changes that have occurred has been the gradual change in the definitions of the problems away from locating them in the individual, through seeing them as a social construction and onto recognizing them as a social creation. Testament to this underlying shift can be seen in the articulation of four broad principles on which subsequent development should be based: by John Fish, formerly Staff Inspector for Special Education at DES, an assessor on the Warnock Committee, and the chair of the ILEA special education review:

(i) Although disabilities and difficulties may be different, and their nature, effects and the needs which result from them should be studied, the handicaps which stem from them have many common characteristics.
(ii) Handicaps are determined by society through its laws, norms and institutions and not by disabilities.
(iii) Handicapping effects result from the nature of the situations met by individuals with disabilities and difficulties in education, social circumstances and employment.
(iv) The degree to which situations are handicapping is determined by the community, its attitudes and its provision for individuals who form part of it (Fish, 1985, p. 5).

Given the individual and social constructionist definition which underpin the Warnock Report, these principles clearly represent a significant shift towards a view of the special need as a social creation, at the policy level at least. However, the fundamental dilemma for teachers at the grass roots remains, for:

> it does appear that when challenged, the education system will defend itself by reverting to innate, individualistic explanations stressing the pupils' deficiencies (Tomlinson, 1982, p. 162).

The development of a pedagogic practice based upon the definition of special educational needs as a social creation, is therefore an urgent and essential task over the next few years.

Notes

1 For a fuller discussion of this, see Oliver (1985 a).

2 It cannot however be assumed that the meaning of this word is unproblematic. Professionals often use it to mean that an individual should be capable of a variety of self-care activities; washing, dressing, eating, toileting and so on. Disabled people on the other hand, use it to mean the ability to take control of one's life; to decide where to live, who to live with, whether to work or not, and how much to rely on others for self-care activities.

3 This is an issue I am currently working on, attempting to look at the way services provided in ordinary schools might reduce the scope of the social control network rather than enlarge it.

4 This is not to deny that there may be changes in the numbers of disabled children who survive as a result of advances in medical sciences, the uses of new technology or the introduction of vaccination programmes. Rather the argument is that the process of educating children, once they have been labelled as disabled, has remained the same.

5 Thus use of the terms disablism and disablist is somewhat clumsy but unfortunately we have no more appropriate terms to describe overt discrimination against disabled people. The fact that we do have such terminology to allow us to discuss issues of race and gender indicates that we have not, up to now, used a similar conceptual framework in order to discuss disability.

6 Kirp (1983) in comparing special education in Britain and America argues that changes that have occurred in the American system occurred precisely because individuals were given certain rights under the law and thus people had access to the courts to prevent discrimination in the exercise of these rights. For a fuller discussion of the issue of anti-discrimination legislation in Britain, see Oliver (1985).

7 A usual criticism of residential care, for example, is that it is organized to meet the needs of staff rather than residents. Thus residents get up, go to bed, eat and are toileted at times which suit the staff rather than when residents wish.

8 This should not be taken as a blanket endorsement of the process of privatization but rather an acknowledgement of it. Clearly, however, one element in privatization has been the inability of statutory agencies to respond to the needs of disabled people as they themselves perceive them.

References

ALTHUSSER, L. (1971) 'Ideology and Ideological State Apparatuses' in *Lenin and Philosophy and other Essays*, London, New Left Books.

BENNETT, A. (1985) 'The Politics of Special Education' in *Socialist Education* Vol. 2, No. 3.

COHEN, S. (1985) *Visions of Social Control*, Oxford, Basil Blackwell.

CREWE, N. and ZOLA, I. (Eds) (1983) *Independent Living for Physically Disabled People*. London, Josey Bass.

DAVIS, K. (1983) *Consumer Participation in Service Design, Delivery and Control*. Clay Cross, Derbyshire Coalition of Disabled People.

DHSS (1986) *Review of Artificial Limb and Appliance Centre Services*, London, HMSO.

DURWARD, L. (1981) *That's the Way the Money Goes*, London, Disability Alliance.

FINKELSTEIN, V. (1980) *Attitudes and Disabled People: Issues for Discussion*, New York, World Rehabilitation Fund.

FINKELSTEIN, V. (1985) Report on World Health Organization Meeting, *Vox Nostra* 2/85.

FISH, J. (1985) 'Community, Co-operation, Co-Partnership', Paper given at International Congress of Special Education, Nottingham.

FORD, J., MONGON, D. and WHELAN, M. (1982) *Special Education and Social Control*, London, Routledge and Kegan Paul.

HALL, P., LAND, H., PARKER, R., and WEBB, A. (1975) *Change, Choice and Conflict in Social Policy*, London, Heinemann.

HARRIS, A. (1971) *Handicapped and Impaired in Great Britain*, London, HMSO.

ILEA (1985) *Educational Opportunities for All*, London, ILEA.

JOHN, M. (in collaboration with BCODP) (1986) *Disabled Young People Living Independently*, Paris, OECD.

KIRP, D. (1983) 'Professionalization as Policy Choice: British Special Education in Comparative Perspective' in J.G. CHAMBERS and W.T. HARTMAN (Eds) *Social Education Policies*, Philadelphia, Temple University Press.

MEACHER, M., BECKETT, M. and MORRIS, A. (1986) *As of right*, Nottingham, Russell Press.

MISHRA, R. (1984) *The Welfare State in Crisis*, Brighton, Wheatsheaf.

OLIVER, M. (1984) 'The Politics of Disability', in *Critical Social Policy*, 11, pp. 21–32.

OLIVER, M. (1985 a) 'Discrimination, Disability and Social Policy' in BRENTON, M. and JONES, C. *Yearbook of Social Policy in Britain*, London, Routledge and Kegan Paul.

OLIVER, M. (1985 b) 'The Integration — Segregation Debate: Some Sociological Considerations', *British Journal of Sociology of Education* Vol. 6, No. 1.

POTTS, P. (1983) 'Medicine, Morals and Mental Deficiency: The Contribution of Doctors to the Development of Special Education in England', *Oxford Review of Education* Vol. 9, No. 3.

SHEARER, A. (1981) *Disability: Whose Handicap?*, Oxford, Basil Blackwell.

STONE, D. (1984) *The Disabled State*, Basingstoke, MacMillan.

SUTHERLAND, A. (1981) *Disabled We Stand*, London, Souvenir Press.

TAYLOR-GOOBY, P. and DALE, J. (1981) *Social Theory and Social Welfare*, London, Edward Arnold.

TOMLINSON, R. (1980) *Disabled People on Supplementary Benefit*, London, DIG.

TOMLINSON, S. (1982) *A Sociology of Special Education*, London, Routledge and Kegan Paul.

TOPLISS, E. (1979) *Provision for the Disabled*, Oxford, Basil Blackwell/Martin Robertson.

TOWNSEND, P. (1979) *Poverty in the United Kingdom*, Harmondsworth, Penguin.

UNION OF THE PHYSICALLY IMPAIRED AGAINST SEGREGATION (1975) *Fundamental Principles of Disability*, London, UPIAS.

(1981) *Disability Challenge No. 1*, London, UPIAS.

(1983) *Disability Challenge No. 2*, London, UPIAS.

WARNOCK REPORT (1978) 'Special Educational Needs. Report of the Committee of Enquiry into the Education of Children and Young People', London, HMSO.

WORLD HEALTH ORGANIZATION (1981) *International Classification of Impairment, Disabilities and Handicaps*, Geneva, WHO.

Chapter 2

From the Other Side of the Wall

Marion Blythman

Introduction

Two reports, both published in 1978, expressed a need for a broader definition of pupils with learning difficulties. The Warnock Committee (UK),
which included representation from Scotland, talked about a continuum of
Special Educational Need, estimating that one child in five would require
some form of special educational provision at some point in his/her career.

Later in the same year a Report, published by HM Inspectors
(Scotland), 'The Education of Pupils with Learning Difficulties in Primary
and Secondary Schools in Scotland', took an even broader view claiming
that up to 50 per cent of the total school population had learning difficulties, and that one of the main causes of these difficulties was the curriculum and how it is presented. The Progress Report as it came to be known
has had a great influence in Scotland on policy, practice, provision for and
training of teachers of pupils with learning difficulties.

The aim of this chapter is to attempt to view the background to this
report and the way it has been implemented as part of an 'ideologically
formed historical process'; that is, to examine these recent developments in a
way which acknowledges that they themselves are not static; that at any one
time they exhibit contradictions and inconsistencies, and that, mainly, their
meaning can only become clear through an examination of particular
instances.

Such an analysis tries to locate these 'instances', however, as part of an
historical process within a context largely determined by the prevailing
political and social ideologies rather than as a series of discrete events to be
interpreted pragmatically in a common sense rule of thumb kind of way.

Education, broadly speaking is a process by which the state ensures
social conformity, political stability and continuity through a system of
checks and balances which often vary with time, place and country. There
are, however, common strands in this process which can be identified and

which clearly have helped to determine and shape the education of children with learning difficulties in both Scotland and England. In effect, the recurring themes show a remarkable degree of agreement. In both countries mainstream education has been built on a 'ladder of merit' system designed to select and provide for a small proportion of the school population, mainly middle-class and/or academic, with only a few places reserved for able working-class children. Working-class education in both countries has been narrowly conceived, very much about 'gentling the masses' and producing a malleable work force, so that the economic needs of society have been put before the social and educational needs of individuals. Pupils who have learning difficulties and therefore special educational needs have not found a real place within either the Scottish or the English system, but have been stigmatized, labelled and either removed from the mainstream system or segregated within it.

Even so, recent developments in Scotland concerned with developing an appropriate education for all pupils including those with learning difficulties in mainstream schools and classes have their own characteristics and have to be described and evaluated for their success and failures within their own historical perspective and as part of the continuing Scottish tradition. To isolate them from that or to view them as a sub-set of a wider UK tradition would be 'to distort, leaving significant elements unexamined', as Bogdan and Kugelmass say (1984, p. 188).

This chapter therefore has been written from a Scottish perspective. Personally, as someone born and educated in Scotland and who has lived and worked there for almost all of my professional life, I always see myself first and foremost as Scottish and rarely even British. Like Viv Edwards, I have always objected when the term 'English' is used as a coverall description for those things which are actually happening within the UK at large. As he goes on to say:

> It is important that such a personal statement should not be dismissed as nationalist paranoia, since it both highlights and challenges certain assumptions (Craft, 1984, p. 80).

Among these assumptions is a view that the political and social ideologies of Scotland and England are synonymous. It can be argued, however, that this is not entirely true for there is in Scotland a unique linguistic, cultural and national identity which has given a sense of peoplehood, quite distinct from that south of the border, often expressed in terms which show both a political and cultural resistance to English dominance.

There does exist and has existed over a long period, particularly since the Act of Union, a political tension in the relationship between Scotland and England. The two populations share a language which allows for communication but which encompasses such a range of variation that the BBC has been known to sub-title reports from Glasgow on the basis that the majority of the English viewers would find the language quite incomprehensible. This does seem ironic when programmes such as 'East Enders' or 'Hill Street Blues' with their linguistic idiosyncrasies are transmitted for popular consumption. The two legal systems and the precepts on which they are founded are quite different, the Scottish system based on practice derived from principle rather than from case law. The educational systems have never been merged despite the fact that they have been shaped by similar forces and subject to similar legislation and regulations homologated at a UK level.

Historical Background

From the time of the Reformation and through the period of the development of mass education, Scots have been proud of their educational system, though it should be said that it has been viewed favourably by the Scots themselves and less enthusiastically by external observers and incomers.

Before 1872

Before 1872, in Scotland, a popular system of education was well established:

> The system of parish and borough schools, substantially augmented by private 'adventure' schools, produced a population renowned for its literacy and what middle class contemporaries called 'intelligence'. The Scots indeed had developed an attitude towards mass education significantly different from the untrusting and hostile attitude of the still dominant rulers of England (Smout, 1986, p. 209).

This is interesting, for the same could not be said about trade, commerce and industry. As far as education was concerned, however:

> The Scottish attitude . . . was destined to win the day in Britain as a whole and thus to form an interesting and little recognised case of the Scotticisation of England (Smout, 1986, p. 210).

The Calvinist tradition allied to a strong philanthropic belief in the value of education as a 'good thing' in itself also influenced the development of the whole system and also what happened to those pupils identified as incapable of meeting the demands of the school system described above. It is within the national silhouette that schools for the deaf, the blind and the 'mentally defective' were first opened in Scotland in the late eighteenth century long before this happened south of the border.

This also reflects a strong sense of social responsibility, for in Scotland education was valued as much for its contribution to the general good, as to the personal development of the individual. There was more economic hardship in Scotland and a smaller middle class. Consequently there was little scope for the kind of system which produced and valued the 'man of letters' educated at Oxford (or Cambridge) and polished by the 'Grand Tour' for example. As in any poor country the benefits of education were highly regarded in Scotland as a means of advancement and as such should not be denied to any of its people.

Much has been made by Scots themselves of the 'democratic intellectual' nature of Scottish education as it developed in the late 18th and 19th centuries, incorporating as it did a romantic view of the 'lad o' pairts', the intellectually able poor boy (rarely a girl of course) who was nurtured by the system and enabled to win through to great academic achievement. It was not until 1871 that this view was reported in England when T.H. Huxley said:

> I conceive it to be our duty to make a ladder from the gutter to the university along which any child might climb.

In Scotland, it was true that the possibility that a select few could and would make it through school to the university was always there, known and valued by the population at large. But in fact as Smout (1986) goes on to point out:

> It is important to realise that neither Smith (i.e., Adam Smith of 'Wealth of Nations' fame) nor anyone else in Scotland actually believed in thorough-going democratic equality of opportunity in education. The common people in Smith's scheme cannot in any civilised society be so well instructed as people of some rank and fortune though they should be assisted to read, write and account at an early age in publicly aided schools. It was never intended that a formal education for the vast majority should 'go beyond the three R's' (p. 210).

While even such limited objectives might have been quite praiseworthy in their day we must question whether the self-congratulatory 'Here's tae us! Wha's like us! Deil the yin' attitudes developed by Scots about the Scottish educational system were in any way justified. Or was this, in effect, a naive and romantic view fired by the nostalgia of the Scots abroad? Forced to emigrate from a country at the receiving end of any UK or world economic depression and still to this day displaying horrifying levels of deprivation, disadvantage and social division, was it all too easy for the Scots to confuse education with the authoritarian and narrow training they had been offered, albeit it was delivered with efficiency mainly derived from the potent and pervasive Protestant work ethic? Or was it, as it was claimed, a system designed to educate a people broadly conceived democratic and open to *all*?

There are undoubtedly conflicting and contradictory strands in Scottish education. There has been in Scotland a national concern to 'square conscience with intellect' (to paraphrase John McLean) and to provide a system of education which unlike the English, would be both democratic and intellectual (George Davie, 1961). There has been a hankering after a system which would produce an educated and 'intelligent' working class. In effect, it can be argued that despite the expressed good intentions, the system has come to be just as much about reflecting social and class divisions, encouraging conformity and a narrow view of education as a means of advancement within:

> the undeniable social hierarchy — in the Kirk, in business, in politics, in sport and the professions (Humes and Patterson, 1983).

In retrospect it is easy to see that education in Scotland became less about liberation and general enlightenment and more about social control, i.e., 'gentling the masses' in effect. There was little doubt that it was ever intended to be anything else. Adam Smith (1776) is quite explicit about the purpose of the system:

> The more they are instructed, the less liable they are to the delusions of enthusiasm and superstition, which among ignorant nations frequently occasion the most dreadful disorders. An instructed and intelligent people besides, are always more decent and orderly than an ignorant and stupid one. They feel themselves each individually more respectable and more likely to obtain the respect of their lawful superiors and they are more disposed to respect those superiors. They are more disposed to examine, and more capable of seeing through the interested complaints of faction and sedition and they are, upon that account, less apt to be misled in to any wanton or unnecessary opposition to the measures of the government (pp. 269–70).

Interestingly this was one aspect of the Scottish system that gained recognition south of the border:

> The knowledge circulated among the common people has the effect of making them bear with patience the evils they suffer from. The

quiet and peaceable habits of the instructed Scotch peasant, compared with the turbulent disposition of the ignorant Irishman ought not to be without effect upon every impartial reasoner (Malthus).

However, at another level, Scotland has always been a nation where traditionally literacy has been highly prized, with schools, particularly in the rural areas where as Lord John Boyd Orr (1966) points out:

> . . . the children of the poor were probably as well educated as those of the wealthy in rudimentary subjects like reading, writing and arithmetic.

And although there were local variations, by 1872, at the point at which education became compulsory, some idea of the national achievement can be gleaned from the fact that only a small percentage of the population could not sign the marriage register.

There was even an early recognition of the benefits of providing an education (of sorts) for all pupils, with local authorities providing schools for the 'mentally defective' as they were termed, from the middle of the nineteenth century. The priority that was given to this, however, can be gleaned from the fact that the 'crippled' children in Glasgow went to school on the fire 'butts' (engines) and so could not go to school when the fire department had to go about its legitimate business.

This gives a small, not uncharacteristic, indication that the early Scottish educational system for all its claims reflected:

> . . . a nineteenth century aspiration which conforms to the first rule of Victorian reform and philanthropy; the alleviation of suffering and injustice up to the point at which further acts of compassion and social justice might begin to disturb the accepted social order and the entrenched privileges of the establishment (Roy Hattersley, *The Observer*, January 4, 1987).

Post 1872

By 1870, in common with England, the main problem was to develop a system which would suit the needs of the employers of the large and relatively neglected working class, who were to be provided with:

> . . . the bare minimum of elementary education combined with adequate social discipline (Smout, 1986, p. 218).

Although, as in England, the intention at this period was sharply focused on the need to provide an elementary system of education as cheaply as possible:

> Scottish critics in the late 19th century felt that their education was being Anglicised, made to concentrate on the simplest needs of one class and controlled from London, rather than being developed along the Scottish tradition of an education that opened a wider range of opportunities for some, at least, in all social classes under local control (Smout, 1986, p. 212).

The difference embedded in the popular mind was succinctly expressed by a Scottish teacher giving evidence to the Argyll Commission (1867)

> The object of the (English) Privy Council is to effect the education of a class, the object of the parochial schools was to effect the education of a people.

As Smout points out, however:

> . . . this was to overstate what the parochial and burgh schools had set out to do even at their best (1986, p. 212)

but which at the same time reveals a recurring theme in popular ideology, discussed earlier, which held that the Scottish education system should be egalitarian, aimed at broad sections of the population. There are always contradictions, however, and despite that, there was a compelling need to do this job at least possible cost. A good example of this is the Scottish-devised pupil teacher training system (one of Scotland's less worthy exports). This was nothing other than a device by which the state tried to ensure a cheap supply of teachers. This so-called 'system' of training lasted for sixty years despite the fact that:

> . . . it was badly conceived and assumed that a child could do two things at once (Kirk, 1985, p. 2, quoted by Bain).

The pupil/teacher system was aimed in effect, to sustain an ethos of control, conformity, continuity, discipline and order in state schools. It reinforced the need to exclude groups of children difficult to manage within such a system and thus ensured their departure from the mainstream system.

Selection and Segregation

As in England, grants to schools depended on the standards of performance of the pupils, standards based on rigid notions of normality and a style of teaching which would enable all children to progress through a lock step curriculum at a uniform rate. Such a system was bound to create failures who then could not be accommodated within the rigid class graded system. Clearly this was at the basis of the development of the separate system of special education fuelled by an ideology which could justify segregation through the labelling of children who departed from the so-called 'norm' as 'idiots', 'imbeciles', 'defective' or even 'different', 'special' or 'exceptional'. This separate system also had the great benefit, of course, that it would simplify and make manageable a mainstream system whose main purpose was to train a workforce at least possible cost. In addition, it is somewhat ironic that although the segregated system was never well or even equally funded as far as the pupils were concerned, nevertheless it provided a 'special ladder of merit' which could be used by professionals to further their own career interests, no doubt at some cost to the state.

By the end of the nineteenth century the myth was well established and legitimated by the pseudo-scientific eugenists and psychometrists that there were qualitatively different sorts of children suffering from 'something' and who were to be offered a qualitatively different sort of education which would provide treatment for that 'something'. The process of segregation of substantial groups of children into special schools or 'backward' classes, based on a system of selection which exaggerated differences and minimized similarities, continued unimpeded for much of the twentieth century.

In Scotland, in addition, working-class children were further devalued in terms of their national identity, language and culture. Once Standard English was adopted as the language of instruction, a form of institution-alized discrimination or even cultural racism came into operation, not always recognized as such within a UK framework.

The message many children received in school was that:

Standard English is the variety of English associated with the socially powerful. It is the most prestigious form of English and . . . educational success and social mobility are dependent upon the ability to use it (Craft, 1984, p. 79).

Not only did most working class children get this message but they accepted it, internalized it and ended up with a sense of inferiority which no doubt contributed to their own view of themselves and their place in the social structure.

It might be thought that the onset of radio and TV would have run counter to this, but a survey by McAulay conducted in Glasgow in the 1970s shows the powerful nature of the message and the extent to which it was woven into the whole fabric of the educational system. It was not only the pupils who were affected, teachers also expressed the following attitudes:

The distortions of Glasgow speech are so associated with inferiority that you feel it is something you have to get rid of.

We are trying to teach English but it is a losing battle.

> The accent of the Glaswegian is the ugliest accent one can encounter, but that is partly because it is associated with the unwashed and the violent.

Little wonder that many Scottish children reported as inarticulate still feel it is cissy to speak English. These feelings and attitudes are well expressed in the poetry of Tom Leonard, quoted below:

From 'Unrelated Incidents'

1. the langwij
   a thi
   intellect hi
   said the langwij
   a thi intell
   ect's English (Extract)

2. right inuff
   ma language is disgraceful

   ma maw tellt mi
   ma teacher tellt mi
   thi doactir tellt mi
   thi priest tellt mi

   ma boss tellt mi
   ma landlady in carrington street tellt mi
   thi lassie ah tried tay get aff way in 1969 tellt mi
   sum wee smout thi thoat ah hudny read chomsky tellt mi
   a calvinistic communist thit thoat ah wuz revisionist tellt mi

   po-faced literati grimly kerryin thi burden a thi past tellt mi
   po-faced literati grimly kerryin thi burden a thi future tellt mi
   ma wife tellt mi jist-tay-get-inty-this-poem tellt mi
   ma wainz came hame fray school an tellt mi
   jist aboot ivry book ah oapnd tellt mi
   even thi introduction tay thi Scottish National Dictionary tellt
     mi

   ach well
   all livin language is sacred
   fuck thi lohta thim

(smout = small person, thoat = thought, hudney = had not, kerryin = carrying, wainz = children, oapned = opened)

3. dispite   dispite   thit fur   it wuzny
thi fact   a long   thi   sitcha
thit   history uv   purposes uv   bad
hi bilonged   poverty n   cultural   day
tay a   thi   statistics hi   tay be
class uv   violence uv   didny really   alive.
people   people n   exist; amaz-
thit hid   positions   in iz it
thir   uv   might seem
langwij   power telln   this
sneered   him his   ordinary wurkin
it   culture wuz   man got
since hi   a sign   up wan day
wuz born;   of his   n
    inferiority;   wuz herd
        tay rimark
        thit;

The selection process as it was practised in mainstream schools in Scotland not only took children out of the system but segregated many within it. It rested on the assumption that it was possible to select the academic from the non-academic and that it was acceptable that the latter would mainly be drawn from the working class. Ramsay McDonald, the stereotypical 'lad o' pairts' (he also came from a one-parent family) was one of the few leading politicians who saw that the educational system had:

> ... nothing to do with the improvement of national education (and that it) ... would fail and ought to fail, if its effect was to form a new series of classes and sub-classes of servants and masters, of sub-ordinates and superiors, determined by the schools through which they had gone (quoted in R.D. Anderson, 1983).

That this way of sorting out pupils was the prevailing though un-acknowledged ideology, however, cannot be denied and any opposition to this was quickly stifled. In 1920 the Advisory Committee had reported:

> ... all save a few backward children are capable of profiting by the same education,

but were smartly brought into line by George McDonald, the then Secretary of the Scottish Education Department, who said:

> They have ignored the fundamental fact that the school population falls into two parts, the majority, of a strictly limited intelligence, and an extremely important minority *drawn from all ranks and classes* (our emphasis) who are capable of responding to a much more

severe call . . . Education must be adapted to their capacities (quoted in Humes and Patterson (Eds), 1983).

In effect, the Scottish education system, including the separate segregated system developed for pupils with learning difficulties was essentially meritocratic rather than democratic. It was more aimed at control than at emancipation; it was about training rather than enlightenment; it was determined by economic considerations and was based on 'a ladder' of merit system of selection and grading and achieved a high degree of sorting and containment derived from the linked processes of minimizing similarities and exaggerating differences. As in England, this led to the denigration and dehumanization of those pupils who were to be excluded from the system. The additional feature, of course, was that the Scottish people had suffered deracination, evidenced by the punishing rate of 'clearance' and emigration, with their language and culture under a sustained attack that caused children at school in the Western Isles, for example, to be subjected to corporal punishment when they spoke in their own Gaelic language. In addition, working class education, as Smout points out:

> . . . was regarded as a low priority once the perceived needs of the middle class had been attended to and once a channel had been opened for a limited number of working class children to use a secondary school and university as a means of upward social mobility (1986, p. 233).

The Onset of Change

Very often a system can proceed based on false assumptions accepted largely because they establish an equilibrium not uncomfortable for those prepared to operate within its constraints. Although the system was patently inegalitarian, there was still a widely accepted view that the Scottish system was essentially democratic and that anyone who wished to could, through his education, advance himself (not herself) to a high position in society. The first raising of the school leaving age in 1947 had caused unease at the time, but had been rationalized away in England through the adoption of:

> a nationwide system based on the distinctive needs of what were felt to be three broad 'types' of adolescent identified by educational psychologists (Craft, 1984, p. 14).

Comprehensive schools taking in almost the whole range of pupils, however, had always existed in the smaller Scottish boroughs and may have been one of the reasons that the 11+ furore was not replicated in Scotland to anything like the same extent as in England. There was no real equivalent of the secondary modern school in Scotland, the majority of children going into undifferentiated secondary schools even in the urban areas. By the early seventies in Scotland, selection had virtually disappeared, while in England a large number of grammar schools had survived and were still, at that late date, creaming off a substantial proportion of the 'brighter' pupils. Ostensibly of course the Scottish school was comprehensive in nature but did in fact largely provide an academic curriculum geared to the needs of the small minority who were destined to go on to higher education.

By the next time round, however, the raising of the school leaving age (ROSLA) was more difficult to rationalize away. By 1976/7, the economic recession allied to the raising of the school leaving age to sixteen was causing many pupils to stay longer within the system. As Michael Marland and others had pointed out, there was, in addition, an expectation that pupils would have to absorb more complex and sophisticated matter from a large number of teachers and over a wider range of subjects. Reading demands were increasing rather than standards going down — which was the popular media view. The political parties and parents were beginning to equate standards with measureable success and the acquisition of certificates and diplomas.

Generally in Scotland the custom of streaming classes in secondary schools was increasingly questioned. It had always been rare to find this practice in primary schools. At local level there was a political commitment to comprehensive education, and by the mid-seventies many secondary schools had mixed ability classes operating beyond the second year of secondary education. Although the rhetoric did not always match the reality, the democratic tradition was still on the national agenda, possibly more than in England, where a 1979 HMI Report indicated 'that most comprehensives preferred streaming, setting and banding and that their curriculum for the less able was narrow and inappropriate'.

Many younger teachers having come through the sixties and feeling themselves committed to a different, more democratic style of teaching and learning, were becoming uneasy and more conscious of the contradictions between the claims that were being made about comprehensive education and the realities of their day-to-day practice. They could not wholly accept a view which saw the pupil as a 'problem' and the response as a 'remedy'. They could not but be aware of the injustice and divisiveness of a system which segregated or withdrew increasingly large numbers of pupils labelled 'remedial', and then gave them a narrow restricted programme which in effect reduced the chances of a return to mainstream.

All of this was exacerbated by the fact that the academic curriculum in Scotland had survived fairly intact, protected as it was by the national system of examinations mainly concerned to meet university and college entry requirements. Schools were still dominated by values which defined success in terms of good results in these examinations, open as they were only to a small proportion of the total school population. That this has continued to be the case can be seen from the recent legislation requiring schools to publish examination results, and the pressure to have such results seen as the measure of success (or failure) of the school.

At the same time, however, assessment procedures were becoming more sensitive. It had become increasingly difficult to ignore or accept the massive degree of failure structured into the traditional 'ladder of merit' system, based as it was on a refined system of selection and grading which had left the vast majority of the school population uncredentialized in terms of certificates and qualifications. As Howell Jones pointed out at the time:

> the real problems of the comprehensive school are not those associated with able, well motivated, examination-oriented young-sters, but those concerned with the effective teaching of the slow learners and children with learning difficulties (Jones, quoted in OU 'Special Needs in Education', 1979, p. 61).

This seemed also to be the case in England where:

> Up to the beginning of the 80s there was little evidence that comprehensive schools had solved the problem for the 'less able' (Tomlinson, quoted in Cohen, A. and Cohen, L., 1986, p. 266).

In particular, the ROSLA curriculum and programmes of the 'Design for Living' variety had not been voted as successful by pupils or teachers. By the mid-seventies there was also evidence of concern for the large numbers of children who were both causing trouble within schools and emerging into the world of the 'disappearing youth labour market' (Tomlinson, 1986), with no qualifications at a time when these were increasingly in demand. In Scotland the Pack Report (1977) had been published, basically saying that the curriculum (not the pupils) was at the root of many of the growing problems of truancy and disruption.

Comprehensive education implies common courses and mixed ability teaching and a concern that 'every child must have the opportunity to come into contact with the breadth of human knowledge' (Grampian Regional Council, 1976). The situation pre-1978 was one of countervailing values and dilemmas of action as Eysenck had pointed out. The conflict between notions of equality and excellence were, and have remained, largely unresolved, not unexpected in a society where, as Matthew Arnold stated 'inequality is almost a religion'. Most schools found it impossible to proceed beyond the idea of equality of opportunity to a situation where they could provide an appropriate and differentiated education. Even:

> the theory of equal educational opportunity was easily translated into economic terms, with human beings being treated as resources which could only be used to best advantage when various market imperfections like artificial barriers to entry to the professions were removed (Roy Hattersley, *The Observer*, 1987).

And of course, in a society where intelligence and academic achievement had become commodities, the needs of the less successful mainly achieved a low priority.

It was abundantly clear that the rhetorical commitment to comprehensive education had not been translated into action. Schools were still largely concerned with the selected few. There was little evidence that:

> the children from the slums, badly fed, badly housed, badly protected from disease and enjoying little or no acquaintance with books could have been said to have acquired any sort of equality with their suburban contemporaries just because they were attending the same schools (Hattersley, 1987).

There was little evidence either that the school system, supposedly conceived on the basis of individual need, could acknowledge the right of the pupil to exercise control and choice or take account of individual or familial aspiration. In retrospect, this required a new pedagogy aimed at recognizing and valuing individual difference and calling for a level of support which could enable all teachers to provide an appropriate curriculum for each pupil as opposed to a general education for all.

Between 1975 and 1980

Between 1975 and 1980, almost every Education Authority in Scotland was in the process of revising their 'remedial' provision for 'slow learners' as they were currently termed. Typical of these is an interim report from the Renfrew Division of Strathclyde which underlined 'the need to examine current practices, provisions, facilities and resources and to invite observation and comments'. They determined 'to assess the effectiveness of remedial education in primary and secondary schools and to provide further guidance, if necessary, to both headteachers and teachers' (Remedial Education in Renfrew Division, 1976).

This activity from so many authorities reflected a ground swell of real concern about what was or was not happening in the comprehensive schools related possibly to earlier notions of the education of a 'people'. While many of the remedial teachers were content to accept the constraints of their traditional roles, there were individuals and groups in Grampian, Fife and Strathclyde particularly who were very much aware of the restrictive nature of their roles and were beginning to move towards a wider interpretation of remedial education, i.e., 'the rapidly changing concept of what remedial education is and what it is attempting to do' (Strathclyde Report 1976).

It was ironic that at the point when there was increasing unease about the segregation of pupils with learning difficulties into separate 'remedial' classes that the numbers should have been on the increase. The numbers of pupils rose by 0.5 per cent in primary and 0.7 per cent in secondary between 1975 and 1976 (SED Statistical Bulletin, 1979), around two thirds of these receiving remedial education under some form of withdrawal arrangement. At one level, this reflected an humanitarian concern since, in effect, little fundamental change had been made in the way mainstream schools were operating in terms of their teaching methods, organization and curriculum.

Many pupils were still being offered a curriculum which harkened back to the 19th century with a strong emphasis on basic literacy and numeracy (with elements of technical education for boys and domestic science for girls). The educational experience of most pupils in this group of low achievers was restricted and impoverished and so 'different' in nature that it effectively and irretrievably reduced their chances of ever getting back into mainstream.

The special/remedial classes and schools had in fact become self-perpetuating ghettos, as much concerned to serve the needs of the system as of the pupils in them, stigmatized as they were by their teachers and peers. In a broad sense these children were the victims of the Scottish meritocratic system showing that many of the high-faluting claims about the open and democratic nature of Scottish education were wearing pretty thin. Their education was 'different but not equal', was afforded a low priority and had been largely ignored as can be evidenced from the fact that it took until 1978 for a national report to appear specifically concerned with their education.

Margaret Clark, then at the University of Strathclyde but later to become professor at the University of Birmingham, gave the following analysis of the position at that time when she gave four views of remedial education. She maintained at a conference that it was:

(a) a hoax
(b) a therapy designed to take the heat off the rest of the school
(c) a euphemism for the teaching of children of low ability with little hope of progress

(d) a certain type of teaching which involved someone 'putting things right' in the short term or the long term, in general, or in specific instances.

Clearly there was unease in many directions with a real concern beginning to emerge about the part played by schools in creating failure and the subsequent effects on teachers and the pupils.

> To the extent that we have ignored cultural differences in patterns and tempos of learning, social and affective differences in the temperaments of children, to the extent that we have set goals of achievement for individual children that are either unrealistically high or low, we have ensured the development of the educationally disordered child, with cognitive and social handicaps, that we relegate to the special classroom. This is not to deny a continuum of competence that may be based on genetic and environmental factors acting together. . . It is to state that the continuum of competence cognitive and social, existing prior to entry to school becomes distorted by the very system that society has devised for the development and measurement of competence. And that distortion is of such a nature that individual, social and ethnic class differences interact with the categorical rigidities of the curriculum, methods of instruction and administrative organization to sort out the children, not solely in terms of the constitutional and environmentally determined differences existing prior to school entry, but to a large extent independently of such pre-school individual differences (Sarason and Doris, 1979, pp. 154–5).

This is indeed a damning indictment of any state school system and one which could not be gainsaid in Scotland where schools, in the broad sense, were continuing to fail to recognize and meet the needs of children who, in the first instance, had been failed by the school system itself.

'The Progress Report'

One of the major influences on the recent developments in Scotland has been the role played by Her Majesty's Inspectors of Schools. While the professional civil servants who make up the Scottish Education Department seem to be prepared to toe the line and accept policies largely shaped by UK economic considerations, traditionally the HMIs have had a concern for the nature of the education offered. 'The Progress Report' is one of a number of reports initiated and written by HMIs, which, despite all the political and economic constraints, advance progressive views and underwrite policies essentially radical in nature.

'The Progress Report' was based on an extensive survey of remedial provision and on information derived from the normal school inspections. These together had revealed a range and diversity of learning difficulty among pupils which went well beyond a failure to master the basic skills. The evidence from the survey showed that all pupils experienced learning difficulties from time to time. It is interesting, of course, that within a framework where the acquisition of the three Rs had been seen as the main aim of education for 'less able' pupils, attention had been concentrated on these and that most teachers as a consequence were not in fact sensitive to the real range and diversity of difficulties experienced by children. The Report emphasized that the response to this wider definition of learning difficulties had to be planned on a whole-school basis:

> Because the range of learning difficulties is so wide and their nature so complex, it is too much to ask that they be tackled by the provision of remedial teachers alone (Progress Report, 4.3),

and that there was a need for a whole-school policy which would involve management, class and subject teachers, and it defined a unique role for what subsequently came to be called learning support staff.

This Report identified two overlapping but distinct groups of pupils with learning difficulties and in this took a different position to that of the Warnock Report which had emphasized a continuum of special educational need. There was some sense in this, for as Tomlinson says, however:

> the notion of children with 'Special Needs' conflates what we have termed 'normative' conditions with 'non-normative'. That is, there can be some normative agreement about certain categories of handicap or need — such as blind, deaf, epileptic, severe mental handicap, etc. These conditions affect children in families from all social classes and occupational groupings (Barton and Tomlinson, 1984, p. 71).

By implication, the Report suggested that the needs and nature of this group of children with 'normative' conditions in Scotland — about 1.2 per cent of the total school population — had overly influenced the training and provision for all children with learning difficulties, including those in mainstream education.

Perhaps the most radical aspect of 'The Progress Report' was its clear move away from a child deficit model. Based on an extensive analysis of the evidence of the survey, the report claimed that one of the major sources of learning difficulty was the curriculum and how it was presented. It stated clearly that the curriculum in fact was at once the main cause and potential cure of many learning difficulties, and that the main agents for change had to be the teachers who dealt with this. It goes without saying that this view did not gain immediate general acceptance. It is also very interesting that this view stemmed from the Inspectorate, who claimed that it came as much from a concern about mainstream education as it did for some so-called set of 'special' needs.

Traditionally, in Scotland as elsewhere, headteachers and other promoted staff had not laid any great emphasis on the responsibilities of class and subject teachers in relation to pupils with learning difficulties or in fitting the work of the 'remedial' teachers into a policy involving all members of staff. In addition, 'remedial' staff had not been encouraged to move out of their closets, many staff feeling both angry and threatened at the time of the publication of the Report which they considered to be devaluing their roles and responsibilities and their real concern for the pupils with learning difficulties.

Although 'The Progress Report' was one of the shortest reports produced in recent years, its influence has been both radical and profound. It is interesting to question why this report did not 'wither on the vine' as so many others had done. The strategy used for dissemination was novel and effective, involving the presentation of the evidence from the survey at a series of seminars for regional authorities, colleges and schools. In fact, the hard evidence from the survey of the range of difficulties that children were experiencing in schools, presented as real life case studies, was convincing and impossible to refute. There was also concern that since these difficulties were affecting the education and therefore the life chances of roughly half of the school population they could not readily be ignored. Finally, the Report was stating clearly that schools were functioning in a way which was not consonant with the so-called 'democratic' nature of Scottish education. 'Facts are chiels that winna ding' (i.e., the power of statistics!) and at the meetings and seminars detailed above, the HMI were demonstrating clearly and factually that all was not well in Scottish schools dominated as they were by a concern to provide a curriculum designed to meet the requirements of a national examination system which was becoming more instrumental, more pervasive and dedicated to individual achievement, competition, grading and the selection of the favoured few. The Report was signalling that the education of pupils with learning difficulties, particularly those experienced by non-recorded (i.e., non-statemented) children in ordinary schools — up to 50 per cent of the total school population, after all — could no longer be regarded as something for a low status minority, additional, different or 'special', but had to be viewed as a central concern of all teachers, schools, regional authorities and the colleges of education responsible for training. The emphasis on the need for a whole-school policy called for changes in the organization and management in schools and for the clarification and definition of a new set of roles and responsibilities for management and teachers. Also a new role had to be found for the specialist remedial teacher which was unique and fitted into this whole-school policy. The report defined a multi-purpose role for the new-style learning support teacher:

(i) acting as a consultant to staff and members of the school management team;

(ii) in cooperation with class and subject teachers offering tutorial and supportive help in their normal classes to pupils with learning difficulties in any areas of the curriculum;

(iii) providing personal tuition and support for pupils with severe learning difficulties in the basic processes of communication and computation;

(iv) providing, arranging for or contributing to special services within the school.

In addition, it was clear that initiating and contributing to staff development was a natural concomitant of these roles, in particular where the aim was to develop a whole-school policy for pupils with learning difficulties.

Following on an unprecedented programme of dissemination involving regional authorities, colleges and schools, the recommendations of 'The Progress Report' were generally agreed, with in-service training seen as the key to implementation.

Before whole-school policies could operate, however, many issues had to be resolved. The notions of consultancy and cooperative teaching meant a move away from the traditional pattern of Scottish teaching with its didacticism, linked as it was to an emphasis on the responsibility of the individual teacher often working in isolation. There was a need to sort out the respective roles of the new learning support staff and those of the regular class and subject teachers. Decisions had to be made about who would have the ultimate responsibility for both curriculum and methodology within schools and classes. There was concern to ensure that other teachers would not see the work of the learning support staff as an intrusion or that they might use the presence of the 'expert' as a way of shelving their responsibilities to this wider group of children with learning difficulties.

A Proposed New Set of Roles for the Learning Support Specialist

'The Progress Report' suggested 'a range of different elements which could go to the building-up of a new set of roles quite different to the singular role of the traditional "remedial" teacher'. Some of the elements suggested were:

(i) offering individualized teaching support for the relatively few pupils who have failed to master the early processes of language and computation, or who have learning difficulties of a degree which may necessitate some of their education taking place outwith the classroom.

(ii) acting as a consultant to individual members of staff on the range of learning difficulties, on the curriculum and on the selection of appropriate methodologies.

(iii) acting as a consultant to school management during any discussions on policies affecting pupils with learning difficulties.

(iv) being a focus for the building-up of relationships between the school and any agency offering information and help on pupils with learning difficulties.

(v) offering, in cooperation with class and subject teachers, extra help to pupils meeting difficulties.

(vi) initiating and contributing to staff development, particularly in relation to the development of a whole-school policy for pupils with learning difficulties.

(vii) offering some form of provision within the school for dealing with pupils who have temporary problems which make it difficult for them to fit into normal classes. Learning support specialists could, for example, provide a temporary haven for pupils 'with temporary emotional upsets' and for pupils being phased back into ordinary schools after a spell in residential or special schools.

(viii) offering a facility in the school whereby pupils can be observed and assessed for a short but intensive period.

(ix) offering special expertise in the use of micro-technology and information technology, particularly in relation to differentiation of the curriculum and the analysis and adaptation of published schemes.

To be effective, the new set of roles had to operate within a stated school policy, known to all members of staff who would be clear about the precise nature of their responsibilities and the specific kinds of help which the learning support staff could offer to management and to class and subject teachers.

This notion of a stated whole-school policy for pupils with learning difficulties known and accepted by all members of staff called for a new level of learning support teacher, trained in a range of consultancy skills, credible and able to hold their own in any school-wide discussion about curriculum, assessment, school management and organization with promoted teachers and members of staff from all departments. What in effect this has meant is that learning support staff have not restricted their attention to those pupils with the most severe difficulties, that their unique contribution has been seen as part of a joint responsibility with class and subject teachers, school management and in many cases local advisers. Where it is working well, learning support staff have become central to, though not in control of, curriculum development, assessment and the whole process of teaching and learning in the school. The selection and training of these teachers has produced cadres, committed 'to informed action aimed to transform'.

As such it is more about 'praxis' than 'practice', in the sense that at best it involves educational and social values and:

> . . . has at its roots, the commitment of the practitioner to wise and prudent action in a practical concrete historical situation (Carr and Kemmis, 1986, p. 190).

As these authors go on to say: 'Praxis is always risky' (Carr and Kemmis, 1986, p. 190.)

It requires judgments and involves values and commitment, in a situation where the reality of contemporary schooling does little to assure us that it is guided by educational values and it is not difficult to find sympathy with those who argue that major transformations of schooling are urgently needed. To reiterate, the recent developments in Scotland, more about 'praxis' than 'practice', could prove to be the first faltering footsteps towards such a transformation. It can only be hoped that this reform, like so many of the goods in Scottish education, will not be stifled. It is, in fact, emancipatory, providing a philosophy which could enlighten a profession increasingly aware of their double role as agents of change and agents of history.

> Praxis is inherently social and political: it embodies individually learned and socially constructed ideas of the good for human kind, expressing the understandings and values of the actor through action (Kemmis, 1987, p. 76).

It is worthwhile and also chastening to recall however, that Scottish 'reformers' have not traditionally been greatly honoured in their own country, as can be evidenced from the treatment of men like A.S. Neill, J. Aitkenhead and R.F. McKenzie.

Conclusion

New policies and practices are products of their history and educational reform has to be viewed as part of an ideologically-based historical process.

The changes in policy in Scotland for pupils with learning difficulties have to be evaluated in this way, the contradictions exposed and the dichotomies examined.

In the century or so since education has become compulsory, we have moved from 'exclusion' to 'reconnection', from 'backward' class to curriculum/learning support and can say that some progress has been made. The emphasis has moved from specialist provisions, compensatory strategies and 'Band Aid' (Elastoplast) solutions to what in effect has been a more fundamental appraisal of mainstream schools, their organization and curriculum. It is interesting to conjecture to what extent this is in line with the Scottish notion of the education of a 'people' as opposed to the development of the system as a means of advancement of the 'few', both aspects of Scottish educational philosophy and practice.

There is more consciousness that schools have not just responded to the inequalities in a divided society but have actually contributed towards these self-same inequalities. 'The Progress Report' at least made clear that the traditional child deficit model was unacceptable and that schools, their curriculum and organization had been a powerful factor in the creation of educational failure. It has become clear that the school experience of many pupils has been hopelessly unrewarding. In fact the system has buried them twice, once because they were labelled, categorized as different and special then taken out of normal education so that their life's chances were subverted by giving them an education which might have been different but certainly was not equal.

Maybe it is to the credit of the Scottish system, that there has been a fundamental shift in thinking. There has been official recognition at a national and regional level that despite quite a high level of political commitment, the comprehensive system has failed a substantial proportion of the school population. There has been a growing awareness of the need for reform and some commitment to seeing it through. All regional authorities for example have policies for pupils with learning difficulties and much support has been given to planned programmes of in-service training.

It is worth noting also that in a paper from McPherson and Williams (Edinburgh University) presented to the American Education Research Association (April 1987), it is reported that Scottish comprehensive schools have increasingly become more representative of the community as a whole. Social segregation, they claim, has eroded fastest in the cities where previously it was more marked. Examination results have improved and the gap in performance and achievement between working-class and middle-class children has been significantly reduced. The apparent success of comprehensive education in Scotland must raise questions in relation to the apparent lack of success in England. It is interesting to conjecture to what extent the new policies and provisions for pupils with learning difficulties are just another facet of a general democratic tendency or whether, in fact, they have been the sharp end of a rather blunt instrument of fundamental change.

It is ironic and contradictory that this has been able to co-exist with unprecedented intervention on the part of the UK Government, where we see moves towards greater control over curriculum and assessment, a more pervasive examination system, (albeit it claims to be more democratic) more control over local authority spending and an 'iron-heel' approach to teachers, particularly in evidence since the success of the Scottish teaching unions during the recent dispute. It is clear also that the government is setting about moving this particular centre of power through the new contracts designed to give more power to headteachers and governing bodies — an increasingly non-democratic form of management.

The question is how to evaluate such developments within a framework shaped by social and political forces. It can be argued that 'The Progress Report' does represent some of the better features of the Scottish tradition. The developments that have taken place since its publication do reflect concern for the well being of individual pupils but within a framework which does not label them as problems and where the responsibility for meeting their difficulties has been shifted to schools, their management, organization, curriculum and styles of teaching and learning; in fact to a model which calls for cooperation, collaboration and open debate about the process of developing and evaluating a curriculum for all.

One contradiction now is that the trend seems to be an increasing concern to see schools servicing the privatised profit-making structures that seem to be all that is going to be left of Scottish (and English) industry. The second contradiction is that schools also seem to be set up to suit the 'providers', concerned with career prospects, protectionism and professional boundaries. The ultimate irony here would be a learning difficulties industry privatised on the American model.

In such a political climate, the question is to what extent these new developments will flourish or even survive, for it is always difficult to divorce such particular 'instances' from what is happening in society at large. If these developments are to continue there are major issues to be resolved including the relationship between equality of opportunity, equality of outcome and notions of standards and excellence, and the relationship between all of these and an acceptance of social, cultural, linguistic and national diversity.

As Roy Hattersley says in *The Observer*, January 4, 1987:

> In the absence of economic expansion, greater equality is more
> necessary and more difficult. But even in the wholly propitious

conditions of continual increase of national income, the achievement of a more equal society requires specific action to achieve that end. Indeed the alleviation of the suffering which comes from relative poverty will not come about without a conscious determination to achieve greater equality. The equality we seek is equality of outcome, the State organized to reduce rather than to accentuate natural differences.

The argument often used against this is, of course, that striving for equality in this sense involves a levelling down. The Ford Foundation in the USA works to expand female and minority equality in these ways, through the programmes it finances, through the make-up of its own staff and through the leverage over the make-up of the staffs of grant recipients. The Foundation sees 'excellence and equity as having a relationship'. Achieving excellence, they claim, demands a broad spectrum of ideas. Excluding significant groups, e.g., one half of the total school population, deprives a school, an organization and a society of the ideas, culture and people that can make it perform at its best.

If our educational policies were to be, in fact, aimed for equality of outcome, then we should be more able to meet the diverse needs of pupils and we should be able to provide an appropriate, not 'average' curriculum, as 'The Progress Report' pointed out. If grading, selection, competitiveness, sorting and containment give way to cooperation, differentiation and diversity, then we should be beginning to move from the notion of the school as a place where failure is an inescapable concomitant. This is an emancipatory perspective which should involve an increase in the participation of teachers, pupils and parents in the school as a democratic community. This is not to be confused, however, with the kinds of parent power which have flowered in recent years, encouraged by the elitist stance of the UK government. As a recent writer in 'The Scotsman' points out in an article entitled 'Parent power or political ploy?',

> Not all parents are expected to exercise their power. If you are white, live in Ealing, and object to homosexual school books, go ahead. But if you are a Bradford Asian protesting against a headteacher you consider racist, you are an anti-democratic hooligan. . . The official emphasis on parental rights is at best a PR exercise and at worst a cynical attempt to mist over the real problem of education underfunding (December, 1986).

The development of the new policies in Scotland has called for an extension of the traditional role expectation of class and subject teachers and role release on the part of the learning support staff. Initially, this was the aspect which caused school staffs to feel anxious and threatened, but it is interesting that as 'remedial' staff have moved from the wings to a more central position prepared to play an integral but unique role as learning support staff, there has been a dawning realization that their 'expertise' was not about making a specialized contribution towards remedying learning difficulties, but was, in effect, about 'good' class and school organization, about flexible and creative teaching methods, and about the need for an appropriate differentiated curriculum better able to meet the diverse needs of all pupils through the development of alternatives, options and choices sensitive to the pupils' needs, culture and social background.

By some unexpected catharsis, the educational inheritance of Scotland, the national ideologies, contradictory as they are, have combined to produce a new emphasis in Scottish schools which challenges the widely accepted view which concentrated attention on the child and his or her characteristics as central to the 'problem' of learning difficulties. Rather, the emphasis has shifted to a close examination of the educational system and the political and social focus which shape and determine its structures. There seems to be some will and commitment to fundamental change of these structures in as much as they are reflected in schools and in how they are managed. It would be all too easy, however, to overstate the importance or success of such a change, radical as it appears to be. There is no doubt, however, that it has engaged teachers, trainers and administrators in a process of appraisal of schools, their curriculum, organization and management. In many respects the changes which have ensued do bear the imprint of the best of the Scottish tradition with its concern for the education of a people rather than a class. The ultimate irony would be to see this kind of development devalued, diminished or distorted by political action from UK government, traditionally unrepresentative of the Scottish electorate, unwilling or unable to recognize its uniquely Scottish character.

References

ANDERSON, R.D. (1983) 'Education and the State in 19th Century Scotland', in *Economic History Review,* second series, Vol. 36, pp. 518–34.

BARTON, L. and TOMLINSON, S. (Eds) (1984) *Special Education and Social Interests,* Beckenham, Croom Helm.

BOGDAN, R. and KUGELMASS, J. (1984) 'Case Studies of Mainstreaming: A Symbolic Interactionist Approach to Special Schooling', in BARTON, L. and TOMLINSON, S. (Eds) *Special Education and Social Interests,* Beckenham, Croom Helm.

BOYD-ORR, J. (1966) *As I Recall,* London, McGibbon and Kee.

CARR, W. and KEMMIS, S. (1986) *Becoming Critical. Education, Knowledge and Action Research,* Lewes, Falmer Press.

CRAFT, M. (Ed.) (1984) *Education and Cultural Pluralism*, Lewes, Falmer Press.

DAVIE, G. (1961) *The Democratic Intellect*, Edinburgh University Press.

GRAMPIAN REGIONAL COUNCIL (1976) *Report on Remedial Education*, Grampian Regional Council.

HATTERSLEY, R. (1987) *The Observer*.

HUMES, W.M. and PATTERSON, H. (Eds) (1983) *Scottish Culture and Scottish Education*, Edinburgh, John Donald.

KEMMIS, S. (1987) 'Critical Reflections' in WIDEEN, M.F. and ANDREWS, I. (Eds) *Staff Development for School Improvement: A Focus on the Teacher*, Lewes, Falmer Press.

KIRK, G. (Ed.) (1985) *Moray House and Professional Education*, Edinburgh, Scottish Academic Press.

LEONARD, T. (1984) *Intimate Voices: Selected Works 1965–83*, Galloping Dog Press.

OPEN UNIVERSITY (1979) *Special Needs in Education*, E241, Vol. 14, Milton Keynes, Open University Press.

PACK REPORT (1977) *Truancy and Indiscipline in Schools*, Edinburgh, HMSO.

PROGRESS REPORT (1978) *The Education of Pupils with Learning Difficulties in Primary and Secondary Schools in Scotland*, Cmnd, Scotland.

RENFREW DIVISION (STRATHCLYDE) (1976) *Remedial Education in Renfrew Division*, Strathclyde.

SARASON and DORIS (1979) *Educational Handicap, Public Policy and Social History*, New York, New York Free Press.

SMITH, A. (1776) *The Wealth of Nations*, Vol. 11, Everyman Edition.

SMOUT, T.C. (1986) *A Century of the Scottish People*, London, Collins.

TOMLINSON, S. (1986) 'The Expansion of Special Education' in COHEN, A. and COHEN, L. (Eds) *Special Educational Needs in the School*, London, Harper and Row.

WARNOCK REPORT (1978) *Special Educational Needs. Report of the Committee of Enquiry into the Education of Handicapped Children and Young People*, Cmnd 7212, London, HMSO.

Chapter 3

The Appearance and Reality of Change within Special Educational Needs

---

Alvin Jeffs

We trained hard, but it seemed that every time we were beginning to form up into teams, we were reorganized. I was to learn later in life that we tend to meet any new situation by reorganizing and a wonderful method it can be for creating the illusion of progress, while producing confusion, inefficiency and demoralization (Petronius Arbiter, 210 BC).

Introduction

It seems highly unlikely that Petronius Arbiter worked within the state education system of this country. It seems even less likely that he had any responsibility for whole-school responses to special educational need legislation and policy recommendations. However, many who do work within that context and have that responsibility will readily recognize the concern that he expressed.

In the wake of the Warnock Report, the Education Act of 1981 and the heightened awareness introduced by the Fish Report, considerable attention has been paid to this aspect of education. The degree to which such attention is facilitated by the roles of local authorities, senior management within schools and those teachers designated responsible for assisting and informing the necessary discussions will be the subject of this chapter.

April 1987 saw the implementation of Circular 6/86[1] and with it the synthesis of three strands of government thinking with regard to in-service training and special educational needs. INSET funding is now to be made available according to schools' perceived needs. The delivery of INSET has gained a sharper focus and training courses provided by institutions of HE are to be 'planned and managed by maintaining or assisting authorities within their allocation for locally assessed needs' (DES, 1986, p. 3). Finally, the INSET emphasis within mainstream schools continues to be placed upon the 'designated teacher' as recommended within national policy documents over the past four years.

It will be the purpose of this chapter to consider in a little detail the possible pitfalls within this approach. Both the ambiguous role of the LEA and the importance attached to the 'designated teacher' will be considered and the question of whether the late 1980s will be a period of structural change within special educational needs or simply one of 'reorganization' will never be far away.

It will be my contention that the gap between government recommendations and the implementation within schools is a wide one. The problems confronting individual teachers as change agents are well documented. The autonomy and, thus, diversity of schools makes change idiosyncratic and unpredictable, while the conservatism of educational institutions suggests that the change agent's initiatives are likely to be at best an uphill struggle, at worst a transient occurrence with little impact on the organizational structure and ethos of the school. Finally, I shall consider a number of features that appear to characterize effective organizational change. My feeling throughout this discussion is that effective policy arises from a clear examination of the *processes* of change and the nature of those forces that inhibit innovation. Unless such an analysis is built into LEA and school policy, lack of clarity will continue to produce ambiguous roles and the appearance only.

SEN INSET — The Hope and the Reality

While attempting to rationalize in-service training 'systematically so as to meet both national and local ... needs and priorities' (DES, 1986, p. 1), Circular 6/86 may well have created at least a short-term and possibly a long-term reduction within SEN INSET work.

There is every indication that both qualification courses and school-based experiential INSET could be reduced dramatically. The reasons for this are not hard to find:

(i)   with the disappearance of the national pooling system the overall sum of money available to many LEAs and, thus, to individual advisers and officers, is significantly less than before;

(ii) money allocated for the nineteen 'national priority areas' is now supported by a 70 per cent grant. This compares with the 90 per cent support under Circulars 3/83, 4/84 and 3/85[2] (those government circulars identifying national priority areas of in-service training). This, in turn, has already led to the demise of many full-time qualification courses provided by institutions of HE. Peter Mittler (TES 3.4.87), quoting a survey carried out by Manchester University across 21 LEAs, indicated a predicted reduction of 70 per cent in one-year full-time training secondments and a 77 per cent drop in SEN-related training overall;

(iii) few LEAs appear to have an INSET infrastructure in place to meet school-focused needs within the field of SEN. Indeed, there are many indications that the very factors that made Circular 3/83 necessary — the low priority attached to special educational needs work and ignorance of the legal and ethical implications — ensure that schools will not naturally develop a coherent and proactive policy within this area;

(iv) despite lengthy consultations between LEAs and schools prior to the new GRIST arrangements, it is questionable whether schools or LEAs have a coherent strategy for INSET provision, whole-school initiatives or differentiated professional development. The sharper focus necessary for the development of a specific dimension of education such as special needs is rarely reported by staff involved in special needs work and one must assume that the focus upon pupils, structures and curricular adaptations envisaged by the Warnock Committee and endorsed implicitly within the 1981 Education Act and 'Better Schools' is, by extension, frequently missing as well.

All of these concerns exist against a backdrop of even greater anxiety relating to an increased centralization of educational control, summed up by the chairman of the Association of County Councils:

> The question would then remain: 'Are LEAs worth keeping, even when financially reformed?' The proposals which have recently emerged piecemeal in press reports would answer the question thus —
>
> 'teachers should be paid by central government; schools should be self-run in an open market; higher education should be "nationalised", ergo, LEAs become redundant with — assumed — large consequent savings in "expensive bureaucracy".' The seductive attraction of such propositions lie in their simplistic nature (TES 20.2.87).

The danger of such propositions also lies in their self-fulfilling nature. The lack of dialogue between LEAs at the inception of the GRIST provision has so far ensured that forward planning at local level in many instances has hardly moved beyond that of damage limitation. Since that time DES and LEAs have continued to indicate very different perceptions of the situation with respect to both the level of funding and its efficacy. Whether or not the anxieties concerning the level of funding and LEA responsibility for developing coherent school-based INSET structures are justified, it is clear that the 'designated teacher' remains at the heart of government thinking 'as a follow-up to the Warnock Report and the 1981 Education Act' (DES, 1983, p. 2). The concept of the 'designated teacher' is at once persuasive and problematic. It is a concept that will bear some examination.

The Developing Concept of the 'Designated Teacher'

In 1967 the Plowden Report recommended 'the nomination of consultant teachers'. This was an interesting phrase in two respects. Firstly, the 'nomination' was separate from the award of graded posts laid down by the Burnham Committee in 1948 and indicated that such responsibilities could be unremunerated. Secondly, the word 'consultant' entered the educational vocabulary with its implication of advisory work rooted in expertise. This was a distinctly different role to the 'post-holder' envisaged by the Burnham Committee. The word has appeared regularly in other major reports, including 'A Language for Life', 'Bullock Revisited' and 'Teaching Quality'. The word 'co-ordinator' later replaces 'consultant' in documents such as the Cockcroft Report and 'Education 5–9'. The latter document indicates a range of responsibilities as basic to the co-ordinator's role:

(i) producing guidelines and schemes of work;
(ii) leading discussions;
(iii) organizing study groups;
(iv) disseminating work done on in-service courses;
(v) working alongside class teachers;
(vi) assembling and organising resources.

The pedigree of the 'consultant' and 'co-ordinator' is long and consistent. It is this concept that has now found its way into special educational needs work within schools following the 1981 Act:

> . . . Nearly all (teachers) will have pupils with special needs in their classes. The government, therefore, accepts the need for each . . . school . . . to call upon a teacher with specific responsibility for advising other members of staff and for those teachers to have some time free from teaching to enable them to carry out these duties (Better Schools, 1985, pp. 44–45).

Specifically, the government has identified the role of such a co-ordinator or 'designated' teacher:

(i) to identify and devise strategies to overcome impediments to pupils' learning

    (ii) to consider the implications for the school as a whole

   (iii) to implement forms of appropriate organisation for additional and supplementary help . . . (DES Circular 3/83).

Its commitment to this role is apparent within the circular (6/86) setting up the GRIST INSET arrangements, where 'training for designated teachers in ordinary schools' is one of the nineteen national priority areas. The only money released specifically to implement Warnock's recommendations and the subsequent legislation within schools is still firmly linked to the designated teacher role.

In considering the role of the designated teacher within schools and in looking at the reality of schools, teachers and resources, a number of clear issues arise:

     (i) The designation of a teacher can be a fiction in terms of creating a role that can never realistically be fulfilled. At both primary and secondary levels special educational needs provision is often an extra duty added to a full working week and other major responsibilities. My own study of primary designated teachers (Jeffs 1987 a) indicated that while 44 per cent of curriculum leaders had that leadership as their one major responsibility, only 25 per cent of SEN co-ordinators were in that position. Similarly, only 24 per cent of this SEN group had a written role description compared with 58 per cent of the curriculum leaders.

    (ii) The very designation can reduce the commitment to whole-school resolution of problems and policy. It is apparent within training courses set up for designated teachers that the difficulty of focusing the attention and commitment of senior management within schools is a matter of chance and likely to be successful only where that commitment provided the stimulus for the staff training in the first place.

   (iii) The problems of overload, time constraint and status mean that national good intentions — seeking effective change through individual designated teachers — produce well-trained individuals with little effectiveness within their own schools.

   (iv) The designation itself can be ambiguous. Designation to what? To 'specific responsibility for pupils with special educational needs' (Hodgson *et al.* 1984)? Or simply to receiving some form of in-service within the general field of special educational needs. The willingness of headteachers and LEAs to second teachers for further training can often be seen as the *de facto* implementation of a coherent policy. Too often it represents merely the staff development of one teacher.

Problems and Constraints for the Designated Teacher Role

The DES itself has recognized the potential limitations within the concept of designation and consultancy:

> Assigning a responsibility has no value in itself, unless the teacher to whom responsibility is assigned exercises a strong lead in planning and carrying out programmes (Schools Council, 1981, p. 29).

Such a reservation is realistic but fails to recognize a range of constraints implicit within the concept of chance through individual teachers.

Studies that have considered change within schools (Stockport LEA; Campbell, 1985) emphasize a range of factors that are likely to produce anxiety and constrain innovation:

(i) *Diversity*

A responsibility within one school may well involve a very different set of duties from that within the school next door. Within one school a post may have a written role specification; elsewhere it may be implicit; in a third setting it may be a matter of conjecture and ambiguity.

ii) *Management style*

The degree to which the headteacher or senior management team is involved and delegates is a crucial variable, as is the professional relationship between head, senior teachers and the designated teacher.

(iii) *Ambiguity*

This exists at two levels. There may be no clear agreement concerning the nature of a vague title such as 'designated teacher' or 'coordinator'. At secondary level this ambiguity frequently arises where a remedial teacher has taken on the responsibility for special educational needs throughout the school. Equally, many teachers find themselves nominated as 'consultant' to colleagues more senior than themselves.

(iv) *Commitment*

The creation of a post may well be in response to a local education authority request. It need not necessarily signify a whole-school commitment to developments within that post-holder's remit.

(v) *Size*

Especially within the primary sector, size of school is a very real constraint. The full-time teaching head experiences the full range of constraints, creating very real problems for innovation, regular liaison and in-service training.

Campbell (1985) points out that the literature has been 'a little ingenuous' in indicating that the nomination of a teacher and the development of a role specification meets the requirement of significant curriculum or whole-school change:

> ... teachers entering upon school-based development without an appreciation of its complexity are likely to experience unexpected difficulties and, in the long term, disillusionment with the process of development itself.

The ambiguity is further confounded when a consideration is made of the LEA interpretation of the phrase 'designated teacher' or 'SEN co-ordinator'. Two contrasting responses quoted by Jeffs (1987 a) highlight the discretionary nature of such role descriptions:

> One LEA contacted indicated an extensive range of duties (for the 'SEN coordinator'):
>
> (a) to provide tuition and support for children with special educational needs;
> (b) to provide a service for children with temporary learning or behavioural difficulties;
> (c) to act as consultant to staff involved with (a) or (b);
> (d) to design and evaluate an appropriate curriculum;
> (e) to offer advice on the suitability of books and other learning materials
> (f) to advise colleagues on appropriate learning activities for pupils with special educational needs;
> (g) to advise on the special needs of individual pupils;
> (h) to assist colleagues in developing learning and teaching strategies;
> (i) to help with reviews of courses, materials and programmes;
> (j) to liaise with colleagues, outside agencies and parents;
> (k) to be an advocate for pupils with special educational needs;
> (l) to have some familiarity with new technology,

while a second LEA responded thus:

> ... schools have not been asked to designate a member of staff to accept responsibilities within the field of special educational needs. We have, of course, asked schools to nominate the responsible person under the 1981 Education Act.

The title 'designated teacher' is one that encapsulates the potential problems, tensions and confusion of expectations that so easily arise from pressure for action in times of recession within such an ill-defined area of educational life as special educational needs.

However, DES circulars and reports do not see this as quite so problematic. Indeed, the designation is not only to the area of special educational needs but, quite clearly, to the role of internal change agent.

What is a Change Agent?

Havelock (1973) defines a change agent as 'a person who facilitates planned change and planned innovation'. This is not too far from the hopes expressed for the designated teacher within Circular 3/83. A change agent within Havelock's typology may have one or more of four roles:

Catalyst — 'Most of the time most people do not want change. For that reason some change agents are needed to overcome this inertia. They do not necessarily have the answers, but they are dissatisfied with things the way they are. By making their dissatisfaction known and upsetting the status quo, they energize the problem-solving process; they get things started.'

Solution Giver — 'Being an effective solution giver involves more than having a solution. You have to know when and how to offer it, and you have to know enough about it to help the client adapt it to his needs.'

Resource link — 'A large part of successful change is **ex**change. Hence problem-solving is in a large part a matter of matching resources in one person or group with the needs in another. Yet most of us have difficulty in asking for help and in giving help. This is why persons with special skills in communicating and relationship-building are important change agents.'

Process helper — 'The process helper can provide valuable assistance in showing the client how to:

recognize and define needs

diagnose problems and set objectives

acquire relevant resources

select and create solutions

adapt and install solutions

evaluate solutions to determine if they are satisfying his needs.'

This fourth role is distinctly similar to the role description provided by NARE (1985).

Similar frameworks have been put forward by Badley (1986) and others. Building on these frameworks, Badley (1986) indicates both the range of roles and the diversity of communication and interpersonal skills involved in the INSET training provided by TRIST. Badley concludes:

> In the real world of the school or college few teachers or heads of department possess all of the skills they need to act as agents or managers of change. The task involves both sharing success if there is success and accepting criticism if there is failure.

The problems implicit in the change agent concept within schools may be characterized thus:

> Dissemination depends on the capacity of large numbers of individual teachers and administrators to absorb and internalise changes of emphasis which together point the way towards modest, incremental change (Becher and Maclure, 1980).

The attractiveness of the concept of the internal change agent must be set alongside the very limited track record of such roles in organizations of both an educational and industrial nature. HMI (DES 1978 b) came to the sombre conclusion that only one in four primary curriculum post-holders had any noticeable effect on the quality of work within their schools. This anxiety is reflected in many works related to non-educational organizational theory:

> The change agent usually has a lesser degree of influence over his client (than might be expected) and, in many situations, no control at all (Marguiles and Wallace, 1973)

The consideration that arises from such anxieties is clear. Can the SEN designated teacher be seen as an agent for organizational change? Documented examples exist of effective organizational change arising through the medium of the designated teacher (Ellis, Jeffs and Smith, 1988; Conlon and Jeffs, 1988), but there is substantial anecdotal and some documentary evidence (Jeffs 1987 a) to suggest that the development of the designated teacher's work by schools and LEAs is far short of the expectations implicit in DES circulars.

It is possible to imagine Havelock's four types combining effectively, to see an identified member of staff, appropriately skilled within an area of pedagogy, inter-personal skills and with a well-developed support network beyond the school. It is possible to see such a practitioner acting as a catalyst, providing a range of solutions, bridging the gap between classroom needs and provisions and facilitating open and structured discussion between staff, support services and parents. However, it is more common to see a resource link, with frequently undeveloped or unused skills in areas relating to the facilitation of discussion and decision-making.

Havelock's typology contains some very real tensions. Those committed to work with pupils experiencing learning difficulties are rarely trained in or expected to become involved in the processes and decisions that relate to full-scale policy change within schools. Once again, it seems inevitable that a contractual obligation on the part of the school should accompany the training of a member of staff identified for the SEN 'designated teacher' role. Without this the training remains a traditional reward or enrichment activity only.

Institutions as Change Agents

A second form of change agent is presented by the external consultant model being adopted by many institutions of HE. This model differs significantly from that of the designated teachers and deserves separate consideration.

The industrial model of the change agent is very much that of the consultant-catalyst, coming in from outside to help things happen. The agent here is a combination of Havelock's 'catalyst' and 'process helper' roles. Within school-focused INSET this concept has already received close attention. Early projects (Nuffield Science and the Schools Council Humanities Project are cases in point) involved such a role and some of the more recent Low Attainers Projects might be seen in a similar light. While many such projects contributed permanently to schools and their curricula, a number of reservations have been voiced with regard to the effectiveness of the consultant role (Macdonald and Walker 1976). The change agent from outside tends to:

> provide too strong a focus on materials and not enough on the new social patterns involved;
> be more concerned with pedagogical processes than the change processes themselves;
> be well acquainted with the project materials and techniques, but at a theoretical level;
> be more involved with implementation and evaluation than sustaining a project;
> be more involved with content and outcomes than processes;
> provide a legitimacy to the project which often deskills those teachers who find change difficult;
> work within a different educational milieu to the teachers involved in implementation.

For the outside change agent it would seem that an awareness of the mechanisms and implications of change is as important as — and possibly more important than — the content of the project itself. Hoyle (1971) in an excellent critique of the change agent role provides a detailed analysis of why such outside agents might fail. Taking the typology developed by Chin (1968), Hoyle emphasizes that some strategies are more relevant than others in the attainment of long-term change within schools. The 'power-coercive' strategy — relying heavily upon authority and hierarchical considerations — is taken as a strategy of last resort. The 'rational-empirical' approach, appealing to the mind of the participants and relating closely to proven research findings and practical examples, carries conviction and typifies many traditional projects. However, it is perhaps the 'normative – re-educative' strategy — seeking to change attitudes through interaction and persuasion — that is highlighted as the strategy with the greatest potential for real and long-lasting change. Crouch (1985) outlines a brief programme of this type, developed by an institution of HE. Opportunity was provided for a school staff group to meet and discuss curriculum matters with an observer present. The emphasis throughout was completely upon the group dynamics and the processes of negotiating change rather than in the organizational routes and content of any specific innovation. The novelty of full participation in decision-making is emphasized by the author:

> For many the idea of redefining identity to include the curriculum-maker role may be as threatening as the behaviour of the pupils (Crouch, 1985).

There are strong indications that an awareness of the processes of change, the interpersonal skills involved and the requisite self-analysis techniques will constitute a large element of any change agent's repertoire of skills. As schools, LEAs and institutions of HE move into an era of predominantly school-focused INSET, such tools of the trade will require as much attention as the issues of identification, assessment and curriculum modification.

The Realities of Change within Schools

Whether the change agent role is taken by a designated member of staff or by an outsider, there needs to be a clear understanding of some of the factors relating to change and innovation within schools. Esland (1972) indicated four major factors that militated against change if they were not articulated and addressed at the outset:

change involves social interaction
change is a process

change disturbs the status quo

change is subject of individual perceptions

Therefore, initially, change is a threat to most participants, frequently presenting more barriers than opportunities to those involved.

Change involves social interaction — any form of change or innovation must alter the balance of relationships and structures within a school, in the same way that a new child alters the dynamics of the most harmonious of families. While attention to the range of interpersonal skills relevant to work settings (Argyle, 1967; Turner, 1982; Hargie, Saunders and Dickson, 1981) may seem abstruse to some and over-elaborate to others, the awareness of what contributes to the existing balance and network of relationships is a vital pre-requisite to considering and accepting new relationships and a new balance.

Change is a process/Change disturbs the status quo — very few innovations involve simply the substitution of one set of materials, methods or procedures for another. Innovations such as in-class support can be readily seen as new processes requiring adaptation. Even basic innovations such as different referral procedures are likely to necessitate subtle changes in the working week and slight alterations to both professional and personal relationships within schools if the change is to take root and become long-term.

Change is subject to individual perceptions — any group of people involved in change will bring to the process not only different value systems — these are possibly easier to deal with — but also differing perspectives and even understandings of the initiative. These in turn will create different expectations. When this consideration is widened to include the expectations and understandings of LEAs, governors, parents and pupils, the range of values and perceptions becomes dramatic. Gross *et al.* (1971) contends that:

> The following assumption made by many administrators needs to be challenged: when an innovation is introduced into a school and teachers are willing to make efforts to carry the change out, it will then be implemented . . . Enthusiasm for an innovation on the part of the staff is not enough to ensure its implementation.

For those who see schools as 'open systems' (Katz and Kahn, 1966), always seeking 'homeostatis' — the biological stability arising from feedback and adaptation to change — the problems of boundary management and internal resource distribution are readily apparent where change is considered. Any school that has experienced the introduction of mixed-ability teaching, in-class support or teacher support from external support services will know that it is not merely a substitution of one set of books by another. In the light of such considerations, the expectation that one designated member of staff can introduce the mechanisms that will allow appropriate identification of pupils with special educational needs, their assessment and relevant curricular responses throughout the school requires a high degree of optimism.

To envisage enough structural change to make whole-school consultation and decisions possible where such things did not exist before requires faith rather than mere optimism. Many of the barriers indicated previously stem from five characteristics identified as related to schools-based change (Hoyle, 1972 and 1986):

(i) the diffuseness of educational goals (academic, socialising and expressive);
(ii) the high degree of authority possessed by the headteacher;
(iii) the control of both goal-setting and school administration residing with that headteacher;
(iv) the low degree of integration amongst teachers;
(v) the privacy and isolation in which most teachers work.

The failure of much training related to designated teachers and curriculum leaders may be seen to lie in the failure to address these five characteristics. Indeed, the danger inherent in any future INSET framework is that these factors may become the very basis for school-focused in-service work.

While school-based INSET may well develop a greater emphasis upon practical curricular provision, this is no guarantee that the boundaries between departments, levels of management within schools or between teachers themselves will be removed. Indeed, with a national curriculum clearly built upon identifiable subject areas and occupying 70 to 90 per cent of the timetable, such boundaries are likely to increase rather than wither away. The reluctance on the part of most headteachers to develop a comprehensive and sytematic staff development policy together with the failure of many LEAs to link INSET funding to contractually agreed and evaluated outcomes forms a powerful combination militating against the sort of coherent structural change envisaged by both the Warnock Committee and the Fish Report. Equally, the unfamiliarity of teamwork within many schools means that any blueprint for change needs to attend to processes rather than content from the outset if any development that touches the full staff is to occur. Finally, the relative isolation of most teachers forms a significant barrier to change and often limits a trained designated teacher to small cooperative ventures rather than full-scale innovatory projects. These factors are strong determinants of the scale of innovation.

The Ingredients of Effective Change within Schools

The present reliance upon the designated teacher as the agent or catalyst of change is at best a gamble and possibly totally misguided in the light of educational management theory and recent experience of national, local and school responses to Warnock, the 1981 Act and the Fish Report. However, enough effective whole-school change has taken place with reference to special educational needs to allow consideration of those strategies and processes most likely to allow this to take place. To begin to consider the conditions most likely to facilitate structural change within schools, it is necessary to consider national as well as local changes.

The national dimension

Galloway (1985) stresses the limited guidance provided by both the legislation and within DES policy pronouncements with regard to special educational needs. He correctly concludes that 'HMI's scope for encouraging innovation is inevitably restricted'. However, he continues:

> The inspectorate's influence through informal visits, through its periodic surveys and through its formal inspections both of LEAs and of individual schools, should not . . . be underestimated.

How much easier such influence would be if HMI were working against the background of INSET funding that was both appropriate and linked to full school initiatives. Four elements of DES and HMI involvement that would immediately produce results are:

(i) the return of the training grant support to 90 per cent for national priority areas;

(ii) the linking of such funds to clearer and more practical criteria than those inherited from Circular 3/83. These might include the recommendation that INSET monies from the national priority area 3 be utilized where schools indicated clear and proactive policies following some form of organisational analysis;

(iii) the use of detailed criteria relating to LEA whole-school advisory policies within the *aide mémoires* of HMI involved in LEA inspections;

(iv) the requirement that local HMIs be closely involved in both the initial analysis and evaluation of such initiatives. The effectiveness of a close LEA–HMI association within this field is highlighted by Booth (Booth and Potts, 1983, p. 55) in the Scottish context.

The LEA dimension

As at school level, the crucial elements within LEA policies are those related to a coherent strategy for advice and support, secondment, INSET finance and availability of informed staff trained in the teamwork and interpersonal skills implicit in whole-school changes. Having access to funds earmarked still for designated teachers, there seems no reason why LEAs should not increase the degree of contractual obligation within the INSET arrangements. Whether such arrangements involve secondment, joint school-IHE INSET or purely internal school-focused INSET would depend very much upon the needs identified and developments projected by the organizational analysis already referred to. There are many instances at individual school and LEA levels where the effort involved in organizational reviews have been supported by specific INSET allocations, the increased availability of support services and the negotiated involvement of IHE personnel in a catalytic or evaluative capacity.

Such worthy intentions presume two fundamental, but by no means certain, factors:

(i) LEAs need to continue as a major part of the British educational scene. Despite many reservations concerning the effect of LEAs upon their constituent schools, many would agree with Merridale: 'Effective responses must, surely, best come from those who live in the midst of those they serve, and whose mandate they must seek. The chairman of the LEA is always only one telephone call away from a problem'.

(ii) LEAs need to present to the schools they advise a good role model in their own ability to work as a team, in an integrated way, taking the advice of their own special educational needs consultants, who — as in the school context — may not be the most senior member of the team.

The school dimension

Kogan (1983) indicates in general terms the model that schools of the 1980s might present to the communities they serve:

They will not be impervious to the demands from outside the school itself and be responsive to social need. They will demonstrate that complicated systems can work cohesively. They will demonstrate that whole-school policies can be formed. They will also show, and how badly needed this is, that due process rather than emotive mass movement and reflex action are the ways in which we can live together.

There is a growing body of experience and example that indicates the constituent elements of any effective whole-school policy. Within a single chapter little more than a list with further reference can be made, but action and effective action can be planned and — as is so often the case — expense need not be a factor and time need only be a consideration while the school needs and new procedures are hammered out. Significant structural change seems within the context of equal opportunities and special educational needs is frequently characterized by

(i) *an organizational review* — the work carried out within the GRIDS framework (McMahon, Bolam, Abbott and Holly, 1984 and 1984 a) has been both detailed and practical. While the literature and processes do not specifically revolve around special educational needs, they do allow the sort of consultative process to take place that allows this dimension full consideration. In its 'Survey of staff opinion' it provides any head, staff management group or quite simply the staff as a whole, with a useful checklist with regard to the health of the institution.

If LEA, head or designated teacher wishes to place structural change upon the school's agenda the employment of such a consultative framework is as good a starting point as any.

(ii) *staff development policy* — the need for and the considerations involved in a coherent policy that seeks to provide realistic and differentiated staff development within the field of special educational needs has been addressed elsewhere (Jeffs, 1987 b). Many examples and frameworks exist to guide staff and heads who seek to consider both the personal and professional development of their staff (Oldroyd, Smith and Lee, 1984).

(iii) *development of teamwork skills* — mention has already been made of the concern felt by many that within training and daily practice teachers are not familiar with the reality of their own roles within working groups and, by extension, the potential for effective change and decision-making within themselves and school-based groups. It is possibly in this sphere that the external consultant has something of value to offer.

(iv) *differentiated responsibilities* — one of the pressures upon any teacher designated with responsibility for any educational matter that has whole-school implications is that of role overload. Too often a designation can be a delegation of responsibility in a very negative way. It is implicit within this chapter that responsibility for special educational needs is universal in its attention to equality of opportunity and access, but quite specific in two — possibly distinct — areas. At primary, secondary and further education levels there is a pragmatic division to be made between the accountability for provision and policy (often residing in head at primary level; often with deputy-head at secondary) and the responsibility for day-to-day provision. It is this differentiation that goes some way to ensure that special educational needs is an issue permeating policy decisions and deliberations at senior management level and also everyday discussions between staff within faculties, departments and staffrooms.

(v) *whole school processes* — if the situational analysis, the staff development implications and the division of responsibility has been considered in detail, the climate should be appropriate for frank discussion of resource and procedural changes necessary for the more effective meeting of specific needs. Often the consultative processes are already in place as the result of previous curricular initiatives (Conlon and Jeffs, 1988). In many cases the constitution of the initial working group is crucial (Giles and Dunlop, 1986). Traditionally — and within many of the designated teacher initiatives — secondment has introduced investigations and fact-finding procedures that initiate full staff participation (Thomas and Jackson, 1986).

(vi) *effective boundary management* — few changes will ever occur in isolation. As has already been suggested, the school functioning as an 'open' system must consider and manage its relationships with a range of external factors. The importance of preparation within integration initiatives has been attested to frequently (Hegarty and Pocklington, 1981 and 1982; Galloway, 1985). The preparation of parents, support services and other institutions is one small aspect of the balance necessary if school-based innovation is not to create imbalance. The Warnock term 'parents as partners' and the 'cluster' concept within the Fish Report both affirm the fact that schools — like any other organization or group of people — function within a web of personal and professional relationships.

These considerations are very real if change is to be initiated by schools rather than be sold to them. Hoyle (1986), having considered the possibility of professionally developed teachers relating more closely to school developments, concludes:

> There are signs that this is occurring as teachers and heads together are confronting the purposes of the school, the skills and resources

needed to achieve these purposes, and how the attainment of these purposes might be evaluated by the school itself.

The designated teacher and change

The concern underlying the whole of this chapter has been the fear that the national strategy for effecting change within the sphere of special educational needs has been rooted in a number of misconceptions. It relies upon attitudes and personalities at LEA, headteacher and designated teacher level. It is a recipe for patchy and very limited change. The more one considers the problems of educational change and the nature of schools and teaching, the more the individual catalyst sinks in a welter of perceptions, expectation and interests. INSET, whether school- or institution-based can have only a marginal effect in this context. However, when attention is paid to the larger issues of an institution's internal health and external relationships, the designated teacher takes on a role that is akin to a realistic change agent. If that person works within a setting that monitors itself, prepares adequately for change and secures consent to those changes that affect the organization as a whole, the designated teacher is less likely to be asked to fulfil the role of solution-giver and more likely to be asked to add the role of process-helper to that of resource-link. Within that setting the designated teacher has an agreed and negotiated role that relates both to the management structure of the school and that person's own professional stage of development. It is in that context that the 'consultant' can listen and advise, the 'co-ordinator' co-ordinate and the 'designated teacher' carry out their agreed remit. It is in that context that the role specifications indicated earlier have meaning. 'What the consultant does not do is to set out to change everything or tell (staff) to do their job differently' (Hanko, 1985).

Conclusion

The fears of many following the 1981 Education Act have been fully realized in some instances. The 'illusion of progress' has produced in full measure 'confusion, inefficiency and demoralisation'. Labels have changed, empires have been renamed and tenuous consultative procedures held up as partnership. In such settings those teachers designated for training and given responsibility for the range of special educational needs within a school have laboured long, but to little avail.

In many other instances, however, the implication of the past eight years has been grasped and planned change has taken place from a baseline of full staff consultation. INSET at LEA and school level has related to the professional needs of staff and strengthened by contractual arrangements. Increasingly, the examples and frameworks of school reviews, individual staff development and whole-school consultation have been tried and found useful.

At a time when the possibility of increased centralization of educational control is rapidly becoming a certainty, it would be a pity if the lessons of such institutions did not help to provide the basis for national guidance with regard to LEA policy towards grant-aided INSET.

Perhaps, had Petronius Arbiter and his colleagues been guided rather than reorganized, they might well have made real progress.

Notes

1 Circular 6/86 was issued in August 1986 and outlines the grants to be made to LEAs for in-service work. The important departure is that of relating all INSET work to the government grant (i.e., no longer is an LEA able to subsidize its INSET work through drawing upon the national 'pool'). Within 6/86 nineteen areas of education are identified for more favourable treatment, the government providing 70 per cent of course costs. Special educational needs within schools is one such 'national priority area'. As 'grant related in-service training', this arrangement is known as 'GRIST'.
2 Circulars 3/83, 4/84 and 3/85 were the predecessors of 6/86. For the period 1983–86, 'national priority areas' were similarly identified and special educational needs in ordinary schools was one such area. These circulars provided for 90 per cent of course costs and ran alongside the 'pooling' system.

References

ARGYLE, M. (1967) *The Psychology of Interpersonal Behaviour*, Harmondsworth, Penguin.
BADLEY, G. (1986) 'The teacher as change agent' *British Journal of In-Service Education*, vol. 12, no. 3, pp. 151–158.
BECHER, T. and MACLURE, S. (1980) *The Politics of Curriculum Change*, London, Hutchinson.
BOLAM, R. (1982) *School-Focused In-Service Training*, London, Heinemann.
BOOTH, T. and POTTS, P. (1983) *Integrating Special Education*, Oxford, Blackwell.
CAMPBELL, R.J. (1985) *Developing the Primary School Curriculum*, East Sussex, Holt, Rinehart & Winston.
CHIN, R. (1968) 'Basic strategies and procedures in effecting change', in MORPHET, E.L. and RYAN, C.O., *Designing Education for the Future No. 3*, Citation Press.
CONLON, J. and JEFFS, A. (1988) 'Sydenham — the whole-school approach to special educational needs', in MOSES, D. and HEGARTY, S., *Developing Expertise: INSET for Special Educational Needs*, Windsor, NFER-Nelson.

CROUCH, C. (1985) 'Curriculum development as process: an approach for INSET programmes', *British Journal of In-Service Education*, vol. 11, no. 3, Spring 1985, pp. 156–159.

DES (1972) *Children and Their Primary Schools (The Plowden Report)*, London, HMSO.

DES (1976) *A Language for Life (The Bullock Report)*, London, HMSO.

DES (1978 a) *Special Educational Needs (The Warnock Report)*, London, HMSO.

DES (1978 b) *Primary Education in England*, London, HMSO.

DES (1981) *Elizabeth II Ch. 60, Education Act*, London, HMSO.

DES (1982 a) *Bullock Revisited*, London, HMSO.

DES (1982 b) *Maths counts (The Cockcroft Report)*, London, HMSO.

DES (1982 c) *Education 5–9*, London, HMSO.

DES (1983–86) *Circulars 3/83, 4/84, 3/85 and 6/86*, London, HMSO.

DES (1983) *Teaching Quality*, London, HMSO.

DES (1985) *Better Schools*, London, HMSO.

ELLIS, V. JEFFS, A. and SMITH, M. (1988) 'Completing the whole-school jigsaw at Trinity', in HEGARTY, S. and MOSES, D. *Developing Expertise: INSET for Special Educational Needs*, Windsor, NFER-Nelson.

ESLAND, G.M. (1972) Innovation in the School, in *Innovation and Ideology*, Milton Keynes, Open University Press.

GALLOWAY, D. (1985) *Schools, Pupils and Special Educational Needs*, Beckenham, Croom Helm.

GILES, C. and DUNLOP, S. (1986) 'Changing direction at Tile Hill Wood', *British Journal of pecial Education*, vol. 13, no. 3, pp. 120–123.

GROSS, N., GIACQUINTA, J.B. and BERNSTEIN, M. (1971) *Implementing Organisational Innovations*, New York, Harper and Row.

HANKO, G. (1985) *Special Needs in the Ordinary Classroom*, Oxford, Blackwell.

HARGIE, O., SAUNDERS, C. and DICKSON, D. (1981) *Social Skills in Interpersonal Communication*, Beckenham, Croom Helm.

HAVELOCK, R.G. (1973) *The change agent's guide to innovation in education*, Prentice-Hall, Englewood Cliffs, New Jersey.

HEGARTY, S. and POCKLINGTON, K. (1981) *Educating Pupils with Special Educational Needs in Ordinary Schools*, Windsor, NFER-Nelson.

HEGARTY, S., POCKLINGTON, K. and LUCAS, D. (1982) *Integration in Action*, Windsor, NFER-Nelson.

HODGSON, A. et al. (1984) *Learning Together*, Windsor, NFER-Nelson.

HOYLE, E. (1971) 'The role of the change agent in educational innovation' in WALTON, J. (Ed.) *Curriculum Organization and Design*, London, Ward Lock.

HOYLE, E. (1972) *Facing the Difficulties in Problems of Curriculum Innovation I*, Milton Keynes, Open University Press.

HOYLE, E. (1986) *The Politics of School Management*, Sevenoaks, Hodder and Stoughton.

Inner London Education Authority (1985) *Educational Opportunities for All?*, London, ILEA.

JEFFS, A. (1987 a) *The Role of the 'Designated Teacher' in Primary Schools*, Bristol Polytechnic.

JEFFS, A. (1987 b) 'Approaches to staff development', in BOWERS, T. *Special Educational Needs and Human Resource Management*, Beckenham, Croom Helm.

KATZ, D. and KAHN, R. (1966) *The Social Psychology of Organizations*, New York, John Wiley.

KOGAN, M. (1983) 'Holding the middle ground: the school as a responsive institution', in GALTON, M. and MOON, B. (Eds) *Changing Schools . . . Changing Curriculum*, New York, Harper and Row.

MACDONALD, B. and WALKER, R. (1976) *Changing the Curriculum*, London, Open Books.

MARGUILES, N. and WALLACE, J. (1973) *Organized Change*, London, Longman.

MERRIDALE, P. (1987) *The Power and the Accountability*, Times Educational Supplement, 20.2.87.

NATIONAL ASSOCIATION OF REMEDIAL EDUCATION (1985) *Guidelines 6: Teaching Roles for Special Educational Needs*, Stafford, NARE Publications.

OOLDROYD, D., SMITH, K. and LEE, J. (1984) *School-based Staff Development Activities*, Harlow, Longmans for Schools Council.

SCHOOLS COUNCIL (1981) *The Practical Curriculum*, London, Methuen.

SPENCER, D. (1987) *In-service 'Threat' to Full-time Study*, Times Educational Supplement, 3.4.87.

STOCKPORT LEA *Specialism in the Primary School*, Metropolitan Borough of Stockport (Education Division).

THOMAS, G. and JACKSON, B. (1986) 'The whole-school approach to integration', *British Journal of Special Education*, vol. 13, no. 1, pp. 27–29.

TURNER, C. (1982) *Developing Interpersonal Skills*, Blagdon FE Staff College.

MCMAHON, A., BOLAM, R., ABBOTT, R. and HOLLY, P. (1984 a) *Guideline for Review and Internal Development in Schools. Primary School Handbook*, York, Longman for Schools Council.

(1984 b) *Guideline for Review and Internal Development in Schools, Secondary School Handbook*. York, Longman for Schools Council.

Chapter 4

Research Practice: The Need for Alternative Perspectives

Len Barton

Introduction

In a book entitled *Research and Evaluation Methods in Special Education* (Hegarty and Evans, 1985), all the contributors support the demand for the necessity of developing new approaches in research for encouraging change. Part of the reason given is the dominance of psychological ideas which have led to the centrality of quantitative methodologies.

The book contains a section on qualitative research, in which the case for investigations of this kind is strongly made. This chapter seeks to support these demands and examines some of the issues in relation to teacher education and research undertaken by students on initial and in-service courses. Further support is drawn from developments within the teacher-as-researcher movement.

Research: Some Initial Observations

In investigations of human behaviour and experience, people are both the medium through which the research is conducted and the subjects of study. Research is conducted at particular historical moments, within specific material circumstances and is a profoundly social act Denzin (1978). However, this fundamental aspect tends to be underplayed in some of the literature dealing with research methods. Concern over instruments of measurement, the precision of scientific language, the question of theory, tend, for example, to obfuscate questions about the relationship of ideology and politics to the research process.

An important paper by Brian Simon (1980) dealing with the issue of the historic relations between research and policy-makers, supports the view that psychometric theory has been the dominant orthodoxy within our educational system generally and in research in particular. He maintains that there is an important link between such research and the demands resulting from the need to administer the public system of education. Discussing the demand which Cyril Burt articulated in the 1920s, for the testing of children's abilities, Simon maintains that:

> This demand provided an important impetus for the development of the whole sophisticated technology of testing of this time and for the application of psychometric testing. So research was turned to providing the principles, and the practical means, required to perpetuate that system.
>
> Once again, then we find educational research, now assuming a modern, 'scientific' form, subsordinated to policy, to the decisions of the policy makers (p. 17).

In a discussion of this nature, we must not therefore underestimate the extent to which, historically, this dominant orthodoxy has supported a narrow interpretation of what counts as legitimate research. This includes what constitutes an appropriate topic of inquiry, the sorts of questions to be examined, the methodology to be employed and the interpretations offered.

I have argued elsewhere (Barton and Tomlinson, 1981) that research directed towards documenting the extent and types of handicap or special needs, as well as the range and effectiveness of service provisions, has featured prominantly throughout the history of research in the United Kingdom. Also, according to Bogdan and Taylor (1982), in the United States, the predominant mode of research has been one in which the causes and consequences of 'mental retardation' have been the focal topics of interest. This has led to the formulation of the following types of research questions;

— what causes 'mental retardation'?
— how many people are 'retarded'
— how can 'mental retardation' be treated?

A number of reasons can be offered about the predominance of this type of approach. They include the dominance of the clinical perspective, the belief that knowledge derived from such research is relatively easily acquired, that the findings appear to have tangible policy and educational implications particularly as they related to the administrative needs of the system, and the fact that this type of research is relatively cheap (Bernstein, 1975).

However, it is not being argued that this form of research is of no value, nor is the intention merely to resurrect polar extremes of studies. That only leads to a counterproductive and sterile debate, which is about as fruitful as Wragg (1984) suggests, attempting to decide whether bacon and eggs beats fish and chips. What is of importance as far as this chapter is concerned, are the difficulties involved in establishing alternative forms of research, influenced by different assumptions and priorities.

The critique offered by Simon is still a timely one because it attempts to challenge the dominant assumptions relating to the position of the researcher, the nature of theory and the purpose of research. He both raises the question of the politics of research and articulates the demand for alternative ways of thinking and working. These problematics are reinforced when consideration is given to the extent to which research findings of educational studies actually contribute towards developing the ideologies and practice of teachers.

Teacher Education

An established tradition within the literature dealing with teacher education is that of examining the relationship between theory and practice. A crucial proposition that emerges from this work is that of the existence of a discontinuity between training and the realities of teaching (Waller, 1932; Musgrove and Taylor, 1969; Lacey, 1977). For example, McIntyre (1980) claims that although reasonable arguments can be offered to support the inclusion of social science courses within teacher education, yet

> . . . it is now clear that the claim of direct relevance or applicability to teaching is not valid for any such course not based firmly on the findings of classroom research (p. 294).

His conclusion is that of the impossibility of '*any* systematic corpus of theoretical knowledge from which prescriptive principles for teaching can be generated' (p. 296). Students are often suspicious and uneasy over the connection between how and what they are taught and the realities of school life. Research questions, it has been argued, are viewed as being too remote from schools and classrooms. Researchers are alleged to be exploiting schools for their own purposes with little if any return for the teachers. Finally, the language in which research literature is couched is often described as incomprehensible (Burgess, 1980).

In an article entitled 'The reform of teacher education through research: A futile quest', Tom (1980) argues that research cannot solve the problems of teachers because:

> . . . any regularities identified through study of the teaching–learning process are limited in generality and likely to shift over time (p. 25).

Other commentators such as Floden (1985) and Elliott (1980) reinforce this type of criticism by maintaining that research-based teacher training — process-product model — is based upon an overly narrow view of education. Accepting the conclusions researchers draw involves accepting their narrow definition without considering alternative ones.

From a variety of sources therefore, criticisms and doubts are being expressed over important issues including:

1. The nature and relevance of educational theory
2. The context in which theory is constructed
3. The purpose for which it is used
4. The nature or style in which theory is presented

Without underestimating the importance of these criticisms, it is also essential to appreciate that many working within these disciplines are themselves extremely critical of the current 'state of the art' and are calling for crucial changes. For example, Peter Woods (1985) argues that:

> . . . sociologists in the main continue to address other sociologists and to contribute to sociology. We have hardly begun to think about how we might communicate the 'sociological perspective' to teachers within a pedagogical discourse (p. 53).

Underpinning this anxiety is a belief that sociology of education[1] on the whole, has not served teachers well.

Of course, this can be seen as a case of special pleading and the extent to which these efforts will cause a radical rethink about the nature of the 'sociological imagination', that will involve a reformation of the relationship between teachers/student-teachers and sociologists working within education, has yet to be demonstrated. It is, however, these very issues that we are strongly committed to, which inevitably involve us in a process of critique and self-critique.

Perspectives on teacher education contain a number of pre-suppositions about what constitutes a proper learning experience, what is the relationship between teacher and taught, what is a good practice, and what is the relationship between individuals and curriculum knowledge. In a series of papers relating to their research on teaching students in the United States, Zeichner (1981–82; 1983; 1986) and Zeichner and Teitelbaum (1982) contend that a consistent finding of research with regard to students on teacher-education courses, is that of a concern with survival. Students approach their course with strong pragmatic interest — 'Does it work or solve the immediate problem at hand?' Their own research explored the students' developing beliefs about teaching and themselves as teachers. They also examined how students acted in the student-teaching roles in the classroom. In a sympathetic analysis (1982) they suggest that:

> Pressures to receive favourable evaluations from cooperating teachers and university supervisors and student concerns about 'getting a job' are just a few of the forces that make a utilitarian perspective understandable (p. 97).

However, they are nevertheless critical, particularly of the impact of behaviourism on pedagogy, which has resulted for them in an unacceptable emphasis being given to *how* questions, including related technical questions of efficiency. In this learning encounter students are essentially viewed as *passive* recipients of professional knowledge.

In contrast, they advocate an *inquiry-oriented* approach in which more emphasis is given to considering *why* questions. Their perspective is premised on the belief that Tom (1980) has captured in his statement in which he claims:

> The effective teacher, therefore, is not the one who has been programmed with theory-based answers to many discrete teaching situations but instead is one who is able to conceive of his teaching in purposeful terms, can size up a particular teaching situation, choose a teaching approach that seems appropriate to the situation, attempt the approach, judge the results in relation to the original purposes and reconsider the original purposes (p. 25).

The preoccupation with utilitarian concerns on the part of students is also claimed to be a feature of student ideology in this country (Lacey, 1977; Denscombe, 1982 and 1985). An emphasis on pre-packaged theories about children, teaching and learning, which students are then expected to apply in their teaching is, as Cave and Madison (1978) point out, particularly applicable to special education. This results in rigid frameworks for understanding and analysing classroom processes.

What sorts of images does involvement by students in this form of pedagogy encourage? A number of possibilities can be identified, including:

1. Theory is that which is created by professional academics and researchers.
2. Teachers therefore need to use the language of theorists both to define problems and understand solutions.
3. Teachers think but they do not think critically.
4. Teachers think but it is low-level thinking.
5. Teachers undertake personal inquiries within their classrooms but these do not constitute proper research (Lampert, 1984).

Thus, the point of contention is not merely as Wragg (1982) argues, that given the nature of teaching it is over-optimistic to hope that many decisions made by teachers will be based on current research findings, but rather, it is the celebration of a crucial mental-manual distinction within this whole debate about theory and practice. This is the distinguishing mark between researchers and teachers.

However, theory is not something that is the particular property of science. People in their daily interactions construct, test and modify theories in order to function (Hammersley and Atkinson, 1983). Thus, teachers theorise, it is an activity they are constantly engaged in as Alexander (1984) so cogently notes:

> Thus the missing ingredient in the traditional theory-practice analysis is acknowledgment of the extent to which teachers themselves theorise independently of the theories created for their use by academics. Teaching in fact is intensely theoretical: it involves deliberate thought and is grounded in assumptions about children, learning and knowledge and so on (p. 147).

It is particularly important to reinforce this perspective of teaching in relationship to special education. Historically, this has often been viewed as 'low-level work' or 'child-minding'. So, it is not now a question of whether teachers theorise but the *status* of their theoretical work.

By positing the issues in the way that I have, it must not be assumed that one is claiming that there is no value at all in research or academic theory. This would be quite misleading for as Alexander (1984) maintains:

> . . . academic theory is neither irrelevant nor unused . . . (and) . . . filters in and out of everyday professional thought and discourse in an elusive manner (147).

Nor does this acknowledgment remove the criticisms and demands for change previously outlined.

Some teachers have responded in very clear and constructive ways by creating their own 'teacher-as-researcher' movement. In a book that has now become prescribed reading for those interested in these issues, A Teachers' Guide to Action Research (Nixon, 1981) traces the antecedants of this movement to the influence of Lawrence Stenhouse and the work of CARE at the University of East Anglia. The writers in the book clearly articulate a demand for new thinking and relationships to be developed.[2]

Supporting this viewpoint, Denis Lawton (1983) writing in the *Times Educational Supplement* on 'The Politics of Educational Research' outlines some of the failures of past research and advocates that:

Most important of all, more teachers should see themselves as part of the educational research community (p. 4).

This he believes would be an important part of the professionalization of teaching.

In a section of their survey of research in special education, Cave and Madison (1978) point to the task of seeking new forms of partnership with teachers. Even the Warnock Report (1978) has a sentence on this question in which it is stated:

The part which teachers can play in research and development is often under-valued and far more encouragement and support needs to be given to them to carry out systematic research (p. 320).

Clearly, if this is to mean more than empty rhetoric, then the list of *Areas in which Research is Needed* that the Warnock Report outlines in Chapter 18 will need to be drastically changed. Finally, in the two surveys reported by Klaus Wedell and others concerning research in Special Education (1982; 1985) strong support is made for research to be carried out by 'practitioners' and reference is made to the value of student dissertations as a resource for insights.[3]

Nevertheless, the task is a difficult one. The ways in which knowledge is institutionalized, coupled with the vested interests and power relations involved, presents advocates of such innovation with an ominous force to be recognized and contested. Teachers-as-researchers may well posit a challenge to the demarcation of boundaries that the labour process of higher education entails. What is distinct is that, unlike researchers, teachers do not have similar *kinds of opportunity and time* to carry out 'systematic research'. The unforgivable possibility must be avoided in which teachers are being encouraged to participate in research, but as Lawn (1984) warns, their involvement will still only be seen as that of an amateur.

Qualitative Research

One contribution that the social sciences can make to teacher education is to provide different approaches for examining educational settings. We have had the privilege of supervising numerous pieces of research undertaken by students. Some of these have been conducted within special schools and have adopted an appreciative stance towards the subjects of study. Qualitative research is an umbrella term that includes a variety of assumptions and priorities. It is easier to state what many researchers working from within this approach are opposed to, i.e., positivism, than it is to clearly identify what they are for (Hargreaves *et al.* 1975). A particular form of qualitative research that has become increasingly evident within the sociology of education, is that of ethnography.

During the 1970s, in this country, sociology of education witnessed a shift of interest which became known as The New Directions. Disillusioned with a great deal of previous forms of research and influenced by Marxism, phenomenology and symbolic interactionism, new questions began to be asked, requiring new methods to examine them. What had previously been taken for granted, the process of schooling, the curriculum, now became topics of key concern. Emphasis was given to questioning the dominant categories within education as Michael Young (1971) points out:

> . . . existing categories that for parents, teachers, children and many researchers distinguish home from school, learning from play, academic from non-academic and 'able' or 'bright' from 'dull' or 'stupid', must be conceived of as socially constructed, with some in a position to impose their constructions or meanings on others (p. 2).

Official categories were no longer to be seen as inevitable, natural or proper. The minutiae of classroom life became a focal subject of research and as Young and Whitty (1976) note, the essential features of this new approach included examining:

> . . . the ways in which teachers and pupils make sense of their everyday classroom experiences, and on how educational 'reality' is continuously reconstructed in the interaction of individuals . . . (p. 2).

Part of this new interest was motivated by a desire for change.

Research interest now focused upon such tasks as:

a) Revealing what constitutes reality for the participants in a given context.
b) Explaining how these participants came to view reality in this way.
c) Identifying the social consequences of their interactions.

A range of research studies were undertaken on such topics as teacher-pupil strategies; pupil perspectives; and the process of classroom interaction.

These ethnographic studies involved participant observation in which the researcher attempts to live or work in the same environment as the subjects of study, over a sustained period of time. A central interest of participant observation is the desire, on the part of the researcher, to understand life from the participant's point of view. This includes their constructs, meanings and interpretations. The ideal to which the investigator aspires is to treat the familiar as strange and what the respondents take for granted as a topic worthy of examination.

An important motivation for the researcher is the belief that as Shotter (1984) notes:

> . . . there is a sense of knowing something from the 'inside' which is quite different from that knowledge we may have of things from the outside (p. 79).

Attention is thus given to understanding and describing the processes by which people make sense of their lives in given settings — what is significant in their lives, their rules and interpretive procedures. For example, Hargreaves, Hestor and Mellor (1975) conducted a participant observation study in order to examine the nature of deviance in classrooms. The research provides us with insights into the nature of labelling and the part typifications and teacher effectiveness play in the construction of pupil identities. They examined the nature of teachers' rules for classroom behaviour as well as the procedures used by teachers for identifying what they considered to be deviant acts. Pupils' views were treated seriously, and such pupil activities as 'having a laugh' or 'mucking about' are as Woods (1985) notes:

> . . . perceived not as irrational, childish, or pathological, but as having deep meaning and some considerable priority in the lives of pupils suffering or practising them (p. 57).

Social interactions involve power relations and the ability of individuals or groups to define a situation as well as to implement their definitions; from this research stance, these now become a topic of interest. This form of research is interested in the negotiations and bargaining that takes place in specific encounters and the ways in which people arrive at a 'working consensus'.

It is essential that research is not viewed primarily in terms of techniques or technical skills. It is fundamentally a *social activity*. This means that in attempting to understand others one inevitably begins to examine oneself. For Hammersley and Atkinson (1983), ethnography is best understood as a reflexive process.[4] Thus the actions and intentions of the researcher are open to examination, in the same terms as those of the respondents. Or, as Burgess[5] (1985) succinctly states:

> . . . the field research process is as much concerned with the hopes, fears, frustrations and assumptions of the researcher as it is with mere techniques (p. 3).

This therefore involves an obligation being placed on the researcher to be self-aware in terms of decision-making and the motives involved.

Researchers are now being encouraged to offer first person accounts in an attempt to demystify the methodology and show:

> What *actually* happened rather than what *should* have happened (Burgess, 1984, p. 4).

The process of research involves difficulties, uncertainties and setbacks and is a real learning experience (Pollard, 1985).

By seeking to discover and understand the cultural knowledge of another group and the ways in which this knowledge is used in daily inter-actions, the researcher is continually faced with the tension of immersing him/herself into the life of the group and being able to maintain some marginality in order to evaluate such insights. So, in attempting to obtain an insider's perspective, stress will be experienced, as Hammersley and Atkinson (1983) note:

> The ethnographer must be intellectually poised between 'familiarity' and 'strangeness', while socially he or she is poised between 'stranger' and 'friend' (p. 100).

Two students,[6] for example, undertaking research in schools, have captured something of these tensions in their accounts of the research process:

> In general, I found that the dilemmas of my identity had almost contradictory effects upon my role. On the one hand I was open to staff talking about the children to me, as somehow I was no novice who first had to be initiated, and also some of the staff passed on tips and 'wrinkles'. So, in a certain sense my identity and status allowed greater access to a participation in some of the mediums of the school. On the other hand, such identity might have made teachers actively aware of my presence as a person who was to judge them on a very vulnerable quality: their 'teaching' (Rogers, 1984, p. 35).

or as Dee (1983) notes:

> However, as I discovered, there is a fine dividing line between participation in the life of the organization and immersion in it. In an endeavour to get an insider's viewpoint, it is possible to get so close to the situation that you become saturated by the everyday events and absorbed in the life of the organization. Thus, you ques-tion the taken-for-granted less and less. . .
>
> I found even when simply observing and not overtly participating, I could be so drawn into the action that I was living in it and through it (p. 14).

This type of research does raise a number of crucial questions, including:

What is the relationship between research and teaching? What is the purpose of the research? What is the relationship between researcher and respondent? What is the status of the respondent's knowledge? Who is the audience for whom the account is produced? Who owns the data? Other important issues are: obtaining access to the participants; the role of an informant; and the difficulties in making sense of a vast amount of material as well as writing the final analysis (Corrie *et al.* 1985). Notwithstanding the difficulties, writers like Woods (1985) are enthusiastic about the value of teachers undertaking this type of work as a means of improving their professionalism. Research of this nature, he maintains:

> ... deals with *teachers'* problems, reflecting a concern not to 'take but to make problems', that is, not to pre-define the problem to be examined, but rather to find out the concerns of the people within (p. 56).

For this type of project to be realized, the use of alternative research methods will be essential.

Special Needs

In the United States, under the influence of such people as Robert E. Edgerton, at the University of California at Los Angeles Mental Retardation Research Centre, and Robert Bogdan and Steven J. Taylor, in the Special Education Department at Syracuse University, participant observation studies have begun to be recognized as an important means of enhancing our understanding of people classified as 'mentally retarded'.

A number of studies have been undertaken to examine the lives of people living within large institutions for the 'retarded', as well as those which studied groups living in various community settings. The sorts of questions the researchers asked included:

> How critical is the problem of stigma in the lives of the participants? Are the participants aware of the stigma-promoting processes that involve them? Do the participants attempt to influence stigma-promoting processes to their benefit? (Dudley, 1983, pp. 12–13).

or

> What are important realities in the lives of these persons? What particular aspects of life concern them? What occupies their thinking? How do they make sense of their lives? (Heshusius, 1981, p. 3).

Recently, Robert Edgerton (1984) has discussed the nature of participant observation in relation to the study of the 'retarded'. One of the respondents in his research is quoted as saying:

> You gotta try to see things from my side too. I know people are trying to do good, but they don't know what it's like to be me (p. 503).

This is a crucial statement that should forcefully remind us of, or provoke us into considering, a number of very serious ideas. Firstly, that people classified as 'mentally retarded' and those with 'special needs' or 'learning difficulties' do have deep feelings and emotions. They do think and have views about their position and experience. Secondly, we rarely approach such people in terms of their important insights, thus we have hardly begun to 'know' or 'understand' them. Lastly, they demand that we recognize them, not in terms of a single dimension, but as people who have rights and deserve our painstaking detailed attention.[7]

The form of qualitative research that I have briefly tried to outline does provide us with an alternative framework in which to think about and discuss a variety of issues connected to our work. Whilst not in any order of priority, nor constituting an exhaustive list, the following insights can be provided from qualitative studies within the field of 'special education' and related contexts:[8]

1) By focusing on the process of social interaction, we can begin to understand how people with 'special needs' interact with others, some whom we call 'significant-others', and the definitions and influences on self that may arise from those interactions.

2) By seeking to get beneath the rhetoric or public views and images that are presented, we can begin to examine the nature of contradiction in specific social encounters. What compromises and strategies are being developed, adopted or changed during the process of social interaction.

3) By attempting to understand the world from the participants' viewpoint we are able to obtain an alternative understanding of institutions. We can begin to see them from the perspective of the people who know them as clients (Bogdan and Taylor, 1982).

4) By emphasizing the social construction of reality and thus the ways in which people in their interactions reconstitute the social order, we can begin to appreciate the ways in which the labels we use to describe people actually influence the way we think about them and act towards them (Booth, 1985). The assumptions and legitimation of official views, particularly those found in case-records, are now

no longer taken for granted or to be seen as automatically a true reflection of the person involved.

5) Finally, a benefit of this type of research is that it highlights the complexity of social experience within, for example, classroom life. It thus provides an antidote to those frequent claims (or demands) that easy answers can be found to the problems and dilemmas facing pupils and teachers in school (Nixon, 1987).

We do have examples of opportunities and encouragement being given to students and teachers to engage in this form of research activity. The new *E806 Advanced Diploma in Special Needs in Education*, at the Open University, encourages students to undertake project work in which observation, interviewing and collaboration are key investigative tools. A significant number of important case studies and insights should emerge from these studies, some of which will be made available to a wider audience. At Bristol, we, like some other institutions, are committed to enabling students and teachers, on initial and inservice courses, to involve themselves in teacher-as-researcher studies. The new funding arrangements for inservice provision could enable more teacher-research based work to go on in schools.

Conclusion

Research is not a value-neutral activity. It is a social experience in which the subjects of research can suffer and perceive particular forms of study as oppressive. This raises a further issue: to what extent are researchers, including teachers-as-researchers, prepared to put their skills and knowledge at the service of the researched? This includes involving them in decisions about the choice of a topic of investigation, as well as the possible use to which findings or insights are put[9].

The importance of this approach for students and teachers is that, although this form of research is often extremely demanding and disturbing, it does provide them with a means of not only learning how to sympathetically attempt to understand others (this includes the learning process involved in observing, listening and interviewing) but with a means of knowing themselves more thoroughly. This process of self-reflection will have some important spin-offs in the ways in which they both think about and interact with their pupils. It will hopefully be a means of enriching the quality of classroom and school life. The more collaboration there is between people in this form of research, the greater the benefits. There is no room for complacency; the task is both difficult and exciting.

Acknowledgment

I am grateful to Rob Withers and Mike Oliver for their comments on an earlier draft of this paper.

Notes

1. Whilst this chapter refers to the issue of sociology of education, a similar argument could be illustrated by reference to educational psychology and philosophy of education.
2. Further literature has now become available, including Hopkins, D. (1985) *A Teacher's Guide to Classroom Research*, (Open University Press) and Hustler, D. *et al.* (Eds) (1986) *Action Research in Classrooms and Schools*, (Allen and Unwin).
3. This is perhaps one of the most undervalued sources of important ideas and references.
4. The issue of what constitutes a 'refective pedagogy' is now receiving more careful attention. For some writers it is inextricably linked to 'issues and questions concerning the teacher-as-researcher' (Carr and Kemmis, 1986, and Pollard, 1986).
5. This book is part of a series that Falmer Press is publishing which should be seen as essential reading for any person interested in qualitative research.
6. These accounts are derived from students on initial teacher education courses. Some of the issues and concerns are therefore different from those of the teacher who attempts to undertake research in his/her own classroom. For example, the question of access becomes less significant and the possible reasons for the research will differ. The issue of developing memorization techniques will become particularly acute for the teacher.
7. For an example of the time and effort involved in research of this nature, see Goode (1984).
8. Some recent examples of this type of qualitative research are: Erting (1985) and Quicke (1986).
9. This does raise a number of important issues with regard to not only the form of the relationship between the researcher and the respondents, but also to what extent does this type of research lead to the empowerment of *all* those involved?

References

ALEXANDER, R. (1984) *Primary Teaching*, London, Holt Education.
BARTON, L. and TOMLINSON, S. (Eds) (1981) *Special Education, Policy, Practices and Social Issues*, London, Harper and Row.
BERNSTEIN, B. (1975) *Introduction to Class, Codes and Control, Vol. 3*, London, Routledge & Kegan Paul.
BOGDAN, R. and Taylor, S. (1982) *Inside Out*, Toronto, University of Toronto Press.

BOOTH, T. (1985) 'Labels and their consequences' in Lane D. and Stratford B. (Eds) *Current Approaches to Down's Syndrome*, London, Holt, Rinehart and Winston.

BURGESS, R. (1980) 'Some fieldwork problems in teacher-based research' in *British Educational Research Journal*, Vol. 6, No. 2, p. 165–173.

BURGESS, R. (Ed.) (1984) *The Research Process in Educational Settings: Ten Case Studies*, Lewes, Falmer Press.

BURGESS, R. (Ed.) (1985) *Field Methods in the Study of Education*, Lewes, Falmer Press.

CARR, W. and KEMIS, S. (1986) *Becoming Critical: Education, Knowledge and Action Research*, Lewes, Falmer Press.

CAVE, C. and MADISON, P. (1978) *A Survey of Recent Research in Special Education*, Windsor, NFER-Nelson.

CORRIE, M. and ZAKLUKIEWICZ, S. (1985) 'Qualitative Research and Case Study Approaches: An introduction', in Hegarty, S. and Evans, P. (Eds), *Research and Evaluation Methods in Special Education*, Windsor, NFER-Nelson.

DEE, L. (1983) 'Ethnography in an ESN(s) School' Dissertation submitted in part fulfilment of BEd (Hons) degree at the University of Birmingham, in *Westhill College Library, Birmingham*.

DENSCOMBE, M. (1982) 'The "Hidden" Pedagogy and its Implications for Teacher Training', in *British Journal of Sociology of Education*, Vol. 3, No. 3, p. 249–65.

DENSCOMBE, M. (1985) *Classroom Control. A Sociological Perspective*, London, George Allen & Unwin.

DENZIN, N. (1978) *The Research Act: A Theoretical Introduction to Sociology*, New York, McGraw-Hill.

DES (1978) *Special Educational Needs (Warnock Report)*, London, HMSO.

DUDLEY, J. (1983) *Living with Stigma*, Illinois, Charles C. Thomas.

EDGERTON, R. (1984) 'The participant-observer approach to research in mental retardation', in *American Journal of Mental Deficiency*, Vol. 88, No. 5, p. 498–505.

ELLIOTT, J. (1980) 'Implications of classroom research for professional development', in Hoyle, E. and Megarry, J. (Eds) *Professional Development of Teachers*, New York, Nichols Publisher.

ERTING, C. (1985) 'Cultural Conflict in a School for Deaf Children', in *Anthropology and Education Quarterly*, Vol. 16, No. 3, p. 225–243.

FLODEN, R. (1985) 'The Role of Rhetoric in Changing Teachers' Beliefs' in *Teacher and Teacher Education*, Vol. 1, No. 1, pp. 19–32.

GOODE, D. (1984) 'Socially produced identities, intimacy and the problem of competence among the retarded' in Barton L. and Tomlinson S. (Eds) *Special Education and Social Interests*, Beckenham, Croom Helm.

HAMMERSLEY, M. and ATKINSON, P. (1983) *Ethnography Principles in Practice*, London, Methuen.

HARGREAVES, D.H., HESTOR, S.K. and MELLOR, F.S. (1975) *Deviance in Classrooms*, London, Routledge and Kegan Paul.

HEGARTY, S. and EVANS, P. (Eds) (1985) *Research and Evaluation Methods in Special Education*, Windsor, NFER-Nelson.

HESHUSIUS, L. (1981) *Meaning in Life as Experienced by Persons Labeled Retarded*, Illinois, Charles C. Thomas.

LACEY, C. (1977) *The Socialization of Teachers*, London, Methuen.

LAMPERT, M. (1984) 'Teaching about Thinking and Thinking about Teaching' in *Journal of Curriculum Studies*, Vol. 16, No. 1, pp. 1–18.

LAWN, M. (1984) Unpublished paper. *Westhill College, Birmingham, England*.

LAWTON, D. (1983) 'The Politics of Educational Research' in *The Times Educational Supplement*, p. 4.

McINTYRE, D. (1980) 'The contribution of research in teacher education' in Hoyle, E. and Megarry, J. (Eds) *Professional Development of Teachers*, London, Kogan Page.

MUSGROVE, F. and TAYLOR, P. (1969) *Society and the Teacher's Role*, London, Routledge and Kegan Paul.

NIXON, J. (Ed.) (1981) *A Teachers' Guide to Action Research*, London, Grant McIntyre.

NIXON, J. (1987) 'Only Connect: thought on stylistic interchange within the research community', in *British Educational Research*, Vol. 13, No. 2, pp. 191–202.

POLLARD, A. (1985) 'Opportunities and Difficulties of Teacher-Ethnographer: A Personal Account'. In Burgess R. (Ed.) *The Research Process in Educational Settings: Ten Case Studies*, Lewes, Falmer Press.

POLLARD, A. (1986) 'Reflective Teaching — The Sociological Contribution'. Unpublished paper, *Department of Education — Bristol Polytechnic, Bristol*.

QUICKE, J. (1986) 'Pupil culture, peer tutoring and special educational needs' in *Disability, Handicap and Society*, Vol. 1, No. 2, p. 147–164.

ROGERS, R. (1984) 'The Invisible Child' Negotiation and Humour: An Ethnography of a 'Special School Class'. Dissertation submitted in part-fulfilment of BEd (Hons) degree at the University of Birmingham, in *Westhill College Library, Birmingham*.

SHOTTER, J. (1984) *Social Accountability and Selfhood*, Oxford, Blackwell.

SIMON, B. (1980) 'Research and Educational Policy' in *Scottish Educational Review*, Vol. 12, No. 1, p. 13–20.

SIMON, B. (1985) *Does Education Matter?*, London, Laurence & Wishart.

TOM, A. (1980) 'The Reform of Teacher Education Through Research: A Futile Quest', *in Teachers College Record*, Vol. 82, pp. 15–29.

WALLER, W. (1932) *The Sociology of Teaching*, New York, J. Wiley.

WEDELL, K. (1985) 'Future Directions for Research on Children's Special Educational Needs', in *British Journal of Special Education*, Vol. 12, No. 1, p. 22–26.

WEDELL, K. and ROBERTS, J. (1982) 'Special Education and Research: A Recent Survey' in *Special Education Forward Trends*, Vol. 9, No. 3, pp. 19–24.

WHITTY, G. and YOUNG, M. (Eds) (1976) *Explorations in the Politics of School Knowledge*, Driffield, Nafferton.

WOODS, P. (1985) 'Sociology, Ethnography and Teacher Practice' in *Teaching and Teacher Education*, Vol. 1, No. 1, pp. 51–62.

WRAGG, E. (1982) 'From Research into Action' in *British Educational Research Journal*, Vol. 8, No. 1, 1982, p. 3–8.

WRAGG, E. (1984) 'Teaching Skills' in Wragg, E. (Ed.) *Classroom Teaching Skills*, Beckenham, Croom Helm.

YOUNG, M. (Ed.) (1971) *Knowledge and Control: New Directions for the Sociology of Education*, London, Collier Macmillan.

YOUNG, M. and WHITTY, G. (Eds) (1976) *The Politics of School Knowledge*, Driffield, Nafferton Books.

ZEICHNER, K. (1981–82) 'Reflective Teaching and Field-Based Experience in Teacher Education' in *Interchange* Vol. 12, No. 4, pp. 1–22.

ZEICHNER, K. (1983) 'Alternative Paradigms of Teacher Education' in *Journal of Teacher Education*, Vol. 34, No. 3, pp. 3–9.

ZEICHNER, K. (1986) 'Content and Contexts: Neglected Elements in Studies of Student Teaching as an Occasion for Learning to Teach', in *Journal of Education for Teaching*, Vol. 12, No. 1, p. 5–24.

ZEICHNER, K. and TEITELBAUM, K. (1982) 'Personalised and Inquiry-oriented Teacher Education: An analysis of two approaches to the development of curriculum for field-based experiences' in *Journal of Education for Teaching*, Vol. 8, No. 2, pp. 95–117.

PART TWO
Examining Key Issues

Chapter 5

Challenging Conceptions of Integration

Tony Booth

Introduction

In this chapter I will try to contribute to discussions about integration by drawing out differences in the way the concept has been interpreted and by subjecting these to critical analysis. As an advocate of integration I have seen my own view as provoking or included within a number of criticisms. In common with other areas of life some are keen to distinguish 'the moderates' (usually themselves) from those they see as 'extremists', who appear to include myself and colleagues at the Open University (see Burden, 1985; Farrell and Sugden, 1985).

It may be that these authors are wary of the political and moral arguments brought to bear on an educational issue supposed, like the rest of education, to lie outside their range of application. There is concern that some academics and researchers do not adopt a sufficiently neutral position. Mittler (1985) claims to have evidence that 'the fervour for integration has taken on something of the language of a religious revival'. He sees this unseemly development as a departure from a proper 'commitment to *better* education for handicapped children in ordinary schools' (Mittler, 1985, p. 9, my emphasis). Here we are meant to trust that the word 'better', like the 'good' of 'good practice', connotes an objectively agreed state of educational efficiency rather than a political and moral preference. For such critics education is to be matched to the 'needs' of pupils which are seen as personal characteristics discovered in the course of 'good professional practice'. How convenient it might seem that just when it became ideologically unsound to perceive learning difficulties and handicaps as properties of individuals, that 'professionals' could switch to the identification of needs, without a flicker of self-doubt about the invention that goes into their discovery.

But if some have felt that a number of advocates of integration have violated the value neutrality of educational debate others have characterized them as politically inept. Thus Barton and Tomlinson argue that the integrationist view may be 'part of a misplaced vision' which 'ignores the inequalities and contradictions that are endemic . . . to both the educational system . . . and the wider society in which it is located' (Barton and Tomlinson, 1984, p. 75). The development of ideas about integration is sometimes seen as a subtle way of perpetuating such inequalities. The intellectual and empirical supports for such a view rest, in part, on Andrew Scull's analysis of the rationale and consequences of community-care policies for people categorized as mentally ill (Scull, 1977). In the 2nd edition of his book, Andrew Scull quotes Peter Sedgewick's assessment of the application of these policies to the situation in Britain which were said to be characterized by:

> the jettisoning of mental patients in their thousands into the isolated, helpless environment of their families of origin, who appealed in vain for hospital admission (even for a temporary period of respite), for counselling or support, and even for basic information and advice . . . (Sedgewick, 1982, pp. 193–4).

For Andrew Scull 'decarceration' was seen as a means for the state to divest itself of financial responsibility for the 'mentally ill'. Martin Söder (1984) applies a similar interpretation to policies for integration of people with disabilities and suggests how arguments about the relativity of handicap, about integration and the decentralization of services can all contribute to obscuring their needs:

> An ambitious and optimistic ideology has created new forms of support for the disabled, but in the future these forms can be used for purposes other than those for which they were intended . . . The invisibility of the needs of the disabled . . . (is) expressed in terms of integration, relativity and decentralization. One could say, without putting too fine a point on it, that the ideology itself bears the seeds of the process of making the needs of the disabled[1] disappear from view (Söder, 1984, p. 33).

Are advocates of integration, at best, dupes of a system designed to perpetuate inequalities? Does their humanitarian rhetoric provide cover for a new means for keeping groups of disadvantaged people in their place? There is a sense in which such explanations are *post hoc*, for, a while ago, it was the proponents of segregation who were fostering the policing of the system through the perpetuation of a disabled and 'defective' underclass (see Tomlinson, 1982). In a society characterized by gross disparities of power between social groups, any movement which appears to increase the power of the disadvantaged will be countered by those whose own advantage is thereby threatened. But does this mean that integration is not to be propounded? Barton and Tomlinson are clear that this is not the case but argue that demands for 'fundamental changes' as well as a critique of current educational inequalities must accompany any such campaign (Barton and Tomlinson, 1984, p. 79).

However, many criticisms of moves towards integration share a common drawback. The word 'integration' may be left undefined as an assumed constant in a critical equation. Yet two advocates of integration may mean entirely different things by it. For me, integration is essentially a political process, it is about the transfer of power (Booth, 1983, p. 3). For others like Mittler it is about the matching of provision to 'need'. In this chapter I will try to illuminate differences in conceptions of integration by examining, in some detail, the use of the term 'normalization' popularized by Wolf Wolfensberger (1972) and often used synonymously with the word 'integration'. I will then explore the use of both terms in a study of the integration of the deaf by Wendy Lynas (1986). Finally I will look at how my colleagues and I have incorporated a conception of integration into a general attempt to describe and reduce discrimination in education.

Props of analysis

In analysing the work of others I employ a rudimentary method based on my experience and reading which involves bearing several particular notions in mind. Some of these are neatly summarized in a novel I read a couple of years ago where the young hero listens to the advice of her 'Aunt' Elsie:

> 'Some folk say I'm a fool, but there's more to this world than meets the eye . . .'

> 'There's this world', she banged the wall graphically, 'and there's this world', she thumped her chest. 'If you want to make sense of either, you have to take notice of both' (Winterton, 1985, p. 32).

The sense we make of an area of life depends on our recognition that there is a personal world and a political world which interact and that neither may be what it seems. We must look beyond the surface of things at the deceptions created by unconscious and ideological forces. Because such processes obscure our thoughts we may be led into contradiction which we fail to detect. It is through an analysis of contradictions that the nature of unconscious and ideological forces are revealed.

Any suggestion that others are prey to self-deception involves a recognition that one's own critical faculties may be similarly distorted. Academics, for example, are as prone to the self-interests of their profession as other groups. Some have implied that the recognition of such interests is a recent observation recorded by sociologists (see Oliver, 1985). Binet and Simon were well aware in 1914 of the opportunity that the new special schools might provide to the emerging profession of special educators:

> Ever since public interest has been aroused in the question of schools for defective children, selfish ambition has seen its opportunity. The most frankly selfish interests conceal themselves behind the mask of philanthrophy, and whoever dreams of finding a fine situation for himself in the new schools never speaks of children without tears in his eyes. This is the everlasting human comedy. There is no reason for indignation. Everyone has the right to look after his own interests, so long as he does not compromise interests superior to his own . . . (Binet and Simon, 1914, p. 10).

Generally speaking, of course, it is easier to detect the contradictions and analyse the conflicting motives of others. We can be incredibly devious in defending our own mental conflicts from scrutiny, particularly from ourselves.

Wolfensberger's Principle of Normalization

I have chosen to start the examination of conceptions of integration with Wolf Wolfensberger's work for a number of reasons. His ideas have been very influential, particularly amongst those working with people with mental handicaps. He has set ideas about integration in education within a broader context for the provision of services for people with disabilities. He has made a clear attempt to link theory with practice and his theoretical ideas are informed by a wide knowledge of the precise details of practice. I am aware too that I and others have made assumptions about the meaning of the concept of normalization without subjecting it to critical scrutiny. In Wendy Lynas's text, for example, there is no reference to the historical underpinnings of her conception of normalization. Finally, I find in Wolfensberger's work a series of ideas which have been previously and subsequently considered by others. It is easy to succumb to a temptation to exaggerate the originality of one's own work.

The notion of 'normalization' was developed in Scandinavia during the late 1950s and the 1960s and introduced to readers of English through Wolfensberger's *The Principle of Normalization in Human Services* (Wolfensberger, 1972). Wolfensberger became and has remained a significant figure for many people campaigning for an alternative to institutional care. Whilst the derivation and elaboration of working principles are fundamental to the work of Wolfensberger and his associates, it is the attempt to describe, promote and establish working and living arrangements which conform to them which is the most important feature of his work. One of the most widely-known projects influenced by his work was that promoted by the Eastern Nebraska Community Office of Retardation which was publicized in England through the Campaign for Mental Handicap (Thomas, Firth and Kendall, 1978). It involved a coherent reappraisal and relocation of services for all people in the Eastern Nebraska area, excluded or under threat of exclusion on the grounds of their relative incompetence.

His book contained a radical critique of the way services for people with disabilities have been developed and controlled. He argued that the professionals charged with caring for people with disabilities misunderstood their own power and the interests they served:

> Many benevolent, humanistic clinicians see themselves as servants of the public, offering themselves and their services in a non-controlling fashion. They see their clients as free agents, free to accept or reject the offered services. Their self-concept — in part due to the indoctrination received during training — is frequently incompatible with action perceived as controlling, directing or dictating client behaviour. Yet here it is where so many human service workers deceive themselves, because their roles are not only almost always societally sanctioned, but in an endless array of encounters between the server and the served, the server is the interpreter of and agent for the interests of society, and wields a truly amazing amount of power and control, even if he may not consciously perceive himself as so doing (Wolfensberger, 1972, p. 1).

Professionals, then, acquire a set of guiding principles, which amount to culturally inherited prejudices, in common with other members of society and in particular through their professional training. Wolfensberger called these prejudices 'unconscious ideologies'. He linked the discrimination against people with disabilities, clearly, to the oppression of other groups through their pernicious application:

> There are few things more vicious, more maladaptive, more inimical to individual and collective well-being than unconscious ideologies. The fact that for 200 years we have adhered, largely unconsciously, to racial discrimination while claiming to adhere to equality is an extreme example, it is a phenomenon that might destroy us (Wolfensberger, 1972, p. 10).

Wolfensberger asserted that those who worked with 'deviants' or people with disabilities needed to make their 'ideologies' or presuppositions conscious and replace them with a new ideology, the principle of normalization. The principle involved a double aim, to end the segregation of services and to make the people receiving services as indistinguishable from the norm as possible. As formulated in 1972 the principle involved the:

> utilization of means which are as culturally normative as possible to establish and/or maintain personal behaviours which are as culturally normative as possible (Wolfensberger, 1972, p. 28).

On the one hand Wolfensberger asserted that 'ideologies are extremely powerful forces' (p. 7) and were 'usually unconscious only because they are "bad"' (p. 7). Yet he believed that people could stop repressing their discrimination against people with disabilities simply by attention to the simplicity and validity of the normalization principle. He shows no awareness of the powerful interests which are used to keep the contradictions of professional practice hidden:

> I firmly believe that the normalization principle, simple and uncomplicated as it is, is the human management principle that is most consistent with our socio-political ideals . . . I further believe that the normalization principle is so self-evidently valid as well as 'right' that it may well become universally accepted in all areas of human management (Wolfensberger, 1972, pp. 41–42).

There seems to be a strange faith, here, in the ultimately caring ethos of the United States which he had certainly dropped by 1980 when he was far less sanguine about the ease with which the principle might be adopted. Yet he portrays this resistance as simply moral, part of a battle between good and evil, and thereby obscures the political processes which might be at work.

> There is nothing good in the world that will not come under attack — and I mean under hateful attempts to destroy that which is good so that something evil will prevail (Wolfensberger, 1980, p. 101).

In particular, in this later text he drew attention to the 'mistaken' view attributed to him that normalization implied conformity to a statistical norm. This he felt was a 'naive and invalid interpretation'. It is clear from his work that he has a strongly-held view that differences should not be devalued. Yet it is easy to see how people would put a narrow interpretation on his views based on the wording of the principle or a reading of the earlier text. As Wolfensberger argued there:

> a (potentially) deviant person should be enabled to emit behaviours and an appearance appropriate (normative) within that culture for

persons of similar characteristics, such as age and sex. The term 'normative' is intended to have statistical rather than moral connotations, and could be equated with 'typical' or 'conventional' (Wolfensberger, 1972, p. 28).

It is apparent that he views society as a unified cultural whole rather than as containing competing groups which are culturally, morally and politically diverse. In assuming that the notion of what is normal is unproblematic he leaves it to be defined by the dominant group of which the advocate of normalization may well be a member. 'Normalization . . . means living in a heterosexual world' is, for example, an elaboration of the principle which Wolfensberger uncritically promotes (Wolfensberger, 1980, p. 43).

He also fails to recognize that the removal of devaluation of some groups might imply the reduction in value of others. His ideal society appears to be one rather similar to our own in which equality of opportunity is established and opportunities realizable. He sees his view of normalization as a working principle for such a society and suggests that 'one would almost have to go to metaphysical systems for more broadly applicable concepts'. One such system, 'idealized socialism', he rejects on the grounds that 'its implications to some devalued social groups would be unclear, or even catastrophic (e.g., in the case of former landowners or capitalists)' (Wolfensberger, 1980, p. 112).

The creation of abnormality

For me, the most positive strand in the normalization work involves the analyses of the prejudices which segregated and specialist services can foster, distorting an aspect of a person until it is seen to determine their whole nature and the reactions of others to them. The subtle 'denormalization' of pupils was brought home to me during two trips I made to schools. The first was to a special class in a primary school for pupils from a next-door school for pupils said to have 'severe learning difficulties'. When I entered I sat down at a table where a group of children were exhibiting various degrees of engagement with the task of the day. In the middle of the table were three dishes, one containing instant coffee, the second drinking chocolate and the third tea leaves. Each child had a worksheet on which they had to record, as best they could, their reactions to the taste and smell of each substance. I turned to the child on my left and asked what he was trying to do. Before he answered his teacher interjected: 'He can't respond to direct questions'. Since I am incorrigibly disruptive I immediately asked him: 'Can you respond to direct questions?' 'No', came the reply. But my attention was mainly caught by the girl next to him. She had Down's Syndrome and her lips were cracked and her face blotchy. She said little, but at frequent intervals would sneak out a finger, dip it into the chocolate powder and then suck it. It was hard not to see her action as determined by, and part of, her 'condition', confirming her abnormal status. When I left the classroom and started to walk out of the school through the playground I heard someone calling after me. I turned to see the 'unresponsive boy' running towards me. 'You've forgotten your folder'. 'Thanks'. We smiled at each other.

The week previously I had visited my daughter's primary school when my turn on the cooking rota had come up. When I arrived I was shown into what seemed like a storage cupboard next to the staffroom. It was fitted out with a cooker and there were utensils, ingredients and a recipe card waiting for me. After a few minutes my daughter, her friend Angela, and Tim Bolder and James Halden were ushered into my care. I had heard about Tim Bolder from Katie before. He was the one who had 'strangled' her three times. Working in pairs they prepared the cake mixture. Every few seconds James would stick out a finger, dip it in one of the ingredients and then suck it. I think he liked the cake mixture best but his fingers also went in the raw egg, the flour and the margarine. Although I found his behaviour intensely irritating it was hard not to see it as boyish devilment.

Countering discrimination

It is also true that whatever the flaws of the principle and its dubious political connotations it is clearly derived from a wish to reduce discrimination against people with disabilities. Thus Wolfensberger rejects the view of one of the Scandinavian originators of the concept who had argued that segregation might be as effective in moving people with mental disabilities towards normalization as integration (Bank-Mikkelson, 1969). For Wolfensberger, societally imposed segregation was discriminatory:

> No good can come of any programme, including normalization that is not based on intimate, positive one-to-one relationships between ordinary (unpaid) citizens and those who are handicapped and who would otherwise be devalued . . . very few people seem to realize that valued people are virtually never segregated from society against their will and that one will only see such segregation when people are devalued. The only times that valued people are segregated is when they segregate themselves in order to increase their own status and value. Therefore, if one wants to do away with devaluation, one will have to come to grips with what is, de facto, involuntary segregation (Wolfensberger, 1980, p. 77).

By 1983 he felt that the misunderstandings that had become attached to the term 'normalization' were detracting from its usefulness:

> Any review of the literature will disclose that once people hear or see the term 'normalization' a large proportion (apparently even the vast majority) assume — usually wrongly — that they know 'what it means'. Even otherwise scholarly persons have published inane critiques of the principle without citing, or apparently having studied or even become aware of the major expositions thereof in the professional literature (Wolfensberger, 1983, p. 234).

He proposed that the term be replaced by the phrase 'Social Role Valorization' (Wolfensberger, 1983). He wished to emphasize further that 'the most explicit and highest goal of normalization must be the creation, support and defence of *valued social roles* for people who are at risk of social devaluation' (Wolfensberger, 1983, p. 234).

I don't think I could ever be persuaded to use the term 'social role valorization'. It is too far removed from my own ordinary language and hence appears to embody the professional mystifications which reduce the power of others to control their own lives. Nevertheless, clearly, it places ideas about discrimination and devaluation at the centre of Wolfensberger's work.

The Normalization of the Deaf; the Denial of Prejudice

For some authors, however, the recognition that people with disabilities may be prey to devaluations finds no place. In her book *Integrating the Handicapped into Ordinary Schools; a study of hearing-impaired pupils* (Lynas, 1986), Wendy Lynas applies the concept of normalization, in its narrowest form, with clear approval. She makes no reference to any other discussion of the principle and assumes that its definition is straightforward, 'making the hearing-impaired as like or as similar as possible to his[2] hearing peers' (p. 63). This involves 'attempting to eliminate as far as possible those differences that distinguish him from "normals" such as poor speech, lack of comprehension, limited language and consequent low academic attainments' (p. 63).

The purpose of normalization is seen not only as giving deaf and partially deaf young people access to the hearing world but also as making them acceptable to it. The key issue here is signing:

> According to the 'normalization' paradigm of integration a deaf child who could talk would be more acceptable than one who could communicate only by means of sign language. One might suggest that the more normal the speech and language, the more

acceptable the hearing impaired child would become (Lynas, 1986, p. 63).

It might seem from this quotation that it is not signing, per se, that Lynas sees as unacceptable to the hearing world but only an inability to talk. Yet she is unable to see that implication. She is locked by her ideological position here into one side of the oral/signing dispute. She leaves a hidden implication that an ability to sign precludes an ability to speak and decode spoken English. Nowhere does she mention the bilingual approach to the education of the deaf which has received much attention in recent years as it has for other minority groups (see Brennan, 1987).

For Lynas 'normalization' is identified with a process of 'assimilation' of young deaf people into the hearing world. Yet, perhaps as a consequence of sequestering herself from the mainstream of educational debate, she indicates no awareness of the critique of the assimilation philosophy within multicultural let alone anti-racist education. She portrays such a process as part of a natural order whereby minority groups conform to the rules of a majority. The acceptance of the minority depends on their willingness to make themselves acceptable:

> Unless there was prejudice against the deaf, in which case little or no acceptance would be possible, it would be likely that the willingness of the majority group to accept would be dependent, to a significant extent, upon the willingness and the ability of the minority group to adapt (Lynas, 1986, p. 63).

Putting pressure on minorities or powerless groups to run their lives according to the rules of the majority or those in power is, of course, just what others interpret as discrimination. But the idea that prejudice against the deaf does exist is dismissed as a fringe view:

> McGrath (1981) even goes so far as to suggest that in a hearing-dominated society the deaf group, because they are unhearing, are oppressed and stigmatized just as other groups are also accorded inferior social status for being 'unrich' or 'unwhite' (Lynas, 1986, p. 67).

There is an echo of Wolfensberger's stricture here, that 'we practice gross discrimination . . . and then we deny it'. Lynas is only willing to give conscious acknowledgment to the existence of prejudice against people with disabilities if it occurred in the past: 'From Ancient Times *right up to the Victorian Age*, handicapped people had characteristically been accorded extremely low status' (p. 2, my emphasis).

When the mind hears

Yet in this book as elsewhere in the field of deaf education as one reads or listens to some of the comments of those involved in the education of the deaf, one feels one has entered a time warp: 'Most educators in Britain', Lynas tells us, 'regard both assimilation and normalization as proper goals in deaf education'. The idea that a deaf person is not *'essentially "abnormal"'* is set up as an alternative to the mainstream of thought (p. 66, my emphasis). Now Wendy Lynas, like anyone else who has been around the world of deaf educators even for a relatively brief period, must have encountered the profound prejudice that exists against sign language and deaf people that is voiced by some educators of the deaf. But the fact that in her writing she shows no awareness of it suggests to me that there are processes of denial and repression in operation. One might predict that this effort to distort reality would lead to contradiction and I believe that her text as a whole reveals precisely that.

When I first became involved in the area it came as quite a shock that prejudice was voiced with less restraint than against any other group within the education system. Thus, while I was gathering material for a TV programme on the politics of deaf education in 1985, one teacher of the deaf referred to the adult deaf community as the 'deaffies' and to one deaf man who had the temerity to challenge her as 'some deaf Jamie'. Another spoke of the use of sign language as akin to 'barking at print for hearing children'; having the surface trappings of a real skill but without the involvement of comprehension. This same teacher of a postgraduate course in deaf education began a lecture to postgraduate students by telling them how the eating of baked potatoes by a group of deaf people in the lounge at a conference she had attended confirmed the relative inability of deaf people to acquire social skills. Another suggested that signing challenged God's physiological acumen: 'If he had meant us to sign, the functions of language would not have been organized in the left hemisphere of the brain'. Another educator, an ex-head teacher of a school for the deaf, went even further. He moved from a discussion of the medieval doubt of the presence of a soul in the deaf to a sudden espousal of his own present views:

> If you look at a Minister signing the Lords Prayer it can look beautifully expressive — but what does that waggling of hands mean to the deaf? No-one knows what they are thinking about. We were not intended to learn the language of signs . . . Faith can only come through hearing . . . isn't it a fact that faith was transmitted orally?

These examples were gathered over a relatively brief period and similar examples must be common knowledge to teachers of the deaf and others involved in deaf education. They have a long history which has been comprehensively portrayed by Harlan Lane in his book *When the Mind Hears* (Lane, 1984). The lecture he gave, based on this book, at the International Congress on the Deaf, Manchester, 1985, stands out for me as a remarkable piece of academic theatre. He recited orally the catalogue of prejudices and mistaken beliefs about the inadequacies of sign language as a linguistic system over the last hundred years whilst these were simultaneously and dramatically disproved by their translation into American sign language, British sign language and Swedish sign language.

The suggestion that in recent years linguists have discovered that sign languages are linguistic systems as fully developed as spoken languages is itself a form of prejudice about who can legitimately possess such knowledge. In another book, edited by Harlan Lane (1984), Pierre Desloges, a bilingual deaf Frenchman writing in 1779 tried to dispel the myth that sign language was a limited form of expression. He described clearly how sign language could represent as complex a set of ideas and relationships as the French language, as well as the combination of manual and facial gestures and body movements of which signs were composed. In particular, he focused on assuring his readers that different religious concepts were readily distinguishable within sign language. He took the abbé Deschamps to task for suggesting, like my ex-headteacher in 1985, that the lack of precision of signing might prevent the deaf from becoming good Christians:

> When I want to designate the Supreme Being by indicating the sky
> . . . I accompany my gesture with an air of adoration and respect
> that makes my intention quite evident. The abbé Deschamps himself
> could make no mistake about it. On the other hand, if I want to
> speak of the sky or firmament, I will make the same gesture
> unaccompanied by any of these auxiliaries so it is easily seen that the
> two expressions 'God' and 'firmament' contain no ambiguity or cir-
> cumlocution (Pierre Desloges, 1779, pp. 37–38).

Desloges was at pains to expose the contradiction in the abbé Deschamps treatise which involved the notion that sign language was not a natural means of communication for deaf people yet it required extremely vigilant and laborious methods to avoid it. He was firm in his conclusion about the place of sign language in education:

> If in the education of the deaf we suppress the use of signs, it is
> impossible to make the pupils anything but machines that speak . . .
> We must conclude that the chief instrument in the education of the
> deaf must be sign language and that like it or not, we will always

come back to the method for the compelling reason that sign is their natural language (Desloges, 1779, p. 40).

Revealing contradictions

Now I do not intend to prove in this paper that arguments against the use of sign language are primarily based on prejudice. That job has been eloquently performed by Harlan Lane as well as the thousands of deaf people through history who in their ordinary spontaneous interchanges show how signing can provide unfettered expression for their thoughts and emotions. But what I can indicate is how one author in her uncritical inheritance of a position based on domination and control unthinkingly reproduces a series of profound prejudices and fails to subject her own data to a proper analysis.

She is certainly led to some strange conclusions. She claims that her findings 'will undoubtedly be much welcomed by those teachers of the deaf who believe their chief responsibility is to teach deaf children to talk'. She also argued that there was a conviction among all the young people with 'hearing impairment' whom she interviewed that 'the acquisition of spoken English was and should be the major goal of their education and of their personal aspiration' (p. 251).

I heard a similar sentiment expressed in a joke told to me by an Irishman and I think it is worth risking a repeat of it here:

> A politician was addressing a large crowd and hoping to impress them with his patriotic principles. He puffed out his chest, adopted a stern expression and began:
> 'I was born an Englishman, I have been brought up to be an Englishman and, when the time comes, I shall die an Englishman . . .'.
> As he paused, there was just time for a member of the audience to call out:
> 'Jesus, have you no ambition?'

The idea that educators of the deaf and young deaf people themselves should lower their educational sights to such an extent that acquiring spoken English is their major educational ambition is absurd. Yet such a view is reproduced by educators as conventional wisdom.[3] If it is successful, education provides a source of enjoyment, a discovery of interests, a knowledge of cultures and the means to continue to develop and control one's own life. The learning of languages may be part of such a process and can be assessed in relation to it but cannot replace it. In their emphasis on acquiring spoken language for the deaf, educators misrepresent the function of language. They portray it as serving only a public function, permitting interchange between the hearing and the deaf. But language is used on our own as a means of thought, as a vehicle of fantasy and a framework for converting wishes and desires into projects and plans of action.

What has been going on in the education of the young deaf people in Wendy Lynas' study if they limit their aspirations for education in the way she suggests? She argues that: 'there was no evidence that I could detect to suggest that those who chose to identify primarily with the normally hearing had been "indoctrinated" to espouse "normality", or compelled to cast off their deaf identity' (p. 251).

My immediate reaction to that comment is to think that Lynas must inhabit a different world to me. In my world everyone seems to be subjected to 'indoctrination' to espouse 'normality'. Lynas' own evidence might lead her to question her conclusion if she had not started out with the assumption that indoctrination to espouse an amorphous normality was a natural and legitimate goal:

> There seemed to be a universal desire among those interviewed to adopt the behavioural norms of the normally hearing in order to be able to adapt to, and be accepted by, hearing-speaking society. These young people . . . wanted to talk as normally as possible, understand the speech of normally hearing people, achieve as near normal as possible academic standards and become socialized into the ways of normally hearing society . . . They hoped that by being in a normally hearing school, some 'normality' would rub off on them (Lynas, 1986, p. 169).

For her to detect an overpressure to appear normal Lynas would have to find some striking evidence. She says that despite wanting to appear normal in every respect this does not mean these young people were 'ashamed or embarrassed about being deaf' (p. 169). Yet interestingly enough Lynas' own evidence straightforwardly includes such sentiments. She reports it and fails to see it and when she sees it, she then denies it. What is going on here? Thus on pages 179–192 she records the strategies deaf pupils use for coping in ordinary classes and many of these involve hiding their difficulties and are 'undoubtedly motivated by a desire to conceal their handicap' (p. 180). Thus they hide their hearing aids (p. 181), pretend they understand lessons when they don't (p. 182) or copy other pupils work (pp. 183–184). Sometimes the belief that hearing pupils had privileged access to the right thing to do belied a deaf pupil's own abilities. A teacher reported of one child, Christine:

> She can paint well, but she always, but always, does what Gail (normally hearing) does. If Gail does a butterfly, then Christine

does a butterfly; if Gail does a snowstorm, then we get a snowstorm from Christine (Lynas, 1986, p. 187).

She leaves her contradictory assertions unacknowledged and unexamined. At the conclusion to the book she is able to report: 'there was evidence that some hearing-impaired pupils displayed on some occasions what might be seen as too strong a desire "to be normal", or at least too strong a desire *to be perceived* "as normal" ' (Lynas, 1986, p. 247).

That some pupils should try to hide their disability was met with surprise by some teachers, as one put it: 'I don't know why they try to hide their aids; everyone knows they're deaf' (p. 181). Whilst some pupils attempt to *pretend* to others that their deafness makes no difference some fall into the trap of believing it themselves.

> These deaf young people did not, on the whole, see their hearing impairment as an insurmountable barrier to their participation in normally hearing society. They therefore did not believe that the acquisition of sign language should be a priority in their education (Lynas, 1986, p. 238).

Their belief that their deafness is not an 'insurmountable barrier' is to be encouraged because it leads them to play down the importance of sign language in their education. But their lack of awareness of their relatively poor attainment is at the same time to be deplored:

> Many, though not all, hearing-impaired pupils in ordinary schools, do not have a strong sense of their academic 'abnormality' . . . it would seem that if hearing-impaired pupils were made more aware of their difference from others in relation to the attainment of academic success, they might be better motivated to aim for higher standards, work harder, and thus achieve more 'normality' in the long run (Lynas, 1986, p. 209).

Here we have the end result of the 'normalization' philosophy. It is propounded by deaf educators but when it is absorbed by young deaf people they are taken to task for succumbing to personal failings. Pupils, like Alison who say 'I hate it if people know I'm deaf' (p. 234) can then receive the stricture: 'Oversubscribing to the idea of being "normal" or affecting appearing to be "normal" rather than acknowledging "abnormality" is likely to be counter productive for the deaf pupil' (Lynas, 1986, p. 248).

Now for part of one page, at least, Wendy Lynas is well aware of what constitutes the barrier to achievement for many young deaf people:

> a severe and profound hearing loss represents a serious barrier to the educational development and normalization of a deaf pupil and is

hence a barrier to his ultimate full assimilation into normally hearing society (Lynas, 1986, p. 240).

The trouble then, acknowledged here, is that young deaf people have difficulty with an education carried out through spoken English because they are deaf. They cannot become hearing and cannot be passed off by others or themselves as if they were hearing. The problem is not that young deaf people cannot acknowledge that they are deaf but that this constitutes a problem for many hearing educators. For to acknowledge that they are deaf means to not only accept that they may need and wish to communicate in sign language but also that a denial of access to sign language represents a severe form of prejudice. But this is a prejudice to be hidden from oralist educators of the deaf by themselves and for those pupils they educate.

A close reading of Lynas' text provides evidence for the counter hypothesis to her own. Young deaf people may be encouraged to espouse a commitment to a 'normality' which is against their own interests. Where this leads them to curtail their freedom and dominate their educational aspirations with the acquisition of spoken English then it is clearly indoc- trination. It is hardly surprising that many deaf people have reacted vehe- mently against this view of integration within deaf education which provides ideological support for their subjugation. It is a tribute to the power of mechanisms of defence that some educators of the deaf can insulate themselves so effectively against the contradictions of their position.

A Short and Partial Self-analysis

It is not only others who find it hard to detect and acknowledge the con- tradictions within their arguments. For the last section of this chapter I will set out aspects of the approach I have taken towards integration which illus- trate the contrasts and comparisons with Wolfensberger's and Lynas' texts and lay my own ideas open for critical scrutiny. As I have attempted to write this section I have realized how difficult and lengthy a process it is to try to trace the continuities and discontinuities between one's own thoughts and the thoughts of others and to document one's own development. In any case, such soul-searching may have limited interest. I will try to be brief.

I have set out elsewhere how my training as an educational psychologist fostered delusions about my expertise and my ability to act in the interest of pupils or their parents and how it was through listening to them that I began to challenge the acceptability of segregated special education (Booth, 1985, p. 39). I drew support to sustain my ideas in this period in the early 1970s as a fringe member of groups articulating their criticism of accepted practice in 'radical' psychology magazines. It seemed almost unthinkable at that time that such ideas might find a place in standard publishing outlets. Criticisms of segregated special education were closely allied with a critique of the value of IQ tests in working with individual pupils and in propping up the processes of selection. They were also spiced with a growing anger from black people about the way disproportionate numbers of black pupils were sent to special schools for 'the educationally subnormal' (Coard, 1971). When I conducted a small survey of the special schools in the town where I worked at the time I found this overrepresentation to exist there too. I could not persuade my colleagues to take an interest since they disputed my premise; that black parents did not relish the overrepresentation of their children. In my colleague's encounters with pupils they did not seem to notice that there was a stigma associated with special schooling, particularly those designated ESN(M), which parents tried to resist. It was much later that I discovered that Binet and Simon had anticipated such resistance and the method for breaking it down in 1914 (Binet and Simon, 1914, p. 36). It was also impossible to gain acceptance for the way biases towards black pupils, which could not be detected at an individual level, could be magnified in the overall process of selection for special schools. It was not possible, I argued, to attempt to treat each pupil on their merits. Of course there are many possible reasons why I found it difficult to persuade others to adopt my ideas and I am predisposed to find only some of these attractive. One of my colleagues used to begin every report on a child with the words 'Routine psychometric testing produced the following results ...'. A student educational psychologist who had been 'on placement' in our area sent me a postcard with these words on one side followed by 'see over'. On the other side was a photograph of a donkey.

I have continued to try to root my conceptions of integration in the understanding of pupils and parents. I learnt much from a group of parents with whom I worked who were struggling to obtain an integrated education for their children with Down's Syndrome as well as by acting as an advocate for the interests of others (Booth, 1981 a). I have been struck by the way the inequalities of power between administrators, professionals and parents are used to enable what is often an inferior knowledge base to dominate the outcome of discussions.

So, in coming clean about the origins of my own ideas I would have to represent the pupils, parents and teachers as well as adults with disabilities and others I have met, for the vast majority of whom a published reference cannot be given. I have formulated a conception of integration which is about the process of enhancing the participation of disadvantaged groups within their communities. People with disabilities are one such group and their involvement in education a particular case. My examination of legislation and integration in the USA, Italy and Norway focused my attention on issues of rights, work and educational philosophy (Booth, 1982; Weatherley, 1979; Ferro, 1981; Vislie, 1981). I was impressed by the way the early introduction of comprehensive secondary education in Norway in the 1920s facilitated the link between a comprehensive and integration philosophy which has been a continuing strand in my own work.

The politics of value

This focus on the enhancement of comprehensive education has led on to an attempt to define in detail the way the curricula in schools might foster the participation of pupils in a series of books, *Curricula for All* (Booth, Potts and Swann, ed., 1987; Booth and Coulby, ed., 1987; Booth and Swann, ed., 1987).

Within this series I have suggested that both an integration principle and a comprehensive principle can be illuminated by reference to a principle of equality of value:

> In schools which operate according to such a principle attempts are made to reduce the devaluation of pupils according to their sex, background, colour, economic or class position, ability, disability or attainment (Booth, 1987 a, p. viii).

The links I and my colleagues have made between segregation, selection and devaluation are very similar to those I find in reading Wolfensberger's work, though until recently I had not given any of it a detailed reading. I am aware that the assertion of a principle of equality of value can appear politically naive in just the way that I have criticized the promotion of valued social roles in the absence of an understanding of the power of the economy to determine the value of people's labour and identity. For me, the links are obvious and I have seen an elaboration of a principle of equality of value as prompting others to make the same links without ramming my politics down their throat. However, if the links are obvious one would expect to see the principle hotly disputed. After all we do live in a society in which people are often obsessed by differences in status and class and the wish to preserve these by differentials in pay. I was surprised therefore when I asked a group of teachers to vote according to the following propositions:

(1) No child should be excluded from a primary or secondary school solely on the grounds of disability.
(2) No pupil should be excluded from a primary and secondary school on the grounds of limited ability or attainment.
(3) Schools should attempt to promote a principle of equality of value.

I had expected the vote to mirror practice in schools. That is, many schools are willing to include pupils with disabilities whilst continuing to exclude pupils regarded as having 'moderate' or 'severe' learning difficulties. Will Swann (1987) has written up an interesting case study, where such conditions are in operation, between a secondary and a special school. Very few schools indeed are willing to address the whole range of devaluations implied in operating a principle of equality of value. However, despite the methodological inadequacies of my opinion survey there was one clear and unexpected result. Every teacher present voted in favour of the principal of equality of value with considerably fewer supporting the other propositions. There are a number of interpretations for this. One surfaced when in expressing my surprise at their vote I asked if they realized the implications for the re-evaluation of pay scales that applying such a principle might entail. One teacher responded immediately: 'of course we realise that . . . it would mean that we would all get a pay rise'. Our discussion had taken place at the time of a long and bitter dispute between teachers and central government over pay and conditions during which teachers were feeling particularly undervalued!

But there is another possible explanation. We may give a reflex-like support for propositions about equality which prevents us from following through the logical implications and leaves deeper prejudices unexamined. As Wolfensberger put it:

> We all claim to believe in equality — and then we practise gross discrimination, but deny it because we cannot admit it and therefore do not realise that we discriminate . . . we claim to render treatment — and then we dehumanize, and yet deny that we dehumanize (Wolfensberger, 1972, p. 10).

Wolfensberger's error at that time was to believe the rhetoric. He felt that people wanted equality but practised discrimination because they did not realize it. I have accepted the argument that a rhetorical commitment for equality in general and equality of opportunity in particular can be an effective way of obscuring one's support for an inequitable society. I have sensed that the rhetoric of integration has served segregative processes in a similar way (Booth, 1981 b, p. 299).

I intended that formulation of a principle of equality of value should point up rather than obscure the nature of inequalities and devaluations in our schools and in society and certainly would not wish it to be linked to a notion of equality of opportunity. As social policy, equality of opportunity is one of the main ideological vehicles for hiding the economic means whereby inequalities are generated. I have drawn on the clear and devastating dismissal of such an idea by Tawney (1931) who characterized it as the Tadpole philosophy as well as an allegory by Kurt Vonnegut in which God berates the souls of dead Americans for failing to grasp the economic opportunities they might have seized. The soul of Albert Einstein attempts to point out the mathematical fallacies involved until he is silenced by the threat to take his violin away 'which he loves more than anything' (Vonnegut, 1979, pp. 188–191). I have tried to make it clear that as long as society and schools provide 'arenas for competing interests . . . the advancement of the participation of one group must be at the expense of the re-evaluation of another' (Booth, 1987 a, p. ix). The advancement of the interests of, for example, people with mental handicaps or black people or women involves a reduction in the power of others by virtue of their characterization as able or white or men. The title of the Fish Report *Equal Opportunities for All* can be seen in this light to be a contradiction in terms (ILEA, 1985). Yet I do not believe people give up their power easily nor without costs though there may be other benefits. As one teacher remarked joyfully after succumbing to the challenge in our course to rethink her position of authority in relation to her pupils and colleagues: 'I have blown my chances of promotion forever'. However, more commonly, people resist changing their working principles and give up their power only after prolonged challenge.

It was partly with tongue in cheek, therefore, that I argued in the preface to the series *Curricula for All* that it was hard to see how 'those who profess a concern for vulnerable and disadvantaged pupils should take any other view' than to regard 'pupils who gain Oxbridge entry as of no greater value, as no more worthy of congratulation than pupils with severe mental handicap' (pp. viii to ix). I am well aware that many would abhor the economic and cultural revolution that this would entail. Yet the contradiction remains that people will profess a lifelong commitment to the removal of the difficulties in learning of pupils in schools whilst adhering to a social philosophy which devalues them, their families and future occupations. One might argue that if such devaluations don't actually lead to the learning difficulties of pupils then they should! Such a set of social attitudes were neatly and pertinently expressed by Mary Warnock in the 1985 Dimbleby lecture when she remarked of teachers who contemplated strike action:

> Teachers on strike get little sympathy, however reasonable their case; and they do their image irreparable harm. They are thought to put themselves on a level with other wage-earners — miners, car workers and those whose jobs are concerned with the production of goods (Warnock, 1985, p. 10).

It is relatively easy to speculate where such a scale of values leaves unskilled workers, domestic labourers and the unemployed, let alone people with mental handicaps. The ways in which the devaluation of pupils can lead to pools of potential or actual disaffection is a major theme of *Producing and Reducing Disaffection* (Booth and Coulby, Eds, 1987).

Integration as challenge

My colleagues and I have attempted to develop, then, a concept of integration which prompts ourselves and others to challenge the social relations and curricula of schools, and to link these to the way inequalities are maintained, reproduced and countered. It is concerned with redefining normality to include diversity and with supporting people to define their aspirations and opportunities for themselves.

Conclusion

In this chapter I have looked in some detail at three conceptions of integration with the intention of fostering the process of criticism. Such a task is a preparation for a more searching analysis of the political underpinnings and effects of the variety of ways in which the advocacy of integration is framed. Like any other area of life competing definitions are the dressing on conflicting views about the nature and future of society. This display of differing conceptions should not impede a careful analysis of any general moves towards community-care. On the contrary this is increasingly urgent as the entrepreneurial spirit consumes ever larger areas of welfare. But I do believe that academics who refrain from making their commitments explicit delude themselves if they believe that their position is neutral in its effects or that their ability to analyse the reality of others or themselves is thereby enhanced.

Acknowledgement

I would like to thank Len Barton for his comments on an earlier version of this chapter.

Notes

1 There has been a growing awareness in recent years that some expressions can contribute to the disadvantage of people with disabilities (see Merry, 1981,

p. 29). I tend to avoid terms where a person's identity appears to be depicted by a disability such as 'an epileptic', or 'the disabled'. However, some people with disabilities use the latter term, themselves, to convey a sense of solidarity and a positive identity. In the case of 'the deaf' I use this term in my own writing because of my acceptance of the arguments from deaf people for an over-whelming need to reclaim their deafness as a positive contribution to their lives.

2 Wendy Lynas uses this sexist language throughout her text, written in 1986. Wolfensberger's 1972 text as well as the quote from Binet and Simon 1914 use male pronouns at a time when the ideological climate on such matters was less accessible to question, though looking back now, some passages look ridiculous. Wolfensberger writes: 'In the next chapter we will review how ideologies have forged man's patterns of response to devalued groups of fellow men (Wolfensberger, 1972, p. 10). Did I really head a chapter I wrote in 1975 *Nature and Change in Man* (Booth, 1975, p. 130)? Some authors writing currently are digging in their heels on such usage. I have analysed the effect that such a deter-mined lack of self-consciousness can have on the way gender roles are ascribed in a review of Cole's *Residential Special Education* (Cole, 1986; Booth, 1987 b).

3 Two examples come to mind immediately but there are many others. Hegarty and Pocklington (1982) report that 'developing pupils' ability to communicate, preferably in an oral way' is the 'central goal' of 'deaf education' (p. 158). Cole (1986) referring to the education of the deaf tells us that 'language development must be the central facet of their educational programme' (p. 85).

References

BANK-MIKKELSEN, N.E. (1969) 'A metropolitan area in Denmark: Copenhagen', in KUGEL, R., WOLFENSBERGER, W. (Eds) *Changing Patterns in Residential Services for the Mentally Retarded*, pp. 227–254, Washington: President's Committee on Mental Retardation.

BARTON, L. and TOMLINSON, S. (1984) 'The politics of integration in England' in BARTON, L. and TOMLINSON, S. (Eds) *Special Education and Social Interests*, London, Croom Helm.

BINET, A. and SIMON, T. (1914) *Mentally Defective Children*, London, Edward Arnold.

BOOTH, T. (1975) *Growing up in Society*, London, Methuen.

BOOTH, T. (1981 a) 'Educating children with Down's Syndrome in an ordinary school', in *Early Child Development and Care*, 7(2), pp. 165–184.

BOOTH, T. (1981 b) 'Demystifying Integration', in Swann, W. (Ed.) *The Practice of Special Education*, Oxford, Blackwell.

BOOTH, T. (1982) 'National Perspectives', *E241, Special Needs in Education*, Milton Keynes, Open University Press.

BOOTH, T. (1983) 'Integrating special education', Chapter 1 in BOOTH, T. and POTTS, P. (Eds) *Integrating Special Education*, Oxford, Blackwell.

BOOTH, T. (1985) 'The Progress of Integration' in *Education and Child Psychology*, vol. 2, no. 3, pp. 39–45.

BOOTH, T. (1987) 'Introduction to the series', in BOOTH, T., POTTS, P. and SWANN, W. (Eds) *Curricula for All*, Oxford, Blackwell.

BOOTH, T. (1987) 'Backwards into the future; residential special education', in *Disability, Handicap and Society*, 2(2), pp. 187–192.

BOOTH, T. and COULBY, D. (Eds) (1987) *Producing and Reducing Disaffection; Curricula for All*, Milton Keynes, Open University Press.

BOOTH, T., POTTS, P. and SWANN, W. (Eds) (1987) *Preventing Difficulties in Learning; Curricula for All*, Oxford, Blackwells.

BOOTH, T. and SWANN, W. (Eds) (1987) *Including Pupils with Disabilities*, Milton Keynes, Open University Press.

BRENNAN, M. (1987) 'British sign language: the language of the deaf community', in BOOTH, T. and SWANN, W. (Eds) op. cit.

BURDEN, R. (1985) 'To integrate or not to integrate: is that the question? Special education needs in the ordinary school', in *Perspectives*, 15, pp. 21–29, School of Education, University of Exeter.

COARD, B. (1971) *How the West Indian Child is Made Educationally Sub-normal in the British School System*, New Beacon Books, London.

COLE, T. (1986) *Residential Special Education*, Milton Keynes, Open University Press.

DESLOGES, P. (1779) 'A deaf person's observations about an elementary course of education for the deaf', in LANE, H. (Ed.), *The Deaf Experience*, Cambridge, Harvard University Press.

FARRELL, P. and SUGDEN, M. (1985) 'Integrating children with severe learning difficulties: fantasy or reality?', *Educational and Child Psychology*, 2(3), pp. 69–80.

FERRO, N. (1981) *The Education of the Handicapped Adolescent: the integration of handicapped youth in normal schools in Italy*, Paris, OECD.

HEGARTY, S. and POCKLINGTON, P. (1982) *Integration in Action*, Windsor, NFER-Nelson.

INNER LONDON EDUCATION AUTHORITY (1985) *Equal Opportunities for All*, London, ILEA.

LANE, H. (Ed.) (1984) *The Deaf Experience*, Cambridge, Harvard University Press.

LANE, H. (1984) *When the Mind Hears*, New York, Random House.

LYNAS, W. (1986) *Integrating the Handicapped into Ordinary Schools: a study of hearing-impaired pupils*, London, Croom Helm.

McGRATH, G. (1981) 'Language competency in the evaluation of integration: a view from Australia', in Montgomery, G. (Ed.) *The Integration and Disintegration of the Deaf in Society*, Edinburgh: Scottish Workshop Publications.

MERRY (1981) in Campling, J. (Ed.) *Images of Ourselves: women with disabilities talking*, London, Routledge and Kegan Paul.

MITTLER, P. (1985) 'Integration: the shadow and the substance', in *Educational and Child Psychology*, 2(3), pp. 8–22.

OLIVER, M. (1985) 'The integration-segregation debate: some sociological considerations', in *British Journal of Sociology of Education*, 6(1), pp. 75–92.

SCULL, A. (1977) *Decarceration*, 2nd edition (1984), Cambridge, Polity Press.

SEDGEWICK, P. (1982) *Psychopolitics*, London, Pluto Press.

SÖDER, M. (1984) 'The mentally retarded: ideologies of care and surplus population', in BARTON, L. and TOMLINSON, S. (Eds) op. cit.

SWANN, W. (1987) 'Firm links should be established: a case study of conflict and policy-making for integration', in BOOTH, T. and SWANN, W. (Eds) op. cit.

TAWNEY, R.H. (1931) *Equality*, London, George Allen and Unwin (fourth ed., 1951).

THOMAS, D., FIRTH, H. and KENDALL, A. (1978) *ENCOR — a way ahead*, London, Campaign for the Mentally Handicapped.

TOMLINSON, S. (1982) *A Sociology of Special Education*, Henley, Routledge and Kegan Paul.

VISLIE, L. (1981) 'Policies for educational integration and its implications for basic education in Norway', in *OECD Study in Basic Education*, Oslo, OECD.

VONNEGUT, K. (1979) *Jailbird*, London, Granada.

WARNOCK, M. (1985) 'Teacher Teach Thyself', in *The Listener*, 28.3.85, pp. 9–13.

WEATHERLEY, R. (1979) *Reforming Special Education; policy implementation from state level to street level*, Cambridge, MIT Press.

WINTERTON, J. (1985) *Oranges Are Not the Only Fruit*, London, Pandora.

WOLFENSBERGER, W. (1972) *The Principle of Normalization in Human Services*, Toronto: National Institute on Mental Retardation.

WOLFENSBERGER, W. (1980) 'The definition of normalization: update, problems, disagreements and misunderstandings', in FLYNN, R.J. and NITSCH, K.E. (Eds) *Normalization, Social Integration and Community Services*, pp. 71–115, Baltimore: University Park Press.

WOLFENSBERGER, W. (1983) 'Social role valorization: a proposed new term for the principle of normalization', in *Mental Retardation*, 21(6), pp. 234–239.

Chapter 6

Who's Moving the Goal Posts and What Game are We Playing Anyway: Social Competence Examined

Andrea Freeman

Introduction

In this chapter I intend to address the concepts surrounding social competence and the ways in which schooling appears to sidetrack common sense expectations that this is a major aim in education. Those children with special educational needs are so defined, in this analysis, through the application of criteria which define them as socially incompetent by the dominant culture in schools and the associated and dominant professions (see Tomlinson, 1982).

Ideas about social competence have been very common in education, but the concerns have been to do with either social control or ways of enabling those seen as very incompetent, because of immaturity or exceptionality to have access to resources for improved coping. In order to undertake this task effectively, it has been assumed via the powerful medical model and its psychological variant, this could only be done through the application of tests, often psychometric. There has been considerable work on the identification of the socially incompetent through an array of formal tests, including those relating to the problems of 'emotional lability', 'maladjustment', 'sensory deficit', 'intellectual deficits', and 'physical disabilities' without any analysis of the assumptions that underpin these processes. These formal tests serve to enable society to identify people, usually children, who will be unable to cope in the world without some form of extra provision. It has been argued that this identification is one of the benefits of labelling: that administrators will be aware of the problems and of the extent of the problems in order to be able to plan more efficiently and effectively. It is also argued that labelling enables power groups to form in order to influence policy making and provision. (This is not to deny that there are many disadvantages of labelling.) However, an examination of the reality which underpins the rhetoric of helping people through the imposition of legitimated labelling is required, and one attempt at reconceptualization follows.

Social Competence

A range of theoretical work has been undertaken on social competence, for example White (1974) who argued that a person, to be socially competent, must be able to conduct successful transactions with the environment, leading to self-actualization and growth. The conditions necessary to conduct these transactions he identified as:

(1) a person must obtain adequate information about the environment
(2) they must maintain satisfactory internal conditions both for action and for processing of information
(3) they must maintain autonomy and freedom of movement — and freedom to use their repertoire in a flexible fashion.

There are many questions raised by this conceptualization, for example, who defines success? The person or the others in the social setting? When can it be said to be successful? There are differences between long and short term effects. How much growth can be considered to be a prerequisite? What proportion of transactions should be successful? For many of us the sorts of transactions that we feel lead to self actualization are few. There are problems with the conditions necessary to conduct such transactions, for although at first sight they may appear straightforward, on examination their complexity and enormity become apparent. Most of us can secure information about the environment, and yet it may not be adequate to enable us to operate successfully in that environment — going to another country for example. Some people are in this position in their own community due to status differences, children may just not be told as they are considered too young, or lack of knowledge about how to find it out, or isolation or even insensitivity. The second condition refers to the ability to cope with stress, by controlling the emotional aspects of life in order to be able to take action, and in addition process information. One of the features of experiencing stress is that information processing capacity is reduced through the preoccupation with those aspects causing the stress. The generality of the condition would include such aspects as health, a sense of well being, and personal self regard, all of which may depend on the three conditions, indicating a circularity of argument. The third condition also appears to depend on the other two, and seems to represent an ideal situation, for most people are constrained by emotional ties or the need for paid employment.

However, the points are made when the lives of the stigmatized are examined (See Goffman 1961, 1963; Edgerton, 1967; Braginsky and Braginsky, 1971). The institutionalization processes and rituals appear to rob the people studied of their limited opportunities to secure adequate information, maintain equilibrium or maintain autonomy and freedom of movement. However White does emphasize the person as a social being, someone who acts in a social world with negotiated meanings.

This is in marked contrast to the approach taken by workers in the field of severe learning difficulties, who have produced a range of assessment tools for the use of workers (and sometimes parents) which are intended to inform decision-making concerning the suitability of the person for placement in a range of residential alternatives. The information can be used to decide whether the incompetent individual can be desegregated on the basis of largely practical tasks, and therefore capable of living in society. An example of this approach is the Chart of Initiative and Independence (Macdonald and Couchman, 1980). This chart involves assessment in ten areas: personal hygiene, medical, domestic, catering, shopping, use of services, finances, social organization of time, leisure, and social interactions. The major criticism of such scales is that they demand higher standards of behaviour from the segregated population than they do from ordinary unsegregated individuals and if the criteria for living in society were applied generally, most people would not meet them. For example Clothes Care, 'This includes the hanging and storing of clothes in wardrobes, cupboards, drawers and clothes stands, etc. Does not include mending clothes.' Many parents would be pleased if their children undertook this! Another example is that of Leisure: Television 'The use of television relates to the modes through the element of choice and the regard for the wishes of others.' There are a number of possible criticisms of this item, firstly exercizing choice, although desirable, is not always possible, either through the particular power of an individual in the family, or through a lack of opportunity for choice. Secondly, there is an implicit valuing of a passive role of deferring to the wishes of others. There is little mention in the Chart of skills relating to being assertive and being able to argue effectively for what one wants. This item also assumes that everyone involved has the same strength of feeling concerning their choice. It may be more important for the individual to be able to judge when a person is strongly interested or slightly interested rather than taking their wishes into account. In addition, the items are largely based on one set of values — white, middle-class and relatively conservative; for example in Use of Services; local facilities 'This includes swimming pools, libraries, parks, leisure centres. It could also include any social clubs, etc., which require social interaction or declared interest'. Would this include any facilities favoured by working class people?

A problem which underpins the whole of the Chart and others like it is the assumptions made about what is 'normal'. Many of the items are implicitly normal, albeit within a particular value system; however this also can be questioned. Would it be desirable for all of the behaviours to be performed? Whilst accepting the desirability of most of the items they are probably not consistently performed by most adults. For example, it may be considered reasonable (and 'normal') to leave the bed unmade if late, and problematic if the bed is routinely made without regard for the circumstances. It can be more important to consider the context of the behaviour rather than the performance of the behaviour. For example, taking one's clothes off is considered normal in certain circumstances, if very young, on the beach or in a sports changing room; however, the same behaviour can lead to custody or commital if very old, it is dark and cold — the social meaning of the behaviour being that the old person is unable to take care of him/herself. Another dimension to the change in social meaning can occur in another culture, including social class and in the differing expectations within a culture of men and women. From Pearlin and Schooler's research (1978) into 'normal' people and how they cope (as opposed to unusual groups such as women awaiting biopsy results), information suggested that women are socialized into different coping strategies which usually increase their stress rather than diminish it. This situation was aggravated by social class differences, in that the lower down the social scale you go, the more the stress experienced and the fewer the coping strategies. Social class differences which produce problems in communication will be discussed later; at this point, however, an example will illustrate the problem of how professionals make judgments using their own notions about normality within their own subculture and misinformation about other subcultures: the use of physical punishment by a middle-class mother is likely to be seen as resulting from stress, whereas the same behaviour in a working-class mother will be seen as normal ('What do you expect from someone who lives there!').

Some programmes in schools for 'leavers' attempt to teach 'life skills', which can be approached variably from the skills of boiling eggs and tying shoelaces (as if these were essential!) to filling in forms, applying for jobs and other clerical tasks. A major component of some lifeskills approaches is basic skills teaching, particularly literacy and numeracy. Some of these programmes are firmly rooted in assumptions relating to deficits which the students have in terms of being able to cope, once they have left the protecting world of the school. Rarely is the school's responsibility in the creation of the identified deficits acknowledged (see Croll and Moses, 1985, for an analogous survey). There are also assumptions about the culture that the students should be initiated into, and who can best do it. The main question is why? and this appears to be unasked in relation to the lifeskills courses — other than because they are 'non-examinable' students. The courses do not appear to be conceptualized in terms of social competence, partly because they are unaware of the available but largely ignored theoretical framework offered by Greenspan (1981) who has produced a taxonomy of social competence which is particularly helpful, and offers not only a description of the areas, which educators would find illuminating, but points out that they can be taught. This is the most important message, that teaching can be undertaken to some effect rather than concentrating on aspects which cannot be readily changed.

Greenspan conceives social competence to be part of personal competence, which has three elements: physical competence, intellectual competence and emotional competence. Social competence is a combination of emotional competence and the social intelligence aspect of intellectual competence. The model below shows the aspects subsumed under social competence.

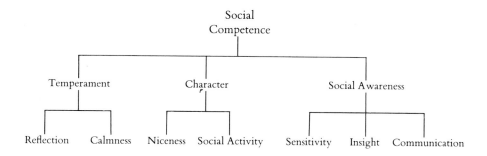

Within social awareness seven areas are delineated:

Sensitivity	— role taking
	— social inference
Social insight	— social comprehension
	— psychological insight
	— moral judgement
Social communication	— referential communication
	— social problem solving

Greenspan's taxonomy is useful for bringing together many differing research findings into a coherent form for investigation. He identifies three types of approaches: the outcome-oriented, the content-oriented and the skills-oriented. White's (1974) analysis is outcome-oriented since to be socially competent the individual must be able to conduct successful transactions with the environment. The approach taken by Macdonald and Couchman (1980) is largely skills-oriented, although most of the items do not fall within Greenspan's taxonomy of social competence but would be seen as 'practical intelligence'. Content-oriented approaches attempt to identify personality traits which contribute to socially successful outcomes.

Greenspan argues that considerable time and effort is spent to little effect in attempting to change children's temperaments and characters to try to make them more socially acceptable, and this is clearly the case with children who are thought to be socially and emotionally unable to cope (so called 'disturbed' children). For example, impulsiveness is one of the aspects of behaviour which is thought to be a serious problem in preventing children from learning — being unable to concentrate one's attention and not acting with deliberation — this is the other end of the dimension of reflection. Similarly, the opposite end of the calmness dimension is emotionality where the individual is unable to tolerate frustration and may become excessively upset. Within the character dimension, niceness refers to the way that children value others, their concern and responsible behaviour to others, whilst social activity refers to the level of gregariousness and boldness of the individual, indicating a valuation of self. These aspects are not put forward as positive and negative ends of dimensions but professionals have used them, in different models, to identify children as 'maladjusted', etc. The aspects subsumed under social awareness are far more amenable to change, since they can be directly taught.

It could be argued that if children learn the three aspects of social awareness — sensitivity, social insight, and social communication — they will inevitably temper their character and temperament through a process of informing, and that direct attempts to 'improve' character and temperament without teaching social awareness is futile, or at best misguided. In addition, the moral and ethical aspects of deliberately setting out to change a child's character must be considered; some teachers have found this notion unacceptable (Freeman and Attfield 1985).

The benefit of using Greenspan's model is that it clearly separates practical intelligence from other aspects of social competence; practical intelligence being the ability to solve problems 'of a physical nature, which are relevant to everyday work and recreational concerns. For example, . . . knowledge of how to get to work, to manage a household, or how to avoid danger' (Greenspan, 1981, p. 30). It also separates social skills from social awareness with the importance of understanding being stressed in the latter. It is one thing to be able to achieve something, it is quite another to understand how one achieved it! The model also offers a framework within which to try to understand special educational needs and how teachers make a social reality out of the concept.

Social Competence and Coping

From my experience, it seems that those aspects delineated in the social awareness aspect of social competence are essential for competent adulthood, and yet it is clear that few attempts have been made to incorporate them into the curriculum of the school. Social competence and coping are linked in common sense usage; it is expected that to cope better, social competence is required, or if a person is not socially competent then stress might be more likely to be experienced, and to some extent the Pearlin and Schooler (1978) research would confirm this view. However the two areas are totally separate in terms of their research traditions, and definitions of each do not necessarily incorporate the other. Within stress and coping research, it is generally accepted that the experience of stress or coping is self-defined, using a process of appraisal in which the person takes into account their social competence as only one aspect of the process; other aspects will include practical intelligence, conceptual intelligence and physical competence as well as resources available (Freeman 1986). However, this is not to deny that social competence as defined by Greenspan (1981) is an integral part of appraisal, and may be more important than other aspects.

There are as many definitions of coping as workers in the field: two examples will be given to indicate the range. Pearlin and Schooler (1978) define coping in terms of what people DO rather than what they ARE, thereby excluding all psychological and social resources and supports. In contrast, Ursin *et al.* (1978) defined coping in physiological terms, in describing physiological changes which took place alongside learning to cope.

In my research into teacher stress and coping, I developed a model of stress and coping which is based upon the two level cognitive processing model explicated by Morris (1981). The two levels are BOSS, which is conscious intentional cognitive functioning such as problem solving, whilst the second is EMPLOYEE, which is unconscious, unintentional functioning such as remembering. The terms used also indicate an executive overall monitoring function for BOSS. When applied to coping strategies, it appears that when coping at an everyday EMPLOYEE level, people are

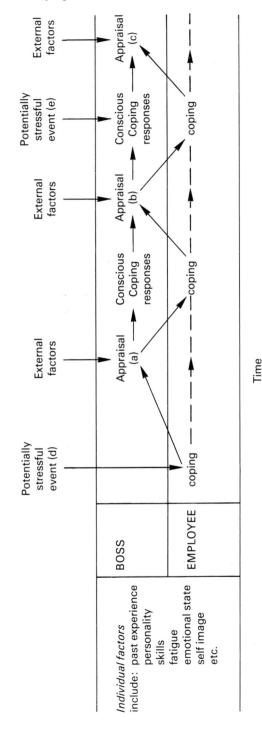

A Model of Coping

Individual factors
include: past experience
        personality
        skills
        fatigue
        emotional state
        self image
        etc.

External factors
include: social support
        hygiene factors
        hobbies and interests
        other resources
        etc.

Conscious coping responses
include: problem solving
        control of emotional responses
        use of ego defences
        reference to self image
        'learned helplessness'
        conscious use of ignoring
        etc.

Time

BOSS

EMPLOYEE

Potentially
stressful
event (d)

Potentially
stressful
event (e)

External
factors

External
factors

External
factors

Appraisal
(a)

Appraisal
(b)

Appraisal
(c)

Conscious
Coping
responses

Conscious
Coping
responses

coping

coping

coping

Figure 1

usually unable to say how they cope, or they can only express it in vague terms, as it is akin to being on automatic pilot. However, as soon as coping moves into BOSS level, it is easy to say how a problem was solved, and the way the thing was thought through (see figure 1). The concept of the threshold has been developed to try to explain the variability of stress that individuals experience. Briefly, a person will define themselves as stressed more frequently when the threshold between BOSS and EMPLOYEE is lowered (resistance is low). When this occurs more BOSS time is occupied with stress matters which leads to a more negative self-image, loss of confidence, self-criticism and self-definition as a person who cannot cope. Indeed, many workers in the helping agencies advise their 'clients' to raise their thresholds in order to promote coping, e.g., don't react to all the trivial matters, only attend to what is important (see figure 2).

COPING and STRESS are closely related. We are aware of stress when coping at the automatic pilot level breaks down, and conscious strategies of coping must be employed.

A. AUTOMATIC PILOT — overlearned strategies (from childhood)
                      — unplanned
                      — often inappropriate in extreme circumstances

position of
threshold
depends on —
personal state
resources and
stressors
i.e. appraisal

B. CONSCIOUS COPING STRATEGIES E.G. PROBLEM SOLVING

                — planned
                — preoccupying
                — limited capacity
                — intentional

Figure 2

A most important aspect of stress is that it is self defined through a process called appraisal. Many different aspects are simultaneously taken into account in the process, including personal factors — how do I feel today? can I do this task? has anything else troubled me? what happened last time? and factors in the environment — who's in the next room? what support can I expect? is it my job to do this? Time is another important aspect, for what may be stressful in the middle of the night may not be so during waking hours.

Many people find it difficult to understand and accept that the experience of stress IS self-defined and think that the non-coper can be spotted easily. But what tends to happen is that some events are thought to be universally stressful, e.g., bereavement, and we all accept that help is required at such times. Indeed, there is a scale of life events which will inform you how stressed you are (see Holmes and Rahe 1967). It is far more likely that we are not going to be able to guess whether someone is coping unless we ask them (and then believe them). Frequently, we misinterpret body language, or we just choose to ignore a worried look because it is more convenient to do so. Another phenomenon is in assuming that a person is not coping because we consider that in that situation we could not cope ourself. Individual differences are a major problem in research into stress for it is figuratively true that one person's meat is another person's poison. Some people engage in activities for fun which others would not do at any price. Misunderstandings may not matter in the long term with friends and families as time can put it into perspective, but it is important when the helping professionals use concepts of coping — *without consulting the consumer*. Blaxter (1976) found that when patients were discharged from hospital the allocation of resources was based on a professional's brief encounter with the patient, sometimes without the appropriate questions being asked. As a consequence, the patients perceived the services as being unfairly given.

This is a further example of assumptions about social competence, individual coping and about disability, often based on the professional's concepts of normality, and what they consider people *should* be able to cope with. Professionals' judgments relating to coping and social competence may be based on social class differences, or upon a communications difficulty between the professional and the consumer, particularly if there is already a class difference and if the consumer is socially incompetent in dealing with powerful professionals. In addition, professionals may define the consumers as incompetent and therefore take less notice of them, making up their own minds about what is required (see McKnight 1977). An insidious problem is that of the frightened or anxious person who knows they have little time with a professional to argue a case. The professional may make all decisions on the basis of the performance of the plaintiff in an extremely stressful situation.

This is compounded by assumptions made that people are essentially untruthful, especially children, and that what they say about themselves is largely untrustworthy unless confirmed by a professional colleague. It is particularly problematic for groups in society who are least powerful, usually women, children and youths and ethnic minority groups. A recent study of Freud's change of mind concerning child sexual abuse delineates the way that the rejection by his colleagues of his original theoretical position — that children do not lie, that child sexual abuse was common, and the basis of subsequent neuroses — led him to change to the position that it was all fantasy (Masson 1984). This appears to have perpetuated a myth in medicine and particularly psychiatry that the patients cannot be relied upon to tell the *real* story (also forgetting that we all have our own social reality).

Some professionals are also required to be legitimizers of definitions or labels of not coping, or lack of social competence, usually so that the person has access to benefits or services. This is certainly the case with the procedures under the 1981 Education Act, where three professionals are required to submit advice concerning the special educational needs of the named child. Most professional workers know that the extent of any disability will not give reliable guidance to the degree of handicap experienced by the individual, and yet the way to get the benefit is to give evidence about the disability rather than the extent to which the disability is translated into handicap. Some disabled people are extremely socially competent, and indeed cope better with life generally than some who do not have disabilities, but who are not eligible for benefits. This is a clear example of the misunderstanding of both disability and of coping. In both cases the medical (deficit) model of the disability as the problem, or the social event as the problem, ignores all that is known about coping, particularly that it is the *individual's response to their social context* which is most important.

Some people are legitimated non-copers without necessarily being aware of it. This may happen when children are placed on an 'at risk' register, where clearly it is the parents who are identified as not being able to cope or as socially incompetent. The registers are intended to protect the children, but often do little more than ensure that any call for help is taken seriously.

Social Competence and Special Needs

In this section I will be considering children with special needs and the way that concepts about social competence are covertly used to identify and segregate children. In addition the assumptions underlying childhood coping will be questioned.

Part of the definition of the status of childhood is that children are not considered responsible for their actions (at least in the early years) and laws protect them from aspects of life which adults have to contend with, such as marriage, work, and jury service; for children, by definition are socially incompetent. They are considered to be unable to care for themselves and are protected from other aspects of life by the need for parental consent (including access by professionals in the helping agencies). A recent public discussion has centred around contraception, and whether parents of children (usually girls) below the age of consent should be given contraception without the knowledge of their parents. In the Lords' ruling, the professionals won the day, with contraception being available on medical grounds of risk (and medical can be very broadly interpreted; see, for example, the Court Report). This focused on two issues which are important when considering the socially incompetent, firstly whether the individual concerned, regardless of their age, understands the issues concerned, and secondly the rights of the parents of the individual. The second issue is of particular pertinence when considering individuals thought of as almost certainly dependent throughout their lives; it is difficult for parents to cease to be parental in their approach even though they may no longer care for their grown-up 'child' at home. And if they no longer do so, to what extent are they still the owners of the problems and responsible for decision making? In addition, the rights of professionals to 'own' problems is very problematic.

If children are, by definition, socially incompetent, then children with special needs are going to be seen as having even greater incompetence, since they require more assistance and different provision from the rest of us who can cope. The definition of special needs is variable; there is the legal definition from the 1981 Education Act, and a range of definitions from government reports and other authors. In practice, most teachers will claim that all children have special needs at some time. There seems to be two competing definitions of special needs which I will briefly mention, which have serious implications for services (see figure 3). The first definition derives from the tradition of caring for the severely disabled, and relies on experts and segregated provision. Within this tradition the need for more and better training has been successfully argued and indeed some teachers are required by law to have specialized qualifications (i.e., those who teach the visually or the hearing impaired). The second tradition originated within ordinary schools, usually remedial or compensatory education, and leads to an acceptance of wide variation within a community, with all participants having a responsibility. This tradition is the one reflected in teachers' claims that all children at some time have special needs. The conflict of interests arises when the differences between the two traditions is not understood and people within the field of special needs argue for more integrated provision and at the same time that only teachers who are highly specialized can teach children with special needs. The two traditions compete for funds at all levels and their advocates often have little understanding of the other side's point of view. School policies may be based on either (or sometimes, confusingly, both) traditions, regardless of whether they are special schools or mainstream schools, in that a special school may have integratory policies, and relate to other schools in the community, recognizing the teaching skills that all teachers have to offer. On the other hand, an ordinary school may practise a segregationalist policy within the school, restricting access, and may view some teachers as having an expert role with others having no expertise.

If we consider what disability means to most people it is clear that the term has implicit in it the idea of a lack of independence, since the individual is unable to care for him/herself, and in addition is not able to do things that others may take for granted. For most people this means a lack of physical movement and control, but also an element of deviance in other aspects of life, such as intellectual ability (see Freeman, in press). This common conception is associated with notions about social competence, since disability is defined by reference to aspects of life which identify people as lacking social competence which inevitably led them to being denied any rights to decision-making about themselves and their lives. The old categories of handicap were similar and indicated to others that the children placed in schools so designated were socially incompetent in particular ways. Children with severe learning difficulties, from very early in their lives, are designated as being unlikely to be able to live independently, and are one group which is officially labelled as socially incompetent. The public image reflects this and parents are usually very concerned about the degree of independence their child may achieve as an adult, and even more worried about what may happen when, through infirmity or death, they are no longer able to care for their child. People categorized as having severe learning difficulties are not expected to be socially competent, and the difficulty may be to convince others that they are. Similarly, children designated autistic, would be viewed as incompetent in that they would not be able to relate socially to others in an acceptable way and further are unable to obtain what they want without recourse to unusual and socially unacceptable behaviour. This may also be the case with some children labelled maladjusted. A different sort of incompetence is expected of those with hearing impairment where the competence of the individual is assessed on the level of communication skills which may not reflect their

COMPETING ASPECTS OF S.E.N.

WHOLE SCHOOL	SPECIAL INTEREST
ALL TEACHERS	SPECIALIST TEACHERS
COMMUNITY	EXPERTS
SAME	DIFFERENT
INTEGRATED	SEGREGATED
RIGHTS	NEEDS
OURS	THEIRS

Figure 3

understanding or social competence, so that the person may be seen as rather stupid, a problem which does not seem to beset the blind.

The old categories were abandoned, largely due to the problem of fitting children into them. A research study in the USA found that very few of the referrals for help to Health, Education and Welfare services were singular problems, but rather they were multi-faceted and required the services of many agencies, e.g., ten specific categorical services for a disadvantaged pregnant teenager (Attkisson and Broskovsky 1978). In this country children could not be slotted easily into single problem categories, and the process was compounded by the manipulation of the facilities by the professionals trying to obtain resources on behalf of individual children. But the procedures under the 1981 Education Act reinforce the idea that the child is the centre of the problem rather than the way the school is organized or the curriculum or the resources available to the teacher. The emphasis on identification and assessment distorts the time available for professionals to offer constructive systemic help to the school and family and children, since there are few requirements concerning intervention other than in placement and facilities. The procedures also serve to enhance the power of the professionals to define problems, usually to imply that the child is not coping, perhaps through social incompetence, and to give children 'spoiled identities' (Goffman 1963).

The question which is more difficult to answer is *who is not coping?* The frequent justification for intervention on behalf of the child is that it is the child who is not coping, or who *may not cope* in the next stage of schooling. This is a difficult position to justify since who is in a position to say with any certainty that this is the case? The interests of the different parties involved will almost certainly conflict. The parents may be the ones who are anxious on behalf of their child and who cannot cope, or the teacher may be unable to cope with feelings of inadequacy in teaching the child, or the headteacher may consider that the teacher is spending too much time with the child to the detriment of the others. The child may be blissfully unaware of the problems that the others are having, feel socially integrated and settled, and that the work they are doing is worthwhile, leading to a sense of achievement. So who can defend the child who is coping? A study by Mercer (1973) shows how different agencies in society use different definitions to select candidates for particular intervention programmes, and that in some cases there was very little overlap in the populations selected. This indicates that different professional groups use quite different criteria, based on differing perspectives and definitions.

How do members of a society cope with individuals that are defined as socially incompetent? Goffman (1963) refers to these people as carrying stigma and describes the consequences he observed from the individuals who were stigmatized and the efforts they made to 'pass' as normal. One way of looking at this question is to discover how people feel when they are in contact with stigmatized individuals and how much social distance they would prefer to have between themselves and the stigmatized. In a survey of undergraduates studying education, they were asked 'How do you feel when you meet someone who is disabled?'. Three sorts of reactions were recorded, and these are consistent with other attitude surveys: the strongest reaction mentioned was unease and lack of confidence about how to behave, including embarrassment; secondly, that it is no different from meeting anyone else — once used to the situation; and thirdly, emotions such as pity, guilt, thankfulness that 'it's not me'. A small number of students said that it depended on the disability (18 per cent) and 3 per cent said it depended on the person's personality. The social distance information revealed a disinclination to share a house, but living next door was acceptable. The surprising finding was the apparent lack of desire to associate with those termed 'mentally ill' compared to 'mentally handicapped' or 'physically disabled'. It appears that some stigmas are easier to cope with, and do not give rise to feelings of alarm or inadequacy which lead to strained interactions between people.

Many people with disabilities are invisible to the general public following many years of segregated provision. The difficulties now are that the prospect of desegregation seems to give rise to feelings of threat and fear which are then disguised as concern for the stigmatized individual. ('Children are so cruel' is a frequent cry, meaning perhaps 'I am fearful and feel incompetent'.)

A threat is experienced by the host group when the stigmatized group oversteps the invisible boundary between what is acceptable and what is not, perhaps in terms of social distance, or unpredictability. The way that society deals with some socially incompetent individuals, for example some school leavers, can be reinterpreted using the idea that it is in some way threatened. That something has to be done with the many school leavers to prevent potential social unrest has been tackled in a number of ways. Redefinition has been used in the area of special needs, particularly by expanding the category to include school leavers who would in the past have had little difficulty in finding work. It has been suggested that all those who are not eligible for further education may be described as demonstrating special educational needs (Webster 1986). Many unemployed school leavers, it is argued, do not have the prerequisite skills for employment, and this identifies them as having special educational needs regardless of whether this was evident whilst they were at school and *regardless of the reality that there are no jobs anyway*. Thus these school leavers can be redefined as socially incompetent since they are unfit for work, and can be accommodated into other categorical programmes. Another form of redefinition is directed towards those leavers who are thought of as delinquent. These individuals are thought of as socially incompetent in the sense that they do not conform to expectations, and in Greenspan's terms are perceived to have either character or temperament defects. The next step in the redefinition is that they are therefore either 'bad' in that they are antisocial, delinquent and likely to commit crimes or they are 'mad' and have some form of personality disorder which makes them antisocial, and likely to commit crimes. Again, the lack of work, particularly in the inner cities and the north, which is a factor in their lack of employment, is overlooked. They are deviant and social controls must be employed. One way that has been instituted to exert social control is the extension of the system of YTS. In spite of criticism the YTS is now compulsory for two years in order to receive benefits and is a very strong form of social control of school leavers who do not have work and who might be seen as a threat to the social order of a society where the crime rate is rapidly rising and where there is said to be an increase in juvenile crime.

Schooling for Social Competence?

In 1985, HMI suggested that there are nine areas of experience that all pupils should have access to (DES, 1985). In a school improvement project to develop the curriculum based upon Greenspan's model of social competence, it was found that social competence totally pervaded the curriculum and could only be separated artificially from the nine areas. But the problem is not so much what is taught, but the implications arising from the model for teacher practices, parents, and the way that schools are run. A brief example will illustrate the difficulty. One of the important areas is that of social problem solving, which would involve teaching assertion skills, to negotiate and argue a case by marshalling evidence. It would be quite contradictory to teach this without changing the structures within the school to enable this to be a normal part of the school's process, otherwise it would be akin to teaching children to bark at print. When the project was underway, these sorts of problems became more and more explicit, so that the structure of schooling appeared to require a total overhaul to be able to incorporate the idea of schooling for social competence. Much of the hidden curriculum is covertly opposed to socially competent pupils, and it is the ideal pupil who conforms and is always interested in what the teacher offers, who is polite and respectful, who is put forward as the requirement, and who is seen as being the most socially competent. If a minority of pupils, regardless of their significance, choose not to conform it is assumed that they are at fault, rather than that they have found what is offered to be wanting and have protested in the only way open to them. In this scenario, socially competent pupils may be quite frightening, for teachers may find themselves in difficulties when justifying their practices, not only as individual teachers but in justifying institutional practices (which is already sometimes the case, for example, why girls but not boys can wear earrings, why lessons are of a particular length, why if you do option A you cannot then do option Y, why toilets are locked). There are also implications for the methods of teaching and learning, the power base and the curriculum. It seems that it is only in the nursery school that there are explicit curriculum areas relating to social competence and where the staff make clear to their pupils the social aspects of the schoolday and what is required of them in terms of social behaviour, for example taking turns, sharing, understanding social roles, negotiating activities and to some extent making sense of their social environment. As the children progress through school the requirements become part of the hidden curriculum without any direct teaching, but rather emphasizing the attempts at social control made by the school. Similarly, it is ironic that those seen as the least socially competent learners (the youngest children) are often given the most flexible and negotiated learning environment, and where, it could be argued, they are more responsible for their own learning than many sixth form pupils. Sixth formers in a school can be an anomaly, where responsibilities are delegated to undertake tasks which some of the staff might find daunting — especially the policing roles — and yet are not accorded the rights to be socially responsible and join in the decision-making, or be expected to negotiate or in general to be socially competent individuals.

The power base would also be threatened. Who would run the schools if the pupils were enabled to learn to become socially competent? Would teachers, parents and other members of society want this to happen or would they fear a situation as portrayed by William Golding in *Lord of the Flies*? The hidden or untimetabled curriculum in schools is very socially controlling, and it does this by means of rituals and procedures which develop conformity and obedience. If children are allowed to practise social competence as they are taught it, the power base in the schools would be threatened since our most revered traditions would be challenged and revealed as the devices they are.

Families would also find their power base threatened. Social competence, as I have said before, must have relevance in real life, so that it is not only in school but also in the home that changes may occur. 'Good' parenting has sometimes been thought of as enabling children to participate in self-determination, although parents facilitate this by offering limited choices. Parents can rarely treat children in the same ways as teachers and succeed; or if they do it is a reign of terror! At the root of it all is the problem of fear of loss of control by the adult, since once a process of negotiation is entered into, there is the risk of being out-manoeuvred by this socially competent youngster and finding yourself in a position that you did not plan for and, even worse, may feel incompetent in. This also begs the question of what the adult's responsibility is, and to what extent it is to maintain the culture through the exercise of social control and the teaching of social rituals.

And would society want all school leavers to be socially competent? The prospect might alarm some employers and politicians since the status quo would probably not be tolerated. But for the most part the social benefits should outweigh the problems. Socially competent young people might be able to bring about significant changes in our society towards greater understanding of personal circumstances, more openness, and more demands for responsibility to be shared.

The consequences of current practices have been frequently written about in the popular education press and in HMI reports, and it can be argued that concerns are reflected in recent legislation (particularly the 1986 Education Act). We have reached a stage in education where the threat–recoil hypothesis can be applied. Many are calling for something to be done, since education is perceived by some as the root of many ills in society, rather than reflecting social problems, indicating that the invisible boundary of tolerance has been breached. The reported consequences of education in the first half of the 1980s has apparently led to school leavers being less socially competent than they were, in that they appear apathetic, disaffected, and with reduced capacity for work. The cycle of deprivation is being reinforced.

What are the possible futures for education for social competence? At present three different developments seem prominent, leading to different forms of competence. The first would emphasize personal competence through individualization of instruction, a process possible with computer technology. But what sort of competences would the individual have and would these be socially beneficial? The second approach is in the increase in vocational training which is gradually filtering down the age range, which would theoretically lead to a more competent work force. The third future is towards increased differentiation and selectivity. This would almost certainly enable more school leavers to be identified as socially incompetent and would assist in social control. In addition, the trend towards selectivity would probably lead to the development of more categorical services, which have been identified as wasteful of resources (Attkisson and Broskovsky, 1978). Whilst some of these notions arise politically, the professionals are also implicated in the process of ensuring that the 'system' is properly oiled and achieves its overt objective of producing the correct number of suitably literate and numerate leavers to enter the job market and maintain the status quo. Each of the three possible futures (and they could be combined) involves acceptance by professionals, some of whom in their social understanding, see themselves as powerless — teachers in particular. But teachers are powerful in the social reality of their students and can use their influence to start them on deviant careers.

Conclusions

Many teachers are pessimistic about education and the role of schooling in society as·they see increased centralization of control over their professional lives. However, some of the difficulties can be seen as arising from within the profession and its stubborn clinging to the modern version of the 'saber tooth curriculum' (Peddiwell, 1984). This book pokes fun at the way that areas of the curriculum are maintained due to their traditional place rather than because of any relevance to the current society and it examines the ways in which new ideas are taken on and adapted to serve the old approach. Teacher education does not escape attack, with Peddiwell suggesting that the greater the academic status of educational disciplines the greater the obfuscation and the less effective the teachers are.

The fundamental question is not apparently being addressed — what is education for? Do we accept that it is a benign force of social control and as such make the best possible attempt to ensure that everyone knows their place? If we do, then the road to follow will be more obvious. Do we partly accept this aspect and temper it with meritocratic notions? One of the most insidious form of rhetoric is in claiming to aim for all children to achieve their potential in all spheres, and to enable them to grow up to be responsible members of society. If this is what schools think they are doing then education clearly fails most children. Even those who are defined as the 'gifted' are not being encouraged to learn, but rather discouraged by an almost universal mismatching of task to capability (e.g., DES, 1977). In my experience, parents have not been taken in by the educational rhetoric, even teachers are more concerned that their children are happy in school than in maximizing potential. The lack of interest that teachers consider is the most important characteristic of parents, may arise not from a lack of interest in their children's development and learning, but from a realistic appraisal of the true role undertaken by schools, which may be of secondary importance compared to the child's life at home, that of the compulsory group experience to ensure conformity, experience of being devalued as an individual and eventually social discipline. We need to be more aware of the relationship between education and society, the ways in which education can change society, but also the way that society is reflected in education via those who have control.

In this chapter I have tried to address the issues of social competence and the ways that schooling either ignores it as a valid curriculum approach or method. I have also drawn the two threads of coping and social competence together to try to unravel the complications within the special needs area and the ways in which both concepts are being abused by professionals in order to maintain a system based on a particular set of values which also preserves their power base. Finally, the consequences of incorporating social competence within the school curriculum were considered and the threatening nature of the challenge explicated. My conclusions are necessarily pessimistic, since I cannot foresee a time in the current climate when social competence will be valued in school leavers, or if it is, it will be very much in terms of skills for particular tasks, and conformity to the prevailing social order.

A salutary exercise is to compare the positive and negative consequences of abolishing schools (a technique borrowed from futures studies, see Slaughter, 1985). When this exercise is undertaken by teachers they rediscover the positive aspects of schooling, when they realize the alternatives and the possibility of less-humanitarian social control. But education is political, and currently teachers often seem to prefer to avoid confrontation with this reality (salaries and conditions of service apart). Teaching is certainly a political activity in a covert way — overt political education now being more difficult — particularly in the exercise of the hidden curriculum and unquestioning acceptance of questionable assumptions about education, schooling, and the nature of pupils. The lack of social competence teaching is also a political act. My feeling is that unless the curriculum and the way the curriculum is delivered is radically changed, education will *only* be a tool for social control.

References

ATTKISSON, C. and BROSKOVSKY, A. (1978) 'Evaluation and the emerging human service concept', in ATTKISSON, C. *et al.* (Eds) *Evaluation of human service programs*, London, Academic Press.

BLAXTER, M. (1976) *The meaning of disability: a sociological study of impairment*, London, Heinemann.

BRAGINSKY, D. and BRAGINSKY, B. (1971) *Hansels and Gretels. Studies of children in institutions for the mentally retarded*, Eastbourne, Holt Rinehart and Winston.

CROLL, P. and MOSES, D. (1985) *One in five: the assessment and incidence of special educational needs*, London, Routledge and Kegan Paul.

DES (1985) *Curriculum from five to sixteen*, London, HMSO.

DES (1977) *Gifted children in middle and comprehensive secondary schools*: a discussion paper by a working party of HMI, Matters for Discussion 4, London, HMSO.

EDGERTON, R. (1967) *The cloak of competence: stigma in the lives of the mentally retarded*, London, University of California Press.

FREEMAN, A. and ATTFIELD, R. (1985) 'Social competence and special educational needs: curriculum implications'. Paper given at the *Education Conference of the British Psychological Society at York University, September 1985*.

FREEMAN, A. (in press) 'Students' attitudes towards disability', in *Mental Handicap*.

FREEMAN, A. (1986) *Coping in schools: a case study of stress and coping in teachers*, Unpublished PhD thesis, University of Sheffield.

GOFFMAN, E. (1961) *Asylums: essays in the social situation of mental patients and other inmates*, Harmondsworth, Penguin.

GOFFMAN, E. (1963) *Stigma: notes on the management of a spoiled identity*, Harmondsworth, Penguin.

GOLDING, W. (1958) *Lord of the Flies*, London, Faber & Faber.

GREENSPAN, S. (1981) 'Defining childhood social competence: a proposed working model', in KEOGH, B. *Advances in special education*, Vol. 3, KAI Press, Inc.

HOLMES, T. and RAHE, R. (1967) 'The social readjustment rating scale', in *Journal of Psychosomatic Research*, 11, pp. 213–218.

MCKNIGHT, J. (1977) 'Professional services and disabling help' in BRECHNIN, A. *et al.* (1981) *Handicap in a social world*, Sevenoaks, Hodder and Stoughton.

MACDONALD, I. and COUCHMAN, T. (1980) *Manual for the Chart of Initiative and Independence (CII)*, Windsor, NFER-Nelson.

MASSON, J. (1984) *Freud: the assault on truth. Freud's suppression of the seduction theory*, London, Faber & Faber.

MERCER, J. (1973) *Labelling the mentally retarded*, London, University of California Press.

MORRIS, P. (1981) 'The cognitive psychology of self report', in ANTAKI, C. (Ed.) *The psychology of ordinary explanations of social behaviour*, London, Academic Press.

PEARLIN, L. and SCHOOLER, C. (1978) 'The structure of coping', in *Journal of Health and Social Behaviour*, 19, pp. 2–21.

PEDDIWELL, J. (1984) *The saber tooth curriculum*, Maidstone, McGraw-Hill.

SLAUGHTER, R. (1985) *What do we do now the future is here?* University of Lancaster Department of Educational Research.

TOMLINSON, S. (1982) *A sociology of special education*, London, Routledge and Kegan Paul.

URSIN, H. *et al.* (1978) *Psychobiology of stress: a study of coping men*, London, Academic Press.

WEBSTER, H. (1986) Introduction to the NARE Conference, Edge Hill College of Higher Education, September 1986.

Chapter 7

Equality, Community and Individualism: The Development and Implementation of the 'Whole School Approach' to Special Educational Needs

Hazel Bines

Introduction

The last decade has seen a number of changes in policy and provision in relation to special educational needs in mainstream schools. Following the Warnock Report (DES, 1978) and the 1981 Education Act, formal categories of handicap have been replaced by a broader concept of 'special educational need' which encompasses pupils in both special and mainstream schools and the number of pupils recognized as possibly having a special educational need has been extended. Integration has been widely mooted and the 1981 Education Act has generated a number of new procedures in relation to assessment, reviews of progress and provision and parental involvement. Such changes have also been accompanied by the development of a new cross-curricular and collaborative model of practice involving special needs teachers offering support to pupils and teachers in mainstream teaching groups as part of a 'whole school approach' to special needs provision. However, much of the debate which has accompanied such innovation has focused on its formal, organizational aspects rather than on theoretical and ideological assumptions and implications. This chapter will thus consider these latter dimensions of change, looking in particular at equality, community and individualism as features of the 'whole school approach' and the potential and problems of developing and implementing associated policies and provision.

Until the development of this new model, special education in mainstream schools was primarily conceived in terms which emphasized the individual assessment and remediation of learning and other difficulties, with provision largely comprising the extraction of pupils from mainstream lessons or their placement in a 'special' or 'remedial' class. Both pupils and their teachers were thus marginalized and segregated from mainstream curricula and teaching (Bines, 1986). In contrast, the new model suggests that special needs teachers should exercise a far broader and more central role, including not only assessment and teaching but also the giving of advice and support to class and subject teachers in order to develop teaching materials and methods appropriate to pupils' individual special needs. They should also give support to pupils in mainstream teaching groups, working alongside class and subject teachers in cooperative or team-teaching situations. This new cross-curricular and collaborative role should moreover be allied to a 'whole school approach' or 'whole school policy' within which all teachers should take some responsibility for special needs and be involved in developing appropriate curricula, teaching methods and organizational structures to facilitate an improved provision for pupils with learning and other difficulties (Bines, ibid.; Gains, 1980; Gulliford, 1979; NARE, 1979, 1985; Sewell, 1982). There have also been changes in the traditional role of the peripatetic remedial service, towards special needs advisory and support work (Gipps *et al.*, 1987; Goodwin, 1983; Laskier, 1985), a reconceptualization of support services which may also include special schools acting as resource and advisory centres for mainstream schools in their neighbourhood (Dessent, 1984; Hallmark, 1983).

There is thus a new emphasis on changing aspects of curricula or teaching which may be generating or exacerbating learning problems, and the content and approach of special needs work has thus been re-oriented towards 'prevention' and towards curricular and institutional change (Golby and Gulliver, 1981). This redefinition has been seen to have a number of benefits for both pupils and teachers, which benefits are in turn related to the reasons for such a new approach (Bines, op.cit.). For example, there has long been dissatisfaction with the status accorded remedial and other special needs teachers (Galletley, 1976) and with the limitations and ineffectiveness of traditional measures and approaches, particularly that short-term gains from remedial teaching may not be maintained once pupils return to normal classes, that there can be a number of discontinuities between the content of remedial and mainstream teaching and that a focus on the remediation of individual difficulties can be narrow in content and fail to tackle some of the root sources of such difficulties as inappropriate curricula or teaching methods or lack of expertise held by mainstream teachers (Clark, 1976; McNicholas, 1976; Moseley, 1975). There has also been concern about the inappropriateness of rigid categories of handicap and the social and educational consequences of categorization and special schooling (Cave and Maddison, 1978; DES, 1978).

The broader concept of special need, more integration of both 'special' pupils and their teachers and the new cross-curricular and collaborative approach have in contrast been seen to offer opportunities to make special education more flexible and more appropriate to 'individual need' and more effective through a focus on the limitations of mainstream curricula and teaching methods. This has also been seen to be less stigmatizing to pupils with special needs and to offer them ways of enjoying the social and academic benefits of common curricular experiences with mainstream pupils. Mainstream teachers can develop expertise through advice from special needs teachers who in turn are likely to enjoy a more stimulating and higher status role through collaboration with mainstream teachers and involvement in policy making within the school (Bines, op.cit.; Daniels, 1984; Lewis, 1984; Lavers *et al.* 1986; Sewell, op.cit.). Moreover, this new approach seems not only to overcome some of the weaknesses of the traditional paradigm of special education but also to offer a positive response to those changes in mainstream education which have forced a new role for remedial and other special education, such as mixed ability teaching and common core curricula (Bines, op.cit.; Golby and Gulliver, op.cit.).

Such benefits could in themselves be seen as sufficient argument for adopting the 'whole school approach'. In addition, however, it could be argued that some further advantages could accrue from such change. Firstly, it would seem to offer an opportunity to alter the theoretical basis of special needs provision, shifting the traditional emphasis from medical and psychological notions of disabilities and difficulties towards an acknowledgement and understanding of their social dimensions. This may then facilitate the development of an educational and political stance towards special education which is concerned not just with the needs of individuals but also with their rights and opportunities, a stance which has been rare in this country in contrast, for example, to the USA (Kirp, 1983). This in turn could raise issues such as status, power and disadvantage which to date have largely been neglected in policy-making and practice. Finally, it could also be suggested that the collaborative and collectivist import of the 'whole school approach' has a number of ramifications not only for special but for mainstream provision. It could provide an alternative to both the traditional individual/psychological paradigm of special education and to the 'cult of individualism' which as Hargreaves (1980, 1983) has argued, has also dominated both primary and secondary schools and marginalized consideration of their social aspects and functions. Such a potential has not to date been rendered very explicit and as will be discussed later, the possibilities of its implementation may well be limited. Nevertheless these are important facets of the whole school approach and will thus now be considered in more detail.

Towards Equality and Community?

Of all the potential developments briefly outlined above, a change in the theoretical framework of special education would seem to be the most apparent. As previously suggested, approaches to special education have largely been medical and psychological in orientation, regarding school and society as peripheral to the major focus on the child and his or her needs. The limitations of such approaches are beginning to be recognized however, with moves towards a more flexible and interactive concept of special educational need which takes into account the educational and social environment available to and experienced by pupils, a development which has been further strengthened by the new emphasis on the importance of curricular, pedagogical and organizational change. Nevertheless, many of the social dimensions of special education remain unexplored. As Barton and Tomlinson (1981, pp. 18–19) amongst others have argued, there is an urgent need to consider the ways in which categories of special need are constructed, maintained and changed, the processes involved in providing for special needs, the functions of special education and the professional and social interests it reflects.

The cross-curricular and collaborative model of special needs provision, within the context of a 'whole school policy', would seem to offer further opportunities for such analysis and discourse. Working across the curriculum for example, in a variety of subjects and teaching contexts, could illuminate the way in which demands of subjects and teaching styles and situations may affect teachers' conceptions of special needs, the learning experiences of pupils and the capacity of current modes of teaching to cater for 'special' or indeed other educational 'needs'.[1] Discussion between special and mainstream class and subject teachers could pinpoint inappropriate materials and teaching methods and highlight those constraints which may impinge on successful learning outcomes, such as lack of teacher expertise, resources and time. Past models of educability have largely focused on individual and socio-cultural difficulties and deficits. The new emphasis on the ways in which curricula and pedagogy may contribute to learning and other difficulties may thus be one way of contributing to the change in model which also recognizes the processes and contexts of schooling as crucial factors in educational outcomes (Bines, op.cit., Evans, 1985). It may also illustrate other aspects of special education and mainstream provision such as professional interests. My own research, for example, suggests that within the collaborative partnership posited between special needs and other teachers, the interests of teachers as well as of pupils may well become more explicit, for instance teachers' concern to preserve professional autonomy and manage workloads and stress (Bines, op.cit.).

Thus some of those factors and processes involved in special needs provision and masked by the traditional accentuation on pupil difficulties may be uncovered and demystified, making it easier to recognize not only the limitations of pupil-based explanations of learning failure but also ways in which change may effectively take place. If teachers recognize, for example, that pupils' reading difficulties may be caused by inappropriate teaching or material conditions in classrooms such as large teaching groups which do not allow for sufficient time to be given to helping individuals, they may well argue for more in-service training and mainstream resources rather than just for remediation of individual literacy skills. Such understanding could thus reinforce one of the major rationales of the 'whole school approach', namely that policy and provision ought not to be directed just at individual pupils and their families but at changing the conditions under which learning and other difficulties are constructed and sustained. This in turn could begin to open up debate on what has been suggested as a second potential aspect of the 'whole school approach', namely a new political and educational stance towards special education which emphasizes equal opportunities and rights.

Paradoxically although those with special needs could be regarded as one of the most disadvantaged groups in society and despite the long-standing debate about equality and education this century, the issue of equal opportunities in relation to special education has been given comparatively little attention by policymakers.[2] For example, only in 1970 were the rights of all children to education recognized, when those diagnosed as more severely handicapped were finally given access to proper educational provision and made the responsibility of local education authorities, whilst the issue of providing equal opportunities in comprehensive schools has rarely been discussed in relation to those considered to have special educational needs. This lacuna of equal opportunities policies has also gone unrecognized elsewhere. As Tomlinson (1982, p. 9) has noted, even sociologists have neglected special education in discussion of the inequities of selection by ability and although equal opportunities policies have been increasingly broadly considered in relation to class, gender and race, special needs have to date been neglected. For example, as a recent report from ILEA suggests, (ILEA, 1985, p. 3) although ILEA was committed to policies mitigating disadvantage arising out of class, sex and race, the committee investigating special needs provision in the authority had no such similar guidelines in relation to disabilities or learning difficulties. A similar point could no doubt be made about policies in other LEAs.

However, the importance of ensuring that the handicapped do have access to education and to society, and are integrated rather than segregated, is becoming more widely acknowledged and could be seen to form one of the major rationales for current changes in special education (Fish, 1985, pp. 2–5; ILEA, op.cit.). Following on from the Fish Report and other initiatives, the 'fourth dimension' of equal opportunities may now be recognized and explicitly linked to comprehensive principles (Potts, 1986). Such an approach offers a political stance towards special education which could be very different from the 'benevolent humanitarianism' which has traditionally been dominant in special education (Tomlinson, 1982). As Kirp (1983, pp. 101–3) has commented, in his comparison of British and American special education policy, the idea of 'rights' can recharacterize special education, giving individuals a recognized entitlement which is not just an artifact of governmental generosity or of professional judgement. It also allows for an assertion of self and a participation in the definition of one's interests. Provision cannot then just be dependent on whether resources are available or on the acceptability of costs to those who do not have special needs. Rather, the burden of adjustment is on the mainstream school and even though resources may be limited, claims to an appropriate education must be met. Similar points could be made about applying the concept of equality to those considered to have special needs. Once it is accepted that such pupils should enjoy the access to common schooling enjoyed by their peers, or indeed that equality of opportunity should be yet further extended, with positive discrimination to try and achieve more equal educational outcomes, as has been argued in relation to disadvantage arising out of race, gender and class, then it is much more difficult to deny integration, or appropriate resources, to make decisions dependent on professional judgement alone or suggest that the interests of those with a particular impairment or difficulty should be subjugated to the perceived interests of others without such apparent handicaps.

The 'whole school approach', by seeking to change comprehensive schools, both primary and secondary, and devlop the opportunities provided within them, could contribute to such a stance and to growing awareness of the political and educational issues involved; for example, the domination of high-status, examinable knowledge, the selective functions of schools and the priority and resources allocated to the most rather than least academically 'successful' of our pupils. However this will involve considerable clarification of what a 'whole school approach' or 'whole school policy' does indeed comprise. There has not been much discussion of such policy despite its apparent importance to change in special provision. It needs to be explicitly recognized that like the collaborative partnership between special and other teachers, the whole school approach is both a strategy or mechanism for change and a means of establishing a particular ethos or goal, that is principles about education (Roaf, 1986). It thus involves value judgements about both special and mainstream education. Butt (1986, pp. 10–11) for example has suggested that the meaning of the 'whole school approach' is 'functional integration', access to the curriculum and 'normalization', a view which would seem to be endorsed by other writers. It would thus seem that the 'whole school approach' can be tied closely to integration and to the extension of equality and the comprehensive principle and that it concerns valuing all pupils equally and not discriminating or segregating on the grounds of learning difficulty or disability. If this is the case, then it is not just a means of changing the curriculum to accommodate special needs but also ensuring a particular type of school and education. The 'whole school approach', when made explicit, could therefore represent a particular political, educational and social stance which could be utilized to foster the rights and opportunities of those who have previously been marginalized and neglected within the education system.

This in turn could facilitate development of what has been identified as a third potential advantage of the 'whole school approach', namely the social rather than individual approach to education with its concomitant emphasis on community and collectivity. As noted earlier, schools have been dominated by the 'cult of individualism'. This has taken a number of forms, but in particular has stressed that education is not primarily concerned with creating a certain kind of society but rather with the promotion of the educated individual. Education has thus been dominated by a concern with the development of individual abilities and aptitudes, moral judgement and personal autonomy. As Hargreaves (1983, p. 92) has noted, this has reduced recognition of the importance of collective experience and learning about group goals and needs within the school community and has also left teachers

> with the impression that they do not need to ask the two key questions — what kind of society do we want and how is education to help us to realize that society . . .

The social and political functions of education are thus ignored. In some contrast, the 'whole school approach' to special needs implicitly challenges some of these assumptions. It suggests for example, that schools should seek to produce a community in which all pupils are valued irrespective of their particular capabilities, that pupils should be socially and academically integrated and have common curricular and social experiences, and above all that individuals with special needs are a communal responsibility, with provision being decided not just in individual interaction between pupil and teacher but by whole school discussion and policymaking. This should in turn help to create a society in which similar attitudes and policies are to be found.

In addition, the 'whole school approach' posits a collective and collaborative approach not only towards pupils but between teachers. As Hargreaves (op.cit.) has noted, the cult of individualism also extends to teachers, as evidenced for example in the stress laid within the occupational culture of teachers on professional autonomy rather than cooperation. The 'whole school approach' in contrast, emphasizes that making provision for those with learning and other difficulties should be a shared enterprise with teachers working together in classrooms and resource areas to share expertise and ideas and develop common approaches and strategies, which partnerships will then be further reinforced by a mutually agreed school policy. Its collectivist import is thus directed at relationships between teachers as well as at provision for pupils and this would seem to be a further way in which the social and corporate rather than individual dimensions of education could be enhanced.

Implementation, Contradictions and Consequences

The 'whole school approach' therefore posits a number of changes to both special and mainstream education which in turn may generate an educational, political and social concern with rights, equality and community as well as needs and individuality. However, despite these apparent benefits, there would seem to be a number of dilemmas and problems, related in particular to insufficient consideration of what this approach may comprise and how it is to be developed, to certain inherent contradictions, to the continuing dominance of the traditional paradigm, and to the conditions and constraints of mainstream schooling. It thus cannot be assumed that the changes posited by this new approach will necessarily be achieved. Moreover, there may be some unintended consequences which are not necessarily beneficial to either pupils or teachers. Indeed a number of difficulties and tensions are already emerging which would seem to illustrate both the potential and the pitfalls of cross-curricular collaboration. These can be usefully illustrated by considering some of the central aspects of the 'whole school approach', namely advisory and support work, curricula for special needs and the development of a whole school policy.

Although support and advisory work is one of the major components of the 'whole school approach', being both content and mechanism of change, there has been a somewhat limited discussion of what it may entail. As Hart (1986) has pointed out, discussion has largely focused on the location rather than the nature of support which has left special needs teachers with a number of dilemmas and difficulties in regard to implementation. However, it would seem to involve support for both the pupil and the teacher, the former through individual help and additional or special resources and the latter primarily through advice on learning and other difficulties and suitable teaching materials and methods (Visser, 1986). Such support however makes a number of new demands on special needs teachers which they may find difficult to meet, including possession of a wider knowledge than previously of mainstream curricula and teaching in large groups in order to make support effective. There would also seem to be a need for new interpersonal skills to foster the collaborative relationship between support and mainstream teacher, skills which the support teacher may not necessarily have.[3] Moreover, even with the requisite knowledge and skills it may be difficult to modify practice or avoid support teachers being used as a substitute for change (Visser, ibid.) or indeed being annexed as a 'coping strategy' to help deal with the exigencies of insufficient time and resources for large teaching groups (Bines, op.cit.). It is also important to note that although discussions of collaboration have rarely admitted such problems, there may be instances of conflict between support and mainstream teacher over lesson content or teaching method and further concern over the preservation of professional autonomy and avoidance of judgements of professional competence (Bines, ibid.).

In addition to these difficulties it has to be questioned whether moves towards 'support' may necessarily change traditional practice in any substantive way. It would seem that in some instances, support may entail little more than the transfer of traditional provision to the mainstream context. As Hart (op.cit., pp. 26–8) suggested in her detailed discussion, there would seem to be two main conceptions of support based on somewhat different approaches to the issue of special needs provision. On the one hand there is what she has termed the 'individual approach' which tends to focus on making lessons appropriate to individual needs and difficulties and is premised on the belief that pupils have unique needs and require a special curriculum. In contrast there is the 'whole curriculum approach' which supposes that there are no radical differences between ordinary and special teaching and which thus primarily seeks change in mainstream curricula and teaching methods with possible ramifications for the teaching of all pupils and not just those with special needs. The two approaches may not be totally incompatible — both, for example, stress the importance of cooperation between support and class teacher. However, Hart suggests that priority should be given to the 'whole curriculum approach' on the grounds that to continue to provide special resources may be to differentiate those with special needs from their peers, that the intervention of a support teacher may draw attention to those with learning or other difficulties and that a focus on individuals is unlikely to generate substantial change in mainstream teaching. It could also be added that the 'individual approach' is symptomatic of continued dominance of the traditional paradigm of special education and only with the 'whole curriculum approach' is the promise of a more integrated and effective provision for those with special needs likely to be ensured.

There is thus the major issue of the degree to which current practice may indeed be implementing the potential of the 'whole school approach' through an appropriate support model. In addition however, the adoption of the 'whole curriculum approach' may not in itself be an adequate solution. Firstly, there may remain problems of mainstream teacher expectation of support roles which may continue to relegate support teachers to the individual model. Support teachers may also not find it easy to resolve the dilemma between ensuring long-term change and giving attention to current learning or other difficulties experienced by pupils. Above all there is also the major issue of the type of change being posited for mainstream teaching. It would seem that the success of the 'whole curriculum approach' is largely to be measured in terms of the degree to which mainstream teachers adopt the tenets and practices of special educators, in particular the emphasis on individual pupils traditional to special provision. Butt (op.cit., p. 12) for example, amongst others, has suggested that it should result in curricular adaptations and greater individualization of work programmes and assessment across the curriculum. However, although it cannot be denied that a sensitivity to individual diversity is important, and that teaching and learning does need to accommodate individual needs and interests, there are a number of difficulties associated with such a conception of 'good practice'. It is for instance questionable whether individual assessment and programmes can be provided given the current conditions of teaching. My own research found that teachers felt they did not have enough time or resources to provide individual help and could thus not implement a more detailed and specialized approach to learning and other difficulties (Bines, op.cit.). A similar point is made by Thomas (1986) who has questioned the applicability of special pedagogy and increasingly complex teaching methods to the mainstream context, arguing instead the need to consider how unrefined strategies can be most effectively implemented. It thus may not be just a question of adopting different teaching content and methods. Even if secondary teachers, for example, could be persuaded to relinquish some of their subject requirements in favour of a closer focus on 'needs', research on primary classrooms, where individual child-centredness has been a major rationale (Alexander, 1984), suggests that a 'match' between pupil capabilities and learning activities is a rarer phenomenon than has been supposed and that individual teacher–pupil interaction is necessarily limited not least because of the size of teaching groups (Bennet *et al.*, 1984; Galton *et al.*, 1980). Attempts to change towards a more individual model of teaching and learning are thus fraught with difficulties due to pupil–teacher ratios as well as the expertise (and teaching models) held by teachers.

This would seem to have a number of ramifications for the new approach to special needs. If teachers believe, for example, that they are successfully providing for special needs even though they are not and pupils still experience difficulties, it is possible that recourse will again be made to traditional explanations of failure, namely individual or socio-cultural deficit. This in itself may well subvert the agendum of curricular and institutional change posited by the 'whole school approach'. In addition, as Ball (1980) has suggested in relation to the use of individual learning methods in mixed ability teaching, particularly the worksheet, these may not necessarily eradicate selection and differentiation. Indeed, paradoxically, they may well facilitate and increase it by allowing the 'faster' or 'more able' worker to cover more curriculum content than when impeded by the lockstep progression of whole class methodology. Such differentiation of pupil progress may then have a number of consequences for future curricular choices, with certain avenues being open or closed according to what work has been completed. Moreover,

> for those pupils who are unsuccessful academically, being seen by their teachers as 'low ability' or 'slow', the experience of mixed ability grouping may involve a process of status socialization and legitimation in that they are continually faced with the individualization of their failure. (Ball, ibid., p. 46)

It would seem therefore that the curricular change posited in the 'whole school approach' may involve a number of difficulties and contradictions. The greater attention to individual differences and needs seen to be a part of ensuring improved pupil learning outcomes may not be easy to realize. Increased differentiation may further segregate rather than integrate those with special needs. It could thus be argued that in certain circumstances little may change from the traditional approach with the exception that the mode of differentiation and segregation will be through mainstream teaching rather than extraction or special classes with the agents being mainstream rather than (or together with) special needs teachers. Pupils may learn basic and other skills 'in context' but through curricular experiences which still remain different from those of their peers and may thus well continue to be marginalized and to be perceived (and perceive themselves) as 'failures' able to cope only with 'adapted' curricula. Thus the equal opportunities this approach was designed to provide may not be realized. Furthermore, individualization may subvert the collectivist import which can be identified in the whole school approach and reinforce rather than modify the traditional paradigm of special educational provision, by maintaining an emphasis on individual needs and experiences and posing 'good practice' in individual rather than communal or cooperative terms. The 'whole school approach' would seem to have gone some way towards breaking down the 'cult of individualism' amongst teachers in a sharing of the teaching enterprise through support and advice. However, for pupils, the academic and social consequences of such cooperation may be very different.

The support and curricular models posited in the 'whole school approach' thus seem to raise a number of difficulties. Equally the development of a 'whole school policy' as part of the 'whole school approach' may be problematic. It is unlikely, for example, that consensus will easily be reached amongst the staff of a school (Boyd, 1985; Bines, op.cit.), particularly if such a policy addresses not only teaching content and methodology but also values about education. Challenges to established practice and changes in resource allocation may conflict with the views and teaching approaches of some teachers, and even if discussion of policy provides a forum for such conflict to be expressed, policy decisions are likely to be seen as a threat to professional autonomy by those who do not agree with a particular outcome. Moreover, difficulties of implementation, particularly material constraints, such as insufficient resources and staffing, may undermine policy realization, even for those teachers who are committed to change. Such a policy therefore may not be able to meet the needs and aspirations of teachers and may also have other unintended and undesirable consequences; for example, the polarization of views and interests as well as or instead of the collective agreement and strategy it was designed to generate.

Finally, it is not easy to predict how cross-curricular support and the 'whole school approach' will affect segregated special provision, particularly special schools. The model has been developed primarily as a means of changing approaches to those pupils already in mainstream schools who may formerly have been placed in remedial departments or have received remedial or other special help and provision. Its principles would seem to be equally appropriate for pupils who might formerly have attended special schools and units and indeed, if the egalitarian and collectivist import of this new model is to be realized, it would seem appropriate that it be extended to all pupils. It is likely, however, that full integration of all pupils with special needs would compound many of the problems of implementation that have already been discussed, particularly in relation to teacher expertise, resources, staffing, curricular differentiation and educational aims and values. Nevertheless, such a development needs urgent consideration, recognizing that currently the 'whole school approach' has been more concerned with the comprehensive nature of schools rather than the system of special and mainstream schooling as a whole, a limitation which it is essential to redress.

Conclusion

Despite its apparent potential, the 'whole school approach' would seem to involve a number of problems and dilemmas for special educators. Nevertheless, there may be a number of ways of attempting to realize such potential which could be explored. Firstly, it would seem that the emphasis in cross-curricular work should not just focus on individuals but on general curricular and pedagogical change. Secondly, the cooperative model posited between teachers could be extended to pupils through a greater emphasis on collaborative, group learning. This could be one way of facilitating functional as opposed to locational integration of those with special needs and reducing their isolation and marginality. It would also seem to be a way of developing equality in learning experiences and relationships and a sense of collectivity rather than individualism.[4]

Thirdly, it should be considered whether current approaches to curriculum are appropriate. This could include considering whether developing provision for 'individual needs' should be the major focus of change, both because of the technical difficulties of implementation and the consequences it may have. It might be more effective to consider those factors which are likely to impede a genuine realization of individuality and diversity which does not deny common experience and interests and does not result in lower status and failure. This could involve attempting to change conceptions of 'achievement', stressing the common rather than different nature of teaching and learning processes for all pupils and also developing the social as well as the academic goals of schools (cf. ILEA, 1984). It would also seem important to question whether curricula should be 'adapted', which presupposes that any starting point should be the 'normal curriculum' for those without 'special needs' rather than one which can involve all pupils. Some of the taken-for-granted curricular assumptions and goals of schools could thus be challenged and possible alternatives developed.

In addition, more consideration should be given to the processes involved in developing policy and collaboration between teachers, including how and whether support can change established practice and how conflict can be resolved. In particular, it will be important for special needs teachers to acknowledge that the perceptions and experiences of colleagues will have a major bearing on change (Bines, op.cit.). It will also have to recognize that the 'whole school approach' does raise political and social issues which need to be elaborated and discussed. To date, it has largely been regarded as a change in structure and methodology, following from a traditional view in special education which has largely ignored its social and political aspects in favour of a concentration on an humanitarian approach to individuals. Development of the egalitarian and collectivist implications of the 'whole school approach' could be one way of broadening the framework of debate. Indeed, it may be crucial given the erosion of egalitarianism and collectivism within schools by such developments as the policy and resource attention being given to GCSE, proposals for age-related curriculum objectives and testing, increasing selectivity and autonomy for certain schools and the probable diminution of the powers of LEAs. The development of the 'whole school approach' to special educational provision, whatever its limitations, does represent a welcome shift in ideology and practice. It will, however, require a critical awareness both of traditional legacies and current and future issues and constraints if its potential is indeed to be fulfilled.

Notes

1 Though much more research needs to be done, it would seem that factors such as subject content and mode of transmission may make very different demands on pupils and thus affect both perceptions and experiences of learning and other difficulties — see Bines (op.cit.) and Evans (1985).
2 There are differences between the liberal and the more radical conceptions of equality and equal opportunities, the former being more concerned with equal access to schooling and the latter more with the equality of that schooling's outcomes (Evetts, 1973, Ch. 4). Both could be considered as aspects of equal opportunities policies in relation to special education, although the emphasis would seem to be increasingly on the latter, for instance, providing positively discriminating measures to overcome disadvantage arising out of impairments and learning and other difficulties.
3 Though there is some debate as to whether such skills are indeed required. See Bines (op.cit.); Visser (op.cit.) and Widlake (1983).
4 See Hodgson *et al.* (1984); Salmon and Claire (1984).

References

ALEXANDER, R. (1984) *Primary Teaching*, London, Holt, Rinehart and Winston.
BALL, S.J. (1980) 'Mixed ability teaching; The worksheet method', in *British Journal of Educational Technology*, 11, 1, pp. 36–48.
BARTON, L. and TOMLINSON, S. (1981) 'Introduction', in Barton L. and Tomlinson S. (Eds) *Special Education: Policy, Practices and Social Issues*, London, Harper and Row.

BENNET N., DESFORGES, C., COCKBURN, A. and WILKINSON, B. (1984) *The Quality of Pupil Learning Experiences*, London, Lawrence Erlbaum.

BINES, H. (1986) *Redefining Remedial Education*, Beckenham, Croom Helm.

BOYD, B. (1985) 'Whole school policies', in *Forum for the Discussion of New Trends in Education*, 27, 3, pp. 79–81.

BUTT, N. (1986) 'Implementing the whole school approach at secondary level', in *Support for Learning*, 1, 4, pp. 10–15.

CAVE, C. and MADDISON, P. (1978) *A Survey of Recent Research in Special Education*, Windsor, NFER-Nelson.

CLARK, M.M. (1976) 'Why remedial? Implications of using the concept of remedial education', *Remedial Education*, 11, 1, pp. 5–8.

DANIELS, E. (1984) 'A suggested model of remedial provision in a comprehensive school', in *Remedial Education*, 19, 2, pp. 78–83.

DES (1978) *Special Educational Needs (The Warnock Report)*, London, HMSO.

DESSENT, T. (1984) ' Special schools and the mainstream — "The resource stretch" ', in Bowers T. (Ed) *Management and the Special School*, Beckenham, Croom Helm.

EVANS, J. (1985) *Teaching in Transition. The Challenge of Mixed Ability Grouping*, London, Longman.

EVETTS, J. (1973) *The Sociology of Educational Ideas*, London, Methuen.

FISH, J. (1985) *Special Education The Way Ahead*, Milton Keynes, Open University Press.

GAINS, C.W. (1980) 'Remedial education in the 1980s', in *Remedial Education*, 15, 1, pp. 5–9.

GALLETLEY, I. (1976) 'How to do away with yourself', in *Remedial Education*, 11, 3, pp. 149–152.

GALTON, M., SIMON, B. and CROLL, P. (1980) *Inside the Primary Classroom*, London, Routledge and Kegan Paul.

GIPPS, C., GROSS, H. and GOLDSTEIN, H. (1987) *Warnock's 18%: Children with Special Needs in Primary Schools*, Lewes, Falmer Press.

GOLDBY, M. and GULLIVER, J.R. (1981) 'Whose remedies, whose ills? A critical review of remedial education', in Swann, W. (Eds) *The Practice of Special Education*, Oxford, Blackwell.

GOODWIN, C. (1983) 'The contribution of support services to integration policy', in BOOTH, T. and POTTS, P. (Eds) *Integrating Special Education*, Oxford, Blackwell.

GULLIFORD, R. (1979) 'Remedial education across the curriculum', in Gains, C.W. and McNicholas, J. (Eds) *Remedial Education Guidelines for the Future*, London, Longman.

HALLMARK, N. (1983) 'A support service to primary schools', in BOOTH, T. and POTTS, P. (Eds) *Integrating Special Education*, Oxford, Blackwell.

HARGREAVES, D.H. (1980) 'A sociological critique of individualism in education', in *British Journal of Educational Studies*, 28, 3, pp. 187–199.

HARGREAVES, D.H. (1983) *The Challenge for the Comprehensive School: Culture, Curriculum and Community*, London, Routledge and Kegan Paul.

HART, S. (1986) 'Evaluating support teaching', in *Gnosis* (Schools Psychological Service, ILEA), 9, pp. 26–31.

HODGSON, A., HEGARTY, S. and CLUNIES ROSS, L. (1984) *Learning Together*, Windsor, NFER/Nelson.

ILEA (1984) *Improving Secondary Schools (The Hargreaves Report)*, London, ILEA.

ILEA (1985) *Educational Opportunities for All (The Fish Report)*, London, ILEA.

KIRP, D.L. (1983) 'Professionalisation as a policy choice: British special education in comparative perspective', in CHAMBERS, J.G. and HARTMAN, W.T. (Eds) *Special Education Policies*, Philadelphia, Temple University Press.

LASKIER, M. (1985) 'The changing role of the remedial teacher', in SMITH, C.J. (Ed) *New Directions in Remedial Education*, Lewes, Falmer Press.

LAVERS, P., PICKUP, M. and THOMSON, M. (1986) 'Factors to consider in implementing an in-class support system within secondary schools', in *Support for Learning*, 1, 3, pp. 32–35.

LEWIS, G. (1984) ' A supportive role at secondary level', in *Remedial Education*, 19, 1, pp. 7–12.

MCNICHOLAS, J.A. (1976) 'Aims of remedial education: A critique', in *Remedial Education*, 11, 3, pp. 113–116.

MOSELEY, D. (1975) *Special Provision for Reading*, Windsor, NFER-Nelson.

NARE (1979) *Guidelines No. 2 The Role of the Remedial Teacher*, Stafford, NARE.

NARE l(1985) *Guidelines No. 6 Teaching Roles for Special Needs*, Stafford, NARE.

POTTS, P. (1986) 'Equal Opportunities; The fourth dimension', in *Forum for the Discussion of New Trends in Education*, 29, 1, pp. 13–15.

ROAF, C. (1986) 'Whole school policy: Principles into practice', in *Forum for the Discussion of New Trends in Education*, 29, 1, pp. 20–22.

SALMON, P. and CLAIRE, H. (1984) *Classroom Collaboration*, London, Routledge and Kegan Paul.

SEWELL, G. (1982) *Reshaping Remedial Education*, Beckenham, Croom Helm.

THOMAS, G. (1986) 'Integrating personnel in order to integrate children', in *Support for Learning*, 1, 1, pp. 19–26.

TOMLINSON, S. (1982) *A Sociology of Special Education*, London, Routledge and Kegan Paul.

VISSER, J. (1986) 'Support: A description of the work of the SEN professional', in *Support for Learning*, 1, 4, pp. 5–9.

WIDLAKE, P. (1983) *How to Reach the Hard to Teach*, Milton Keynes, Open University Press.

Chapter 8

The Curriculum: Some Issues for Debate

Bunty Davidson

Introduction

Articulating the school curriculum has become the *bête-noire* of teachers heavily engaged in addressing the day-to-day requirements and pressures of working with a wide range of pupils in a variety of settings. Pressure from central government, through local education authorities, for documentation of curriculum philosophies, aims and content and the requirement for them to be provided for and accessible to parents has increased pressure on teachers to review their roles and the nature of their practice. In the case of teachers who are responsible for, or involved in, identified 'special educational' provisions or related support work, this has been an opportunity for them to become a part of mainstream educational practice. The historical roll call of government committees and reports relating to 'special education' began with the first provision for separate classes in the late nineteenth century. Emphasis on the nature of the curriculum rather than the content and purpose of special programmes or 'treatment' began in earnest in the 1970s. While the Schools Council surveys concerning special education (Brennan 1979; Leeming *et al.*, 1979; Wilson and Evans, 1980) followed by Wilson's curriculum paper (Wilson 1981) identified some lack of documentation about intentions for practice in schools and other provisions, it was also pointed out that the existence of such documentation was not necessarily related to good practice. It was clear that there was a need for special educators to develop an understanding and awareness of curriculum theory and development in mainstream education, but as examination and evaluation of curriculum became more sophisticated it became clear that many mainstream teachers have an inadequate grasp of curriculum studies. They also lack knowledge of the nature of special educational provisions, and the rationale and historical and political background which influences decisions on identification, assessment and placement or provision for a wide spectrum of learning difficulties. Indeed, all practitioners require to develop a professional strength which allows them to reflect critically on their own practice and context and then to act on their findings. This cannot be an isolated process; partnership and collaboration with colleagues has to be integral to it. In providing education there is a need to work in multi-disciplinary teams and with parents but classroom and school dividing lines have not yet been dismantled. The existence of the separate world of 'special' education with its own research field and professional associations emphasizes this lack of cohesion within the education system. Progress towards a less divisive educational service can only be achieved through new approaches to professional practice. Under pressure from government and media, teachers in all public sector provisions have become increasingly defensive about their roles and hence more likely to want to defend their known 'expertise'. It is unclear at present what will be required in the way of documented material given the move to a National Curriculum (or more accurately the Public Sector Curriculum). Certainly the increased powers given to parents and governing bodies could mean an elaboration of written material to which teachers will be held accountable.

Constructing a written curriculum may generate discussion but does not necessarily provide the kind of self-evaluation which can lead to the type of change and development needed to demolish the invisible as well as visible barriers, whether in special or mainstream settings, set up by teachers and the educational establishment. As long as there is no real commitment by politically influential bodies to implement a more open system and teacher education continues to be forced into a position of maintaining the status quo rather than generating more demanding and questioning pro-fessionals who are capable of and allowed to initiate new approaches, then the issues which concern those engaged in providing the support for pupils who have at present no real place in the system except as 'non-conformers' is unlikely to be resolved.

This chapter will make some comments on those parts of the active curriculum which may be included in written documentation but are not always seen as being central to the delivery of the curriculum. These are: context, teacher and pupil interaction and method. The aims of a school and the content and experiences to be provided, have usually been the starting point for curriculum evaluation or planning, but because the provision of special educational support is increasingly focused around goal planning and projects, there is a need to be concerned with the nature of the 'where' and 'how' as well as the 'what'. The 'for what' is a matter for conjecture. Who, for example, could have foreseen the introduction of Japanese industrial methods and philosophy into the North East of England in a substantial form, and what effect does this have on planning the school or college curriculum? Consideration of context, method and teacher and learner style is necessary for the identification of the attitudes underlying the ethos of a school.

Context is more often than not seen as the physical environment in which teaching and learning takes place. Decisions are made about the physical environment which are influenced by underlying attitudes and political expediency and may bear no relation to the needs of pupils but which may generate other contextual influences. The interactions of teachers and pupils are the subject of considerable research in the mainstream but knowledge gained from this is not often reflected in planning and organizing classrooms and schools. Although there is a growing awareness about issues of gender and race in interactional behaviours and the relationship to categorization and achievement, implementation of policies and practice has hardly begun and is not aided by political and media hype.

The segregated sector is still an area lacking in substantial enquiry into interactional behaviours, although interest in integration has led to some literature on the subject (McEvoy, Nordqvist and Cunningham, 1984, among others) and use of language in classrooms has been the subject of some interest, although mostly with respect to language development. Method may be described in written documents and is usually considered as the teacher's personal affair but it is increasingly being influenced by professionals who are not based in the classroom. Before exploring these areas it is worth noting the present climate in which demands for schools to clarify their aims and practices are being made.

The period between the publishing of the Warnock Report (DES, 1978) and the third report of the Education, Science and Arts Committee on the implementation of the Education Act 1981 (Select Committee, 1987) has been one of expansion and change in the training of teachers in the field of special education. At one level, increasing understanding of the nature and complexity of the causes of learning difficulties and under-achievement has led to exciting challenges for the work of all professionals and parents with a substantial growth in the literature associated with these. At another, as the latter report confirms, the lack of resources stemming from the government's decision in 1981 not to provide extra funds to this area, and consequent as well as existing confusion in local authorities about policy, has led to a situation in which the constructive development of curriculum and the implementation of change has been seriously impeded. During this time there has also been a switch away from initial training of specialist teachers. While the lobby for the sensorily handicapped had the stronger voice, initial training for teaching children with severe learning difficulties ended with a final intake of students in 1987.

The 1980s have seen the school curriculum and performance of pupils brought to the forefront as a major political issue. This has had implications for approaches to the planning and teaching of curriculum content in both inservice and initial teacher education courses. From the point of view of special education, advanced professional courses traditionally have approached this in a prescriptive way, looking at the child as having deficits and problems which required remediation with adjustments to the curriculum content in line with the approaches identified by Brennan (1979) in the Schools Council survey. Courses in initial education have considered 'special educational needs' as being provided for as an option which could be taken as an adjunct to the mainstream course offered. This has slowly begun to change and new innovations have been made in courses in higher education. Students are being encouraged to move away from a concentration on the specific identification of children's needs as an end in itself to an examination of organizations and their part in generating a climate of failure. Surveys of institutions by HMI together with the nature of courses offered by HMI between 1985 and 1987 confirm that these traditional approaches have not been sufficient to alter attitudes and that the development of clear policies in departments of education are a pre-requisite for the identification of targets for action. These would include an examination of the concept of special needs, justifications for integration and segregation, development of skills in teachers, and, most importantly, approaches to attitudinal change in order to enable positive environments for learning and teaching to be created (HMI 1987).

A number of initiatives are taking place which are designed to shift the traditional patterns of secondary education to a more appropriate and relevant model for the demands of increasingly technologically-based workplaces. Some of these are seen by some as interferences by industry in the traditional world of education but are nevertheless providing resources and new forms of planning for learning. This is providing a framework for increasingly restrictive practices unless an informed dialogue with those responsible for implementing the broad curriculum containing opportunities for aesthetic and personal development is insisted upon and maintained with required practical application. Other initiatives which are arising from collaboration with local employers are directly relating the school context with the world of work and Youth Training Schemes (Youth Award Schemes, Brockington and White, 1987)). The new GCSE examinations are designed to improve the quality of thinking of all pupils and universities are pressing for changes in the 'A'-level format to enable academically-able pupils to operate from a broader base of knowledge and experience (Report of Vice Chancellors 1987). At the same time as those engaged in the practice of education and post-school education are attempting to provide opportunities for the whole range of abilities, there is a whole new package of assessment of achievement about to be imposed on schools by central government which will have implications for those people for whom the years of formal schooling may not be the period when they actively pursue academic achievement. Evidence of the development of potential in mature students is available throughout further and higher education. A return to the system of identifying so-called 'failure to achieve' will be unhelpful to the large proportion of school pupils who will not be part of the top 10 percent of the academic range.

Within this scenario, the literature of 'special needs' has multiplied. Tomlinson (1981), Barton aand Tomlinson (1981, 1984) at the start of the 1980s began to shift attention away from that of remedial methodology or interventionist proposals to that of sociological enquiry into the conceptual bases underlying practice and provision. The most recent publications consider the nature of the practical application of, for example: placement (Galloway and Goodwin, 1987); method (Solity and Bull, 1987); linkage (Booth, Potts and Swann, 1987); language (Beveridge and Conti-Ramsden, 1987). These and the established literature on curriculum and special needs (Wilson, 1981; Brennan, 1985) and teacher and learner style, has provided teachers with a direction to follow. It is unclear how policies for placement and provision may develop and it may be that in spite of increasing centralization of control over education in general, in practice the area of special education may continue to be tackled piecemeal, leaving the experiences of pupils and their curriculum to be unchanged. This provokes the questions, where and in what way can teachers take actions which are personal to their own practice and not dependent on the employment of systems constructed by others?

Context

The aims and objectives of schooling have been seen as the starting point for planning, although there is increasing emphasis to make the characteristics of the pupils the key to establishing priorities. The fact that the extent and depth of the majority of learning difficulties are relative to any given situation means that the teacher has to be particularly aware of the climate generated by him/herself and colleagues in the school or other setting.

Contextual influences on the curriculum are extremely strong. Contexts are normally seen as physical environments. There are clear messages from surveys of schools (HMI 1987) that paucity of resources in general is the cause of deteriorating school fabric, and the deployment of teachers into situations with which they are neither familiar with, nor necessarily willing to enter has had a deleterious effect on a whole range of provisions. This can only contribute to an increase in pupils with some kind of motivation or learning problem. Emotional factors and the emotional context are also fundamental to the types of negotiations that take place and the behaviours that occur within the physical context. There is no doubt that attitudinal bias stemming from deep-seated emotional reactions to 'handicap', morality and mental health encourages the establishment and continuation of segrated provision. Personal anxieties about loss of employment, devaluation of property and dislike and fear of 'differences' are fuelled by ignorance. Current work on stigmatization and labelling confirm the existence of negative attitudes. Unless every school pupil becomes informed about the range of human variety, is encouraged to help and support their peers and be involved in a total educational process, these attitudes are unlikely to change. Teachers themselves have to be helped to confront the issues and to work alongside colleagues who may work in segregated settings. Until there is a positive professional move to initiate change by influencing the political apparatus which is used to set up, support and maintain structures and thus legitimize the underlying attitudes, then there can be little advance made.

Emotions and feelings may be well disguised behind rationalized justifications for decisions. Motivation governed by a drive for power can over-ride professional judgements if there is not a rigorous system for controlling personal profit and self interest. Inadequate resources may be a 'reasonable' externalized excuse for the failure of the Education Act 1981 in the eyes of the bureaucrats, but resources are frequently inappropriately and inefficiently located within the local authority or governmental structure. Money may be tied up in compartmentalized budgets and while virement may sometimes be possible, it is usually the case that funds are not used as they could be. Resources may dictate but they don't account for decisions to house the least-able in the worst classroom, or in the hut across the playground; the most-handicapped in the most-inaccessible building; school refusers in rotting housing stock; the nursery for handicapped infants in the local health centre. Underlying this is a need to maintain the status quo for those who are already in positions of strength.

The emotional drive governing parents of severely mentally handicapped children can result in high levels of resourcing in schools and this can be compared with the difficulties a special class tacked onto the local primary school on a poor urban estate may have in raising funds. This force for positive or negative action is encountered everywhere and the effects can be found in all cultures.

In Portugal, for example the poorest country in the EEC, there are similar reactions to those who do not fit the required model for educational attainment. Children in the poorest area of a residential suburb of a major city (blacks of Cape Verde descent, gypsies from the country and poor whites), are misfits in the mainstream school, and a social nuisance for the rapidly growing tourist industry. They are provided with a derelict building for a centre for alternative activities and a social educator (not a teacher) to organize it. Schooling is part-time for the rest of their peers as well as for them but these pupils form the deviant class and therefore get special provision. Despite the condition of the building in which they operate, the warmth and emotional drive of the organizer and her helpers, some of whom are voluntary and come from the immediate vicinity, has generated an environment to which the youngest and oldest (five to twenty-plus years) return day after day and throughout the official school vacations. Activities are project-based, art, craft and self supporting enterprises (dancing traditional dances to raise money) using the methods we associate with our own good primary schools. There are numerous examples of this kind of context here in the UK, and abroad wherever the established system fails to support those who do not fit in.

Another EEC country (Denmark) illustrates how an alternative system can operate alongside established schooling with government support and encouragement. The main virtue of this is that all abilities can enter this system and unlike the British independent sector does not produce an elite aiming towards the professions, City-based financial enterprises, and government. It genuinely provides an alternative system for learning and teaching. In the area of special needs, however, there is the same questioning of segregation and integration with sufficient reservations on the part of one community area to vote out proposals for the reorganization of special provision on an integrated system. Personal relationships in both these countries are valued and in their different ways they seek to preserve the principles of a decision-making process based on discussion. Yet there still exists the stigma associated with low achievement, particularly when accompanied by disturbed or disruptive behaviour. Apparently democratic decisions are made between the able-bodied and -minded for maintaining existing structures. The relationship between those capable of work and thus contributing to the economy and their 'handicapped' peers is similar in the different economic situations of the three countries (UK, Portugal and Denmark). In each of these the special needs industry is firmly established with separation in teaching, professional development (research) and training. The contexts in which people live are only just beginning to change with a firm policy of small groups in family-sized units in local residential areas. These are difficult to set up because of ignorance in the general community resulting from years of segregation. Attempts to break down barriers are left to enthusiastic individuals who in the end have to operate within the separate system and there is no formalized policy to encourage those who 'have' actively to engage in mutual enterprises with those who do not.

It seems that alternative contexts are a necessary antidote to the established system however enlightened the mainliners maybe. Good resources and low pupil–teacher ratios (as in Denmark) do not prevent parents seeking some other educational context, nor does it encourage integration of the severely handicapped more fully into the mainstream. But whether teachers are operating in the established or an alternative provision the values that the pupils will take away will be governed by the attitudes of those teachers and the nature of the context that they create.

If the contexts within which special needs will be met or prevented from becoming more severe, are to be effective for the participants, whether adult or pupil, then teachers need to be able to identify the emotional connotations of their role and its relationship to the environment they provide. While most teachers will say they teach because they like children and special teachers are usually particularly well-motivated towards the child with probelms and get drawn towards that aspect of the work, there is no doubt that a large number of teachers accept the context in which they are located, and find it difficult to initiate change in either physical or emotional environments even when they are aware of the need to do so.

This is due in part to the enmeshed behaviour of teachers and pupils to each other. Contexts are constructed by the participants so in the prevention and support of special needs the role of the teacher as an interactor with the pupil requires more analysis than simply the analysis of functional language or an observational narrative about classrooms. Categorizing teacher styles is also illuminating, but while these contribute to understanding classroom behaviour, we are still only at the beginning of the exploration of inter-personal operations in teaching and learning.

Teacher and Pupil Interactions

This is a difficult area for teachers to analyse for themselves. It is where collaboration between professionals can produce the kind of data which can enable change to take place. Development of 'teacher as researcher' strategies goes some way towards encouraging reflexivity and should allow teachers, whether in training or in service, to work with colleagues on analysis of interactional practice. It is a resource intensive activity and requires considerable knowledge of the nature of linguistic structures to be useful.

The special needs support teacher's role focuses on the traditional view of intervention and remediation for the pupil. While the number of skills that these professionals require are numerous and complex, they do not necessarily include an understanding of social and linguistic interactions at the kind of level which could be useful, although they may be aware of the issues involved. The support teacher could be used to help the teacher to identify those intuitive actions which underlie practice. This would mean a reassessment of this role and a marked change in status for it. The special needs sector suffers considerably from the low status labelling which has traditionally been given to those working in this field whether as trainers or teachers. Some means of changing this needs to be found if there is to be any progress made in the unpacking of the stigma attached to segregated and non-segregated provisions. The subject specialist in the secondary school in the main does not encourage the use of co-teaching, although there are some examples of it working effectively in, for example, mixed-ability environmental sciences classes. A minority of teachers may plan with their teaching colleagues, but the purposeful use of the support teacher in such a role is very rare.

Even special schools and classes, where it might be expected that a sharing of expertise might occur more easily, contain the insularity, insecurity and lack of imagination which sabotage those more open and sensitive approaches that some teachers are working towards.

The research focusing on the nature of teacher–pupil interactions and their learning and teaching styles has been developing in range and type since the early 1970s. Ethological studies have been paralleled by the work on adult-child language and learning through interaction (Tough, 1976; Wells, 1981). Aspects of secondary schools which could be construed as the special needs area, ('deviancy' in classrooms for example) have long been of interest. Other studies on adolescent behaviours and reactions to schools are extensive, i.e., Hargreaves, 1981; White, 1980, White and Brockington, 1983; Delamont, 1976, 1983, and Stubbs and Hillier, 1983 and long-neglected areas such as gender and race are now included (Spender and Sarah, 1980; Whyld 1983). Primary schools are increasingly being analysed, both regarding teacher and pupil styles (Oracle Project, 1980), the social behaviour of primary pupils (Pollard, 1985) and pupils' perceptions of the learning game.

Interactional behaviour of pupils with identified special needs in units and schools have not received the same attention until recently and as a result of integration programmes. Most studies with children with special needs have focused on interventionist programmes such as those on language intervention with children with severe learning difficulties (Berry 1976, Leeming *et al.*, 1979). Hackney (1981, 84) examined the relationship of children's levels of functioning to teachers' perceptions about such children. In Davidson (1979, 1984, 1987) and Williams *et al.* (1981) it was suggested that the language functions of children and adults had crucial effects on the learning context and process. There is a need for teachers to be aware of factors such as the learners' receptivity styles (and what these might be) as well as their own patterns of verbal and non-verbal behaviour. The nature of the curriculum in action is dependent on the action of the participants, but while language as an issue in education is seen as primarily to do with literacy and oracy as disciplines, and behaviours between people in mainstream provision and 'special' provision are seen as separate concerns, structural modifications that are needed to prevent communication failure between peers and between adult–learners in classrooms will not effectively occur. Certainly programmes for integration will need to be informed by work such as that by McEvoy *et al.* (1984) and Tiffany Field (1982) among others and the literature of social psychology.

It was suggested at the beginning of this section that special needs support staff could play a role in the analysis of teacher–pupil interactions and styles of approaching learning and teaching and that the low status of the role makes it difficult for them to enter into such a partnership with the regular teacher. As long as regular teachers see the support teacher as the person who will deal with their 'problem' pupil(s) a working partnership will be impossible. They need to have a positive training in the use of such extra staffing for monitoring and evaluating the classroom so that change can take place *in situ*. It is clear from curriculum projects done by inservice teachers using situational analysis techniques in the classroom that the skills exist to investigate these contexts in an informed way. What is required is for the regular teacher to be an equal participant. The kind of constructs that teachers formulated about themselves in, for example, the Ford Teaching Project (Elliott, 1976) identify the role issues to be tackled. The problem lies in finding ways to enable this to happen in the present climate.

Method

The third aspect for discussion, method, is one which is central to successful delivery of the curriculum. While contexts and interpersonal behaviours may be indirectly affected by external influences, methods of teaching pupils with 'special needs' is increasingly becoming directly influenced by psychologists. In particular, behavioural rather than cognitive psychologists, are able, because it is possible to produce packaged teaching programmes using a structured behavioural approach, apparently to fulfil teachers' 'needs' for coherent and sequential materials to intervene in practice. This is not to say that teachers are uncritical of these structured packs. Constraints of time make it difficult for detailed analyses to be made. It is also the case that many teachers do not have a deep understanding of approaches to learning which would enable them to evaluate these materials at other than an intuitive level. There is a possible conflict between the teachers' desire to have help in the teaching task and their intuitive dislike of such tailored programmes. Frequently they adapt them to suit their needs. They are not well equipped to counter effectively the behavioural psychologist's case. It is this lack of informed professionalism which puts teachers into a vulnerable position. Critics of the way curriculum is planned and presented are able to 'appraise' practice in a destructive but convincing way. Emphasis by the popular media on the negative attributes of schools makes work with pupils with seriously disadvantaged backgrounds extremely difficult and does not encourage teachers to have faith in their own methods, particularly where it is clear that the pupils need to learn through a slower process of experience, negotiation, decision-making and individual counselling than the product model of the skills training approach. (Cooper 1987) gives a useful analysis of the difficulties facing providers for special needs students in further education with the conflict between government-backed schemes which emphasize training rather than initiative.

Swann (1983) provides a useful critique of the behavioural approach and its relevance to the delivery of the 'curriculum'. He points out that the specification of objectives is no guarantee that the teaching will be appropriate. Stenhouse (1975) had already provided a critique of the behavioural approach in mainstream education but this has not discouraged the behavioural psychologists from viewing the special sector as an appropriate place for the introduction of these methods. A balanced and extremely useful overview of the advantages and disadvantages of cognitive and behavioural approaches is given by Fontana (1985) and illustrates the commonality of needs that teachers have.

To conclude, education happens through easy and uneasy alliances between teachers and pupils and pupils and their peers. Legislation has provided the way for those other than teachers to prescribe how the pupils should be taught, while teachers are put under pressure to extend their range and type of skills. Shortage of speech therapists, art and drama specialists and special needs support staff along with the growing number of children with adjustment difficulties does not encourage the most productive atmosphere for curriculum development and implementation and moves to desegregate. Yet stimulating and productive environments exist, activities encouraging integration are being initiated by schools, and materials and methods are being evaluated and modified. The teaching profession requires a supportive framework within which to tackle the complexity of the job and consideration needs to be given to the nature of training required for the variety of demands being made on schools.

Some schools may indeed be able to produce clear and descriptive accounts of the intentions and content of their curricula and have curriculum review panels and committees and identified curriculum specialists on the staff. Nevertheless many do not, and those that do often are not able critically to evaluate the congruence between intention and reality nor what needs to be done to change situations. Confronting students with strategies for engaging in reflective and investigational studies enables them to confirm what they may feel — that the practice of schooling may cause, as well as exacerbate, learning difficulties even in situations where teachers are doing their utmost to improve pupils' self-esteem and achievements. They also become more able to understand that the threatening nature of self-evaluation prevents curriculum development from taking place. Just as the development of policies for coherent and sensitive approaches to provision are still in an embryonic and inequable state, so approaches to curriculum development while often seriously aproached, are apparently dependent on individual enthusiasms and strengths of advisors, headteachers and teachers. Initiatives by the Department of Education and Science to provide short but intensive one-term courses for inservice training in special needs may go some way to providing a more informed teaching force and keyworkers for staff development in schools. This in itself, however, cannot provide sufficient grassroots power to change systems which are antipathetic to other than the deficit model of special need. It is the unfortunate case that some courses reinforce the very concepts that are responsible for identifying differences rather than similarities between pupils.

Views about curriculum are based on differing and conflicting ideological viewpoints. Primarily they focus on the function of schooling and the way in which schools will prepare the citizens of the future for the needs society will have. In a climate where the strong are encouraged to develop their strength and those who have few or no resources are regarded as ineffective but nevertheless requiring punitive measures to be controlled, then the education system will be geared to encouraging the best endowed to succeed while discouraging independent thinking from anyone. In addressing the curriculum and particularly that for the pupil who is experiencing difficulty the teacher is faced with an increasingly difficult task because the biggest constraint of all to the development of effective learning and the potential of 'slow developers' will be the imposition of time barriers in the form of regular assessment. It will be necessary for those working in curriculum development with teachers in the 'special education field' to develop alternatives which will enable all pupils to make their contributions to their communities, but most of all, to extend themselves in the face of increasingly unequal opportunities.

References

BARTON, L. and TOMLINSON, S. (Eds) (1981) *Special Education: Policy, Practices and Social Issues*, London, Harper and Row.

BARTON, L. and TOMLINSON, S. (Eds) (1984) *Special Education and Social Interests*, Beckenham, Croom Helm.

BERRY, P. (1976) *Language and Communication in the Mentally Handicapped*. London, Edward Arnold.

BEVERIDGE, M. and CONTI-RAMSDEN, G. (1987) *Children with Language Disabilities*, Milton Keynes, Open University Press.

BOOTH, T., POTTS, P. and SWANN, W. (1987) *Preventing Difficulties in Learning*, London, Blackwell.

BRENNAN, W.K. (1985) *Curriculum for Special Needs*, Milton Keynes, Open University Press.

BRENNAN, W.K. (1979) *The Curricular Needs of Slow Learners*, London, Evans/Methuen.

BROCKINGTON, D. and WHITE, R. (1987) *Organising a Negotiated Curriculum*. Youth Education Service Publications.

COMMITTEE OF VICE CHANCELLORS REPORT (1988) University Entrance 1988: The Official Guide. Association of Commonwealth Universities.

COOPER, B. (1987) *Curriculum Study*. Unpublished Paper, Bristol Polytechnic Diploma in Professional Studies (Special Education).

COUPE, J. and PORTER, J. (1986) *The Education of Children With Severe Learning Difficulties*, Beckenham, Croom Helm.

DAVIDSON, R.E. (1979) *A Comparative Study of the Verbal and Non-Verbal Interactions Experienced by a Down's Syndrome Child, his Mother and his Teacher*. Unpublished Dissertation Diploma in Advanced Studies in Education, University of Bristol.

DAVIDSON, R.E. (1984) 'Styles in Teaching and Learning', in British Journal of Special Education Journal 11, 1. pp. 19–23.

DAVIDSON, R.E. (1986) *Aspects of Classroom Interaction in Teaching Children with Severe Learning Difficulties*. Unpublished paper presented at British Educational Research Association Conference, Bristol.

DAVIDSON, R.E. and AVON TEACHER'S RESEARCH GROUP (1987) *Classroom Interaction in Classrooms for Children with Severe Learning Difficulties*. Unpublished paper presented at the International Conference: Social Psychology and Language, Bristol.

DELAMONT, S. (1976, 1983) *Interaction in the Classroom*. London, Methuen.

DES (1978) *Special Educational Needs (Warnock Report)*, London, HMSO.

ELLIOTT, J. (1976) *Ford Teaching Project*, North Dakota Study Group on Evaluation, University of North Dakota.

FIELD, T. (1982) 'The Play of Handicapped Pre-School Children with Handicapped and Non-Handicapped Peers in Integrated and Non-Integrated Situations; Australia Topics in Early Childhood', in *Special Education*, 2.3.

FONTANA, D. (1985) *Classroom Control*, London, Methuen.

GALLOWAY, D. and GOODWIN, C. (1987) *The Education of Disturbing Children*, London, Longman.

HACKNEY, A. (1981) *Problems of Language and Communication in Severely Educationally*

Retarded Children. Unpublished Doctor of Philosophy thesis, Oxford University.

HACKNEY, A. (1984) *Learning Together*. Windsor, NFER-Nelson.

HARGREAVES, D. (1982) *The Challenge for the Comprehensive School: culture, curriculum and community*. London, Routledge and Kegan Paul.

HMI (1987) *Special Educational Needs in Initial Teacher Training*. Course organised by Her Majesty's Inspectors Newman College Birmingham 1987.

HOGG, J. and RAYNES, N.V. (1987) *Assessment in Mental Handicap*, Beckenham, Croom Helm.

LEEMING, K. *et al*. (1979) *Teaching Language and Communication to the Mentally Handicapped*, London, Evans/Methuen.

McEVOY, M., NORDQVIST, V.M. and CUNNINGHAM, J. (1984) 'Regular and Special Education Teachers Judgements about Mentally Retarded Children in Integrated Settings', in *American Journal of Mental Deficiency*, 89, 2 pp. 167–173.

ORACLE PROJECT (1980) in GALTON, M., SIMON, B. and CROLL, P. *Inside the Primary Classroom*. London, Routledge and Kegan Paul.

POLLARD, A. (1985) *The Social World of the Primary Child*. London, Holt Rhinehart and Wilson.

SELECT COMMITTEE (1987) *Special Education Needs: Implementation of the Education Act*, London, HMSO.

SOLITY, J. and BULL, S. (1987) *Special Needs: Bridging the Curriculum Gap*, Milton Keynes, Open University Press.

SPENDER, G. and SARAH, E. (1980) *Learning to Lose*. London, The Women's Press.

STENHOUSE, L. (1975) *An Introduction To Curriculum Research and Development*. London, Heinemann.

STUBBS, M. and DELAMONT, S. (1976) *Explorations in Classroom Interaction*, London, John Wiley.

STUBBS, M. and HILLIER, H. (1983) *Readings on Language, Schools and Classrooms*. London, Methuen.

SWANN, W. (1983) 'Curriculum Principles for Integration', in BOOTH, T. and POTTS, P. (Eds), *Integrating Special Education*, Oxford, Basil Blackwell.

TEYBER, E.C., MESSE, L.A. and STOLLAK, G.E. (1977) 'Adult Responses to Child Communications' in *Child Development*, 48, pp. 1577–1582.

TOMLINSON, S. (1981) *A Sociology of Special Education*, London, Routledge and Kegan Paul.

TOUGH, J. (1976) *Listening to Children Talking*. London, Ward Lock.

WELLS, G. (1981) *Learning Through Interaction*. Cambridge University Press.

WHITE, R. (1980) *Absent with Cause*. London, Routledge and Kegan Paul.

WHITE, R. and BROCKINGTON, D. (1983) *Tales Out of School*. London, Routledge and Kegan Paul.

WHYLD, J. (1983) *Sexism and Racism in the Secondary Curriculum*. London, Harper and Row.

WILLIAMS, V., DAVIDSON, B., HAMMOND, J., JOHNSON, H. and SILVERMAN, S. (1981) 'Teachers Greeting Children in ESNs Schools' in *British Journal of Mental Subnormality*, Dec 27. pt. 2. (53).

WILSON, M. and EVANS, M. (1980) *Education of Disturbed Pupils*, London, Methuen Educational.

WILSON, M. (1981) *The Curriculum in Special Schools*, York, Longman.

Chapter 9

Power In Disguise

Rob Withers and John Lee

Introduction

The word 'assessment' is now commonly used in such a variety of educational contexts that it is easy to forget that it has acquired this key role in
educational discourse only very recently. All kinds of qualities and
personality traits are said to be assessed, yet the use of the term carries with it
the implication that the process of selection is scientific, neutral and
benevolent. In this chapter we will examine contradictions which underpin
talk of assessment, and the assessors' understanding of their practices.

'Assessment' of pupils within schools is the exercise of power by those
who arrogate the functions of assessors, yet it is constantly acted out as an
unthreatening natural activity. Assessment which is claimed to be scientific,
including the use of special instruments, such as tests, profiles and such
procedures is *at the same time* nothing but an extension of ordinary judgments
which any teacher makes of her pupils. A process which alters the future
treatment and life chances of children, and which is sometimes the means by
which pupils are selected for special provision, is somehow presented as con-
templative and advisory, as if the judgment were made elsewhere, independently of the practices of the assessor. The basis of the process, especially the
norms on which it is based, is nevertheless inaccessible to those who are
'assessed' and whose futures will be altered as a result. We will explore these
paradoxes in the rest of the chapter in order to discover and expose the
means by which the threatening, powerful aspect of assessment has been
hidden from assessed and assessors alike, and how critics of examinations and
testing have been disarmed by talk of assessment.

The practice of educators, in differentiating the performances of pupils
produces those who are certificated successful and those who are in the
extreme case leading to segregation, the least successful receiving separate
provision. Unable to solve this contradiction in our practice, a solution has
been provided by the benevolent and humanitarian discourse of assessment.

Thus the discourse has an ideological function in the sense that the unacceptable contradictory practice of educators in reproducing the unequal social relations of society, can be 'solved' in consciousness where the connotations are of a scientific, natural, technological activity. The unacceptable *practices* are rendered into natural *activities*, and the domination of the powerless who are assessed by the powerful assessors is legitimated. The *means* by which contradictions are overcome in discourse, and practices legitimated, is what we refer to as an ideological mechanism. How assessment comes to have this function cannot be explained adequately by examination of changes in the use of the term, nevertheless it is worth noting the passage of changing signification. The use of the expression to stand for the process by which tax liability is decided is no longer clearly related to its educational use, but elements of the original connotations have been retained: the assessment of qualities and abilities now appears to be as unproblematic and objective as the assessment of someone's ability to pay. Just as the assessment of tax liability was seen as a practical matter, a kind of calculation based on estimation of values of goods which could be realized in the market, so too is the estimation of a person's ability now seen as a practical task without conceptual difficulty. So complete has been the pervasion of educational discourse by the notion of 'assessment procedures', that educationists find it difficult to see what is wrong with this picture of a practical calculation. Such inurement to a process of change affecting the lives of a large proportion of the population must be brought about by a powerful ideological mechanism.

Assessment as Ideology

The success of the discourse depends on much more than acceptance of an extension of meaning and acquired connotations. What has to be explained is why it is that testing and examinations always provoke fierce criticism now, while 'assessments' do not, even when the procedures used are known to involve the giving of tests. Our particular concern in all this will be to account for the acceptance of assessment as benevolent and humanitarian in the highly divisive and political selection of pupils for special schooling (by which, we mean segregated provision of school and segregated provision within school). While it has come to be recognized that tests are constructed to produce positional results and are acknowledged instruments of selection, (part of its technology), assessments of ability or of degree of special need, or of suitability for a particular kind of schooling, are seen as necessarily motivated by a concern for the interests of the individual. By extension, assessment itself is a profoundly ideological process. Testing and examinations are recognized as means of providing restricted gateways to serve a function in a positional society, yet assessment escapes this kind of analysis, even when used to identify those who will be called 'the bottom 20 per cent', and assumes a very different analysis of society as humane.

In the first half of the 20th century, testing became established as a neutral and scientific activity through the claims for standardization and objectivity. Objectivity was predicated upon the construction of shibboleths, most notably the IQ test. The notion of 'intelligence quotient' has proved systematically ambiguous. The testers themselves warn that IQ is not to be thought of as a quantity, yet at the same time they talk of 'its measurement' and they acknowledge that IQ is constructed with reference to particular test items while insisting on the word 'intelligence'. The ambiguity has been encouraged by trading upon the confusion between the shibboleth as a mere device, a sieve, and its basis in a particular ability, e.g., the ability to make the sound 'sh': Judges XII 4–6. Despite the success of critiques of IQ testing, which have largely ended its use in national selection procedures, it seems that teachers are still confused and held captive by the ambiguity. Croll and Moses (1985) reveal that IQ is regarded as a cause of special educational need. IQ is a numerical description of a test result expressed as a quotient; chronological age is used to compare a child's test result with a norm of success. Since it is not a characteristic of the child but a construction, it cannot be a cause, not being the right kind of thing. This confusion is evident in the work of Jensen who, in offering a critique of the possibility of boosting IQ accepts it as a cause of educational underachievement (Jensen 1969).

The power of the new concept of assessment is that it has been able to incorporate the claims of tests to be scientific, objective and neutral, yet it has been able to do this while largely abandoning the use of the shibboleth and the ideal of standardization. For example, those who continue to use standardized tests often claim that they are not interested in the results of tests, but in the way in which the testee completes them. (It is, in that case, difficult to see why they use such tests in preference to materials designed to allow the tester to explore the child's methods of working.) 'Assessors' also say that they gather factual information about the subject which is neither norm-referenced nor criterion-referenced. Such is the power of the ideology of assessment that it apparently goes unrecognized that such 'assessments' must therefore be *evaluations* of methods of working, and *interpretations* of this 'factual evidence'.

The emergence of assessment, filling the space left by the demise of testing, is a phenomenon which demands to be explained by means of a powerful general mechanism. There seems to be little difficulty in accounting for the decline of IQ testing. Many studies have been published drawing attention to the cultural bias of the tests, the convergent nature of the 'answers' which are accepted, the attitudes of the pupils who have been required to sit down and answer questions which they may see as irrelevant, boring and silly, and the norm-referencing that underpins the structure of the tests (see Rose, 1979, for instance). During the period from 1944 to the late 1950s, one would find children being tested each week in their primary schools, practising the 11+ selection as well as completing yearly tests for streams. During the period it was openly acknowledged that children were being selected for specific kinds of schooling within the tripartite system. Although the scientism of testing was sufficient to keep the IQ test central to this process of selection for twenty years, the attack from the advocates of comprehensivization, based upon a variety of principles connected with equality and fairness, (some of which, such as meritocracy, were illusory) eventually proved irresistable. The nature of selection, and the inherent power of the relationship, were demystified as parents saw their children consigned to what they believed to be inferior schooling. Middle-class parents fuelled the attack on IQ tests with their anger. They found their own children labelled as 'secondary moderns' and not 'grammar' on the basis of tests held in the course of a morning, and without the possibility of using the system by exercising any right of appeal. With comprehensivization the need for a national selection process disappeared and new needs took its place. Schools wanted formal records of progress for individuals, and so demands for measures of achievement continued. In place of testing and selection we were offered the more informal sounding 'assessment'. On this basis pupils were nevertheless placed in sets, units, or moved to special schools. What has to be explained is why assessment was siezed on as an acceptable alternative, apparently free of the vices of discredited testing and selection.

In the 1967 Plowden Report on primary education, *Children And Their Primary Schools*, the most significant post-war official expression of primary educational philosophy, the transition from the criticism of methods of selection to the promotion of assessment is evident:

In the past fifty years, persistent efforts have been made to refine methods of selection (para 413).

Selection at eleven is coming to an end, a trend we welcome in view of the difficulty of making the right decisions and the effect on the curriculum in the primary school. This does not, however, get rid of the need for assessment of primary pupils before they leave (para 418).

What is not clear from this early statement is how 'methods of selection', that is tests, are likely to differ from 'methods of assessment'. An example of 'assessment' gaining ascendancy over selection is provided by the example of an LEA which assessed fourth-year juniors in order to *ensure* a fair spread of abilities across all secondary schools. Here selection and assessment were taken to be the same thing, but the expression used was 'assessment'. The acceptance of assessment throughout education cannot be explained by a change of name alone, yet we seem forced to acknowledge that just such a change has taken place and has been important. There is now a general preference for the term 'assessment' even when the intention is solely to administer tests. For example, a recent book about testing and varieties of testing is entitled *Assessment In Schools* (Satterly, 1981). Similarly, asked to make an assessment, educationists may be satisfied to administer a test, or to refer to a test result. Croll and Moses (op.cit.) found that teachers in primary schools believed that poor reading was a cause of special needs. When he asked them to make an assessment of their pupils' reading, Paul Croll found that most turned to the results of standardized tests. Teachers, well aware that reading tests have important shortcomings, and who warned that the Burt and Schonell tests require pupils to 'bark at print', commonly said that particular pupils were poor readers because they had low test scores.

Our task is to produce a recent archaeology of assessment, uncovering the way in which this disguising ideology functions. Assessment is now most generally held to be an evaluative process, while tests are abstracted from the kind of activities which pupils might undertake. (The shibboleth is the extreme of abstraction.) Assessment is constructed as an examination of the activities themselves. In this dominant view, the assessment of quality, that is evaluation, is located as paying close attention to what the pupil produces, rather than requiring him/her to complete a test devised to use standard items abstracted from their usual contexts. Thus, in this its primary usage, it appears as a natural and inescapable human activity.

Description and judgement are linked to evaluation in the following way: what we pick out as features of objects reflects the interests which we have. Interests are given by what we would choose or reject, what we would pursue or avoid. The choices which we make are, then, reflections of values. Thus, as has been remarked often enough and in a number of scientific traditions, observation is value-laden, and description and judgement are evaluative, reflecting the kinds of choices which we make or might make. Assessment understood as a necessary feature of everyday life appears unthreatening. We are, in consequence, presented with a model of social persons as assessors. It is this account of assessment as a natural activity arising out of our social existence which has predominated in educational discourse. However, this natural activity involving no necessary power relationship, needs to be distinguished from developed institutional forms of assessment. It is our thesis that this second developed form, which for convenience we will term 'Mode Two Assessment', involves an intrinsic power relationship, but its problematic and political nature has been disguised ideologically by the failure to distinguish it from the natural activity of evaluation which we call here 'Mode One Assessment'. To use Barthes (1973) terminology, the process we have called 'Mode One' naturalizes 'Mode Two'; the discourse of assessment, signifies a single or common process, and thereby constitutes a disguising ideology, hiding from the assessed, and from the *assessor*, the nature of the 'Mode Two' process. As the quotation from Plowden makes clear, the use of tests as methods of selection was not disguised, and tests were acknowledged to be designed for particular purposes. The items were intentionally selected to produce distributed results, and so reflected our class society and its consequent educational rewards. It will be recalled that Burt set out to construct a test which would select children not merely for differential schooling but for adult roles in the economy. 'Mode Two Assessment' can lead to selection, such as selection for a special school, and may even involve administering tests, but unlike undisguised selection and testing it appears naturalized and unpolitical.

Assessments are made using criteria. Criteria are employed to judge something against an example to see if it is of that kind. Assessment in its essentials is a judgement of kind, of category. We have criteria for picking out objects, including, of course, people. This means we can recognize them as different from or similar to each other. In this sense it can be argued that assessment is a natural and necessary activity which we all engage in. We do not wish to deny that such natural assessments are made. The aim is to try to distinguish these 'Mode One Assessments' from 'Mode Two Assessments', despite the common feature that both forms involve the use of criteria.

Criteria and comprehension are linked in this way: features of something by which we identify it, consitute criteria, and our employment of criteria is a function of our interest in, and our understanding of, that something. And so it is that criteria connect learning and understanding. We learn the criteria for seeing this as an example of that, and hence for classifying this as that. (See Hamlyn, 1978, for an extended examination of these relationships.) So 'Mode One' has a clear and important learning function. It is, for example, the kind of assessment which enables a student to see what counts as an essay, or as an answer, or as a solution, or as a project of the appropriate kind. In all this one can see the importance of convention and the social nature of learning.

It can be argued that 'Mode One Assessment' does not have to involve a power relationship, since such a relationship is not a necessary feature of commonplace judgements made in day-to-day life; 'Mode Two' is linked with a power structure and serves particular purposes, having become institutionalized. These purposes, in the case under discussion, will include the separation of troublesome pupils from the mainstream, the preservation of a clientele for a group of professionals, the satisfaction of a need of professionals to be seen as coping in their teaching in the mainstream, and so on. (For further examples of the interests served by assessment in special education, see Dyson, 1986, and Brisenden, 1986.)

However, it is not sufficient to show that there are two distinct modes of assessment here, 'Mode One' naturalizing and thereby disguising 'Mode Two' functions. For the analysis to be successful it is necessary to show further that there is a relationship between the two modes which allows a 'slide' between the two positions, and an eliding of distinctions between them. A clear 'switching' would be obvious and clearly inconsistent to anyone who found themselves engaged in assessing others. We have to demonstrate the possibility of a naturalizing ideology, of the kind revealed by Barthes, in which the assessors themselves have the nature of their activity disguised from them. For this it is necessary to show a principle linking what are otherwise distinct modes. The connecting principle which we find is that 'Mode Two' similarly involves criteria and can demonstrate connections with learning. The important difference, however, is that the criteria are, in this case, norm-referenced. This will appear to be confusing, and possibly confused, since it is usual to talk of 'norm-referenced tests' in contrast to 'criteria-referenced assessments'. It is here, however, that the nature of the ideology is most clearly revealed. The criteria employed in assessments are means by which a judgement is made of how nearly a sample compares to a standard example. In this form of assessment, a comparison of measure, for instance, would be made by checking the example against a standard to see how closely it approximates to the paradigm. In the case of measure, the paradigm was the standard metre which was kept in a case under standard conditions. In the case of school abilities, however, the paradigm will be something like an idealized model of what it is to be able to read, to calculate, to write a sentence or a coherent story, and so on. Or in the case of behaviour, it will be what it is like to behave appropriately, and so on. Two points need to be borne in mind about this: the conceptions of what it is to be a reader, and the like, are themselves norm-referenced in the sense of being drawn from age-related norms (see Croll and Moses, op.cit.); the 'criteria' are imaginary in the sense that each assessor carries in her head a conception of what each child needs to be like in order to be said to be a reader, or a conception of what it is to be 'adjusted', and so on. That the criteria themselves are norm-referenced is apparent when one considers that our interest in this child not yet being able to read relates to the fact that she is 7-years-old and not 7 months, for at 7 months the criteria get no application. Similarly, in the case of writing and being a good writer, the particular features of 'writing' used as 'criteria' derive from an appreciation of the role of sentence formation as a norm in writing and the population of writers. In the case of 'acceptable' behaviour habitually shuffling around the classroom on one's bottom is appropriate behaviour at 1, but not at 41. The criteria employed by assessors in 'Mode Two' are therefore imaginary, not just in the sense of being held intentionally 'in mind' while assessing a particular child, but also in the sense of being constructed as a norm, an imaginary object. It is this deployment of imaginary criteria by assessors in 'Mode Two Assessment', under the guise of performing a natural form of judgement, which serves to allow them exercise of great uncheckable power. It is uncheckable and unaccountable since the criteria are imaginary and not accessible to the uninitiated. Thus the experts are able to defend their power, and the assessed have no independent redress.

The connection between criteria and learning is similarly discernible, yet once again there are differences between the modes, as is required if the analysis is to be convincing. The checking of something to see to what degree it matches the paradigm presupposes an appreciation that it is appropriate to make a judgement of approximation in this respect. The appropriateness of comparison invited will be determined much more explicitly by conventions, since, for example, in order to measure something against a standard metre it is necessary to recognize the category of length and the appropriateness of measuring the object in respect of length. (This is not to say that it is necessary to learn something about length first, before 'measuring'. As Hamlyn (op.cit.) demonstrates, logical pre-conditions and conditions are not temporally ordered but may be met *at the same time*.) Thus the child who attempts to learn about deafness might do so by carefully observing a hearing-impaired child and making comparisons with a norm. In this way she could learn something of what deafness is, but she would be unaware that normal hearing is an imaginary construction. The importance of hearing impairment is relative to the interests and demands of a society constructed around the 'normal', and so deafness is not 'a something' she could learn about, but is a conventional notion. The paradigms constructed in 'Mode Two Assessments' are all of this kind, and the conventions in which the paradigm and criteria are located become institutionalized.

Our argument illuminates the way in which medical models of disability use paradigms drawn from 'medicine' where the power of the professional to shroud their speculative, imaginary nature from public scrutiny is exceptionally strong, based as it is on powerful institutional defences and invisible colleges. Assessments for the purposes of special education are able to take on the mystique of diagnosis, the protection of the expert professional, and the secrecy and power of the clinician. When the naturalizing function of assessment comes into play, this appears to be a natural matter. Particularly important here, however, is the connection with Foucault's argument about surveillance. Until 1971 those classified as 'mentally handicapped' were confined under the care of health authorities in hospital and were outside the educational service. The change in responsibilities marked a commitment to the possibility of educating these children, but at the same time increased and extended the possibilities for surveillance of individuals, inherent in hospitalization, to a wider population through the organizational forms, but more particularly through the increased demands for assessment. Coupled with the moves away from the use of the shibboleth of tests to procedures more nearly resembling everyday school work in assessments, and the increases in the subjects to be assessed from 10 per cent to 20 per cent, this constitutes a massive increase in surveillance. By making the assessments connected to all facets of the child's activity and production in school, the technology of power imported from hospitals is able to reach deeper levels of personal conduct. It is to the massive extension of this powerful, isolating gaze of assessment (Rabinow 1986) which we will shortly turn.

Although we have concluded that thinking involves categorization and the deployment of criteria in the 'Mode One' manner, it would be foolish to argue that we could state precisely when such pristine use of criteria occurs in educational settings when people are being assessed. Nevertheless, this in no way weakens our argument since all that is required is acceptance of such assessments as occuring at specific times and as a possibility.

Our analysis and account hinges on the ideological nature of assessment, the way in which what is a public political act is treated as a private matter. There is, we believe, no escape from this. It is the disguised power of the assessor that must be laid bare in order to demonstrate its political nature. It should also be noted that in the case of assessment treated here, power extends beyond surveillance of bodies since the act of assessment also involves the direction of scarce and valuable resources.

Profiling provides a powerful and succinct example of how assessment works ideologically, of how power relations are hidden by appeals to naturalism and humanism while the claims to objectivity and efficiency are nevertheless retained. In the case of profiling, the headings and listed criteria are presumed to provide an unproblematic description of the abilities and capabilities of the assessed. The assumption is that such criteria do not relate to norms, but it is clear that the collection of criteria on the profile are not arbitrary: they relate to what the assessors believe a person can and should be able to do. In the creation of the profile, assessors surely must relate criteria to an idealized person, in the sense of a person able to match all the criteria laid down. As we argued above, this is a function of imagination and not empirical analysis. The profile is constructed on a powerful norm. Broadfoot (1985, p. 206) finds the same process underlying the French system of 'orientation':

> Orientation is based on the idea of a norm. It is a measure of conformity to this norm as adjudicated by corporate decision which, if it prevents the operation of individual prejudice, nevertheless disguises value judgements under a bland objective technocratic facade in which the individual is powerless to challenge the norm.

The profiling process in the French system is one of continuous and benign surveillance. We argue that precisely the same process operates in England in the assessment of children for special educational provision. Inevitably, despite claims to 'assess the situation' rather than the child, the focus is not on the abilities of the assessed or the social character of schooling, but rather on their inability to perform certain tasks. When public examinations, or compulsory norm-referenced tests, are used, the power relationships involved in assessment are undisguised. However, the use of checklists for the purposes of making special educational provision effectively disempowers the assessed, because there is no established norm for the person assessed to appeal to.

A Case in Point

The points made here can be demonstrated in an examination of published 'assessments'. In *E241 D12*(1984), the Open University published responses to the course material of *Special Needs in Education*. In his responses to Will Swann's remarks about the role of educational psychologists, Geoff Lindsay shows to what extent the assessors themselves can be taken in by the disguising ideology of 'assessment'. He says (p. 11) that he is asked 'to advise' on a very wide range of 'problems', providing 'information and opinion about a child's needs'. He then unconsciously places the responsibility for exercising power elsewhere, believing that he merely gives 'information' to other people, and that they make the decisions. What is particularly instructive is his reiterated claim to be 'dispassionate', in analysing problems (p. 11) as a social scientist (p. 12), and his supposition that as such he is not acting in a self-interested way, but only in the interests of the child.

Bearing in mind the consideration that the 'assessment' is proffered as evidence that psychologists do not use IQ tests on the scale suggested by Swann, and in view of his characterization of his work as providing a thorough appraisal of the child and his problems making use of many areas of knowledge and commonsense, it is surprising to find a highly general description of poor handwriting and spelling followed by references to the results of standardized tests. Of course, his description of the 'problem-solving approach', which he sincerely espouses, can only amount to a brief sketch. Nevertheless, it is important to note that the example was carefully chosen by Lindsay to show a psychologist working in the interests of the child and providing detailed objective assessment. That is, he is reassuring us that he simply engages in the natural activity of judgement, yet at the same time he claims to do so in a specially scientific or dispassionate manner. The institutionalized form of assessment is naturalized, and so his general practice is defended to himself. We are not trying to disparage his evident sincerity; the aim is to show how the naturalizing function of assessment operates even in the case of examples offered in a conscious spirit of self-defence. For Lindsay, 'assessments' can be constituted by administering tests and considering the results. He says that he 'did not try to measure Mark's IQ, but try to assess a range of Mark's abilities using a variety of techniques which included normative tests'.

Unit *E241 NL* includes a report on a boy attending a nursery school which was made by Lindsay 'following the checklist for advice on special needs proposed by the DES in Circular 1/83'. It is said to reflect the changes in the concept of special educational needs and their assessment underpinning the 1981 Act. The detailed 'advice' which is contained in Part II of the report (p. 10) begins with a 'description of the child's functioning' and moves on to explain 'the aims of provision', thereby casting further doubt on the claim that factual information is provided in a manner which keeps it separate from decisions. It also raises the issue of the relationship between the 'information' which the assessors choose to provide and the recommendations made.

By contrast with the previous example, in this case Lindsay says that he was asked to advise on David's needs, and on the child's subsequent school placement. His recommendation is that David 'requires the continued support and help available in a school for children with mild or moderate learning difficulties'. This is based upon a view which is expressed in terms of what he considers the child to be, and the difficulties which the child has: 'I consider David to be a child who has complex learning difficulties, and whose performance at school is significantly below the optimum shown at home'. The profile of the child (an expression used explicitly on the Scottish Statutory Form of Record of Special Needs) is broken down as a checklist under eight headings: Sensory; Mobility; Emotional State; Cognitive Functioning; Communication Skills; Perceptual Motor Skills; Approaches and Attitudes to Learning: Behaviour. This is very much a checklist in that several of the sections contain statements that the child is 'functioning adequately', with, for example, 'evidence of satisfactory memory', hearing and vision adequate for the tasks he was completing, and satisfactory perceptual skills. Running throughout the report there is evidence of the use of a powerful norm of what a nursery child should be like at school, when tested, and when receiving speech therapy. It is stated that he knows the main colours, can count (though not perfectly) to ten, can complete sentences 'deliberately left blank', and showed good strategies on an inset board, matching pieces to spaces, and vice versa, in a task involving about twenty-five pieces 1 cm long. He could also answer the 'phone. Concern is shown because the clinical psychologist reported that this 5-year-old boy 'appeared to be functioning in the low average range overall'.

The main thrust of the report is to pick out a significant difference in the way in which the child behaves at home and in schools. This is not, however, as a prelude to a consideration of the nature of the school and the child within it, but as the basis for recommendations about a particular form of special schooling. At home he came across as a happy friendly little boy, well dressed and well cared for. He met Lindsay at the door, led him in, sat on his lap and tried to talk and play with ease. He was smiling, playful and interested in all his surroundings. Also at home he was capable of 'a good deal of appropriate language', and chatted easily and often. He was able to sing a nursery rhyme, and *I am Sailing*, 'almost perfectly'. The only problem in this repsect was that his 'articulation was slightly impaired', though exactly what form this took, or how the educational psychologist made this judgement, is not revealed. In terms of behaviour at home, he showed good resistance to distraction, persistence on tasks, and concentration of 'ten minutes plus'. Whilst talking, he was able to respond to the start of a jingle and tell the psychologist that this was the start of Radio Hallam News. This, then, is part of the situation, the home situation, of a child whom Lindsay assesses as being a child who has complex learning difficulties.

At home David appears to be, then, a socially well-adjusted and competent child. If assessments are, as we are assured, of situations, then David's very different 'behaviour' and 'attitudes' in nursery and language group should provoke an interesting and powerful critique of these other situations from someone who claims to make use of a variety of different theoretical perspectives. But 'assessments' are of the subject, the person whose name appears on the form and of whom a profile is constructed. David does not meet the norm of acceptable behaviour for a nursery child employed by Lindsay in his assessment. At $4\frac{1}{2}$-years old, during a visit by the educational psychologist, (length of time unspecified) he moved around the nursery 'almost exclusively' by bottom shuffling. It is not clear whether this is what is meant by the 'various odd movement patterns' which he has said to 'have shown' at nursery. The power of the assessor to be selective in what is described and how it is presented is evident here. He also appears to be 'relatively withdrawn' at nursery (once again the 'objective' assessment contains important but unspecific qualifications), displaying no interest in visitors and does not play well with other children. Lindsay 'rarely' heard him make any conversation, though his teacher reported that on occasions he will produce quite long, appropriate sentences. All this appears to have more bearing on his response to the social situation of school rather than on his alleged complex learning difficulties. The ground for that assessment seems mainly to lie in the claim that his drawing ability is 'immature', a transparently normative judgement. He spontaneously drew a large square which was firm with good attempts at right angles, but the lines were 'wavy'. Particularly telling, it appears, was the fact that this child, who in many countries would not yet have started school, was unable to draw a number 1 with consistent accuracy, some being squiggles and others horizontal.

The role of parents in assessment procedures has recently been much discussed (see Moses and Croll, 1987). A common claim is that involving the parents of the child in the assessment process necessarily leads to a fuller assessment. Once again, the presupposition is that a neutral and natural process of information gathering and description is in operation. However, the assessor decides what is relevant, or accurate, and makes a selection from that information as a basis for recommendation. The power of the assessor to select and interpret is disguised by the assumption of a neutral 'dispassionate' process. Lindsay says that 'David's mother has had difficulties, as one would expect, with coming to understand, and to terms with David's problems'. Some of us would sympathize with her in this. It is asserted that she was concerned that people may have believed him to be mentally handicapped, but there is no indication who these people might be. Since the behaviour of David at home is known to be that of a socially well-adjusted and normally functioning child, it may be that the people she refers to must have some knowledge of his response to school, or to the language group, and may even be teachers or therapists. Certainly the omission of this information creates an impression of a child who gives rise to comment from the public at large, which is quite inconsistent with the account of him outside school.

It is on the basis of assessments such as this, then, that selection is made for special schooling. The air of objectivity is coupled with the assumption that the process of assessment is unproblematic, and this disguises the power of the asessor to choose what to record and what use to make of it, and how to justify the recommendation. In the example, Lindsay makes use of a norm of maturity and an idealized profile of nursery school child. On this basis he recommends attendance at a day school for children with mild/moderate learning difficulties for a period of about two years. After that time, he says, David 'may have developed enough to enter mainstream' (p. 11).

Conclusion

We have argued that, because assessment operates as a disguising ideology, both assessors and the asessed have its true nature hidden from them; this is a profoundly pessimistic political situation. If the argument is concluded in this way then teachers must be viewed as powerless dupes caught in structural forces not merely outside their control but of which they can have no knowledge. We believe this sort of political pessimism can be rejected and that teachers can be both aware of the nature of their actions as assessors and develop critical stances to both assessment and selection. It would be possible, for instance, for an educational psychologist such as Lindsay to accept responsibility for his involvement in the process selection and to recognize that the powerful norms which he invokes serve as a means of segregation. It could be facile to pretend that teachers do not stand in a power relationship to the taught and that in the day-to-day business of teaching and learning, assessment does not go on. It is precisely this that teachers must recognize; that the job is one redolent of power and that there is no escaping from it. What is needed is not escape but a grounded critical analysis of assessment. Such an analysis would not merely question the results of assessment as occurred with 11+ selection, nor the mode, but its political and social function. We suggest the following will provide a way forward.

In many circumstances teachers are themselves assessed. The current political struggle in Britain over teacher appraisal and the historical struggle over payment by results show clearly that assessment's ideological function can be decoded. Here, teachers have not only the experience of the raw power of assessment at the receiving end but have formulated strong critiques of the whole process. What is needed here is both simple and very difficult. First, a recognition that the struggle of those designated for special education against assessment is the same as the struggle that teachers are engaging in over appraisal, and second, an application of their own critique of appraisal to their actions as assessors. In the teachers' struggle against their own assessment, they insist upon the right to negotiate. The process of negotiation is one key to the decoding of assessment. If a similar right were extended to those assessed for special educational placement, the calm unproblematic surface of the assessment process would be at least ruffled. Negotiation, of course, makes the power of the assessor obvious but cannot remove it. Finally, the role of imagination in the construction of assessment needs to be honestly recognized. Curiously, teachers, perhaps more than anyone else, have experienced this in their own training, particularly over the question of 'Teaching Practice'; the imaginary norm of the ideal teacher they know from their own college experience to have been almost entirely dependant on the whim of an individual tutor.

References

BARTHES, R. (1973) *Mythologies*, London, Paladin.

BRISENDEN, S. (1986) 'Independent Living and the Medical Model of Disability', in *Disability, Handicap and Society* 1, 2 pp. 173–178.

BROADFOOT, P. (1985) *Selection, Certification and Control*, Lewes, Falmer Press.

CROLL, P. and MOSES, D. (1985) *One in Five*, London, Routledge and Kegan Paul.

DES (1967) *Children And Their Primary Schools*, (Plowden Report), London, HMSO.

DYSON, S. (1986) 'Professionals, Mentally Handicapped Children and Confidentiality', in *Disability, Handicap and Society*, 1, 1 pp. 73–88.

HAMLYN, D. (1978) *Experience And The Growth Of Understanding*, London, Routledge and Kegan Paul.

JENSEN, A.R. (1969) 'How Much Can We Boost IQ and Scholastic Achievement', in *Harvard Educational Review*, 39, 1 pp. 1–123.

MOSES, D. and CROLL, P. (1987) 'Parents as Partners', in *Disability, Handicap and Society* 2, 1 pp. 75–84.

Open University (1984) *E 241 NL. The New Laws On Special Education*, Milton Keynes, Open University.

RABINOW, P. (1986) *The Foucault Reader*, London, Peregrin.

ROSE, N. (1979) 'The Psychological Complex: Mental Measurement And Social Administration', in *Ideology And Consiousness*, 5 pp. 5–68.

SATTERLY, D. (1981) *Assessment In Schools*, Lewes, Falmer Press.

Chapter 10

Parents: Whose Partners?

Sue Wood

Introduction

In the wake of the burgeoning literature concerned with parental involvement in the education of children with special educational needs, Pugh (1987) is one of the few who add a cautionary note and a hint that all may not be what it seems. She asks:

> Whether the current emphasis on parental involvement always implies a more open relationship ... or whether sometimes responsibility for children's education ... is being shifted from professionals to parents and self help groups ... are we simply supporting a cutback in expenditure on state support for families?

She comments:

> Participation of parents can just be a way of passing problems back to those parents (p. 103).

'Parents as partners' and the concept of parent–professional partnership appear almost old hat in terms of their ready acceptance, now, as 'good practice' in the sphere of education of children with special educational needs. There is little questioning of the why's and wherefore's of parental involvement. On the other hand, there are an ever-increasing number of descriptive reports of successful projects, and a growing literature concerned with methodology and tips for improving parent–professional relationships. The meaning of 'successful' and 'improving' in this context is unclear — by what criteria, on whose terms, for whose benefit, for what purpose, are questions begging to be answered. The aim of this chapter is to contribute to extending the debate once more.

I believe the discussion which follows is relevant to the subject of parent professional relationships in general in special education, and to the understanding of 'parents as partners' in particular. However, my comments are made having specifically in mind the expansion of educationally based pre-school services for children with special educational needs, where the rhetoric of parent–professional partnership is continuously and directly invoked.

My purpose is threefold:

1. To map out some of the main arguments and positions taken in this sphere.
2. To draw attention to conflicting premises and positions, to question some key ideas underpinning present practice, and to argue that the concept of parent–professional partnership must be placed in the context of the politics of special education if the debate is to be extended beyond tips for teachers and recipes for professionals in establishing links with and utilizing parents in their own work with children.
3. To argue for more open exchanges between and amongst professionals and parents, and that parents' perspectives be given serious consideration alongside professional perspectives on special educational needs.

I hope that the chapter will be of use to those coming into the sphere of special education, but that it will also prove thought-provoking to practising teachers and other professionals. I hope it might be useful to parents.

Much has been written on the subject of 'parents as partners' in special education in the past 10 years, the vast majority by professionals for a professional audience. The Warnock Report (DES, 1978) devoted a whole chapter to the subject. Numerous books and articles have been published (Mittler and Mittler, 1983; McConkey, 1985; Lunt and Sheppard, 1986).[1]

There is a wealth of material describing parent–professional involvement projects, with frequent suggestions for developing good relations (Thomas, 1986; Wolfendale, 1986; Mittler and Mittler, 1983). Various definitions of partnership have been put forward and differentiations made between parent involvement, parent participation and 'true' partnership. Pugh (1987) gives a useful breakdown of dimensions of parental involvement, developed to describe the different ways parents relate to pre-school services. This offers some insight into the notion of partnership within the context of parent–professional relations and is summarized below:

Dimensions of Parental Involvement (following Pugh, 1987)
1. *Non-Participation* — where parents are unlikely to be involved or do not participate for whatever reason.
2. *External Support* — where parents support from the 'outside', e.g., fund-raising activities, attending social functions.

3. *Participation* — where parents participate under the supervision of professional staff in any variety of ways, e.g., providing an extra pair of hands, servicing the group by mending toys, decorating buildings, running mother and toddler groups, toy library, attending case conferences, participating in users' committees or on governing bodies.
4. *Partnership* — 'a sharing of power, resources, knowledge and decision making between parents and professionals' (Pugh, 1987, p. 97). Pugh sees this occurring in three different ways, which relate to different levels of action:

   a) *between one parent* (or set of parents) *and a professional*. This can be described as basically a 'grassroots' partnership and has as its focus the development of the child

   b) *between parents in general and a particular group or scheme*, that is where parents are partners in running the service and are therefore involved at the level of management, with the proviso, as Pugh points out, that '. . . whether or not this (parent representation on management committees/governing bodies, etc.) can be defined as partnership depends very much on whether anyone listens to what they have to say' (Pugh, 1987, p. 98)

   c) *between parents/clients/consumers and policy makers* and therefore at the level of planning and policy making, e.g., involvement in District Handicap Teams, working parties, local council committees, community health councils.
5. *Control* — where parents both determine and implement decisions and are ultimately responsible and accountable, e.g., in community playgroups and nurseries, mother and toddler groups and in some voluntary organizations.

It is clear from Pugh's (1987) analysis that there may be many variations in arrangements concerned with parental involvement, operating singularly or together, with individuals and groups of parents involved in a specific service system or institution such as a school. It is also clear that different sets of arrangements for parental involvement, participation and partnership may result from differing perceptions of roles and underlying assumptions about the rationale and desirability of parental involvement and parents rights. However, despite the many attempts at defining partnership and the general acknowledgement that some kind of equality and sharing is involved in the relationship (Mittler and Mittler, 1983), the term is frequently invoked as a vague ideal teachers should be working towards. It is also applied as a descriptive term to any one or mix of the situations Pugh (1987) notes above, often without definition, without critical analysis and indeed without reference to the various dimensions and levels of parental involvement and partnership which might be involved. For example, Moses and Croll (1987, p. 67) note that:

> The idea of 'parents and partners' has come nearest to fruition in the case of children with severe learning difficulties.

They cite the '. . . many individual examples of successful schemes such as Portage and parental training in behaviour modification' (Moses and Croll, 1987, p. 76). It is unclear, however, in what ways such schemes relate to the concept of partnership. Indeed, the parent–professional relationship in Portage is frequently held up as exemplifying 'partnership' (Wolfendale, 1985; Philps and Jones, 1985; Pugh, 1987) without the detailed clarification and analysis which might justify such a claim.

It remains the case that the emphasis on parental involvement within special education has been almost exclusively in the dimension of participation and partnership at the grassroots level, between one individual parent and one particular professional. In this sense Portage and 'parent training' are representative of parental involvement. Pugh (1987, p. 101) comments:

> Most parental involvement is dictated on professionals' terms — 'you help us in the ways we think fit, and we will help you bring up your children better'.

The position adopted in this chapter is that the concept of partnership implies full involvement of parents and/or parent representatives in the planning, development, policy making, implementation and evaluation of services, and therefore in a sharing of power and control, at all levels of action. Professionals and parents need to be clear and honest about the boundaries involved in their relationships, what is on offer and what is not, rather than invoking 'partnership' as a global description open to misinterpretation and misunderstanding.

The concept of 'parents as consumers' in the education of children with special educational needs, and their rights to information and involvement in decision making, has been influential in extending the debate about partnership beyond the individual relationship a teacher may develop with a parent for the direct and immediate benefit of the child (for example, in developing consistent responses to a child's behaviour at school and at home). Mittler and Mittler (1983) describe three phases of parental involvement having occurred and still occurring as a process of evolution. They suggest that in the first phase, parents were left largely unsupported and uninvolved with the professionals and service systems working with their child. In the second phase, the 'transplant phase', professional skills were implanted into the home, with professionals training parents to use particular techniques, and gaining parents' cooperation in extending a child's training or educational programme into the home. The third phase (which Mittler and Mittler saw us entering in the early 1980s) is the 'consumer phase', in which parents are offered a range of information and, ideally, services from which they can select according to their current needs.

It remains the case at present that many teachers, and other professionals involved in the education of children with special educational needs, find the idea of 'parents as consumers' who therefore have a right to pick and choose, and the concomitant concept of partnership as parental involvement in policy making, planning and so forth, as 'democracy gone mad'. As Croll and Moses (1987, pp. 76–77) note:

> . . . it seems likely that many professionals would find a true partnership difficult to reconcile with present working practices.

The Parents' Perspective

Parallel to the wealth of material, written by professionals, describing parental involvement projects and approaches to partnership, is the set of literature describing parents' perspectives and frequently, from the parents point of view, unsatisfactory relationships between themselves and professionals (Shearer, 1981; Fox, 1975; Hannan, 1975; McCormack, 1978; Turnbull and Turnbull, 1979; Family Focus, 1983; Wylie, 1986). Comments like 'I know they get this training but they don't really know how you feel' and 'they don't tell you anything' (Fox, 1975, in Potts, 1983, pp. 183–184), are still as relevant today as they were over 10 years ago.

Feelings of hesitancy and helplessness, when fearing that to comment or act will

> . . . put the backs up of the professionals concerned as well as run-(ning) the risk of being written off as someone who could not accept (her) son's difficulties (Family Focus, 1983, p. 27).

are also frequent. Parents often feel ignored, patronised, fobbed off. One parent notes how 'the current concept of "parent training" is extremely insulting' (Schulz, 1979, p. 33).

Furthermore, parents may feel forced to accept demeaning relationships with professionals because of the scarcity of services and the lack of choice involved, as well as expectations that professionals, by definition, have something positive to offer. A parent recently told me how the pre-school home teacher for children with special educational needs in her area, enters her home with a look of despair at the possessions and decor, proceeds to demand a room, table, chair, child, quiet and parent out of the way, and then, sometime later, leaves without so much as a comment about what the child (or she) does in the session. The parent continues to accept the service despite her anger, for fear of losing her access to the system altogether.

Akerley (1979, p. 40) speaks of her discovery of the false gods who reign in the sphere of services for children with special educational needs:

> . . . one potentially redeeming feature may be realized if the parents react with sufficient anger to take charge, to assert their right to be their child's 'case manager'. Unfortunately . . . it takes more than one false god to make us give up religion entirely. And when (or if) we do manage to assert ourselves, our behaviour is viewed by professionals as the final stage in our own pathology.

Perhaps there is some justification in professionals feeling that often, especially in the child's pre-school years, they are scapegoated by families and that expectations of professionals are unrealistic. Furthermore, it may seem that professionals as a group have to pay dearly for the insensitivity or lack of time and skill of one of their number. Russell (1986) has pointed out the importance of how parents are told about their child's difficulties or disability, and how this may colour their feelings towards and subsequent involvement with professionals. Others (Wylie, 1986; Cameron and Poidevin, 1985) have highlighted the importance of parents being able to offload their feelings about their child and the fact of their disability before being capable of entering into more constructive relationships with professionals and child.

However, the self-gratifying flavour of the majority of reports and discussions of parental involvement projects and parent–professional partnership strongly contrasts with parents' comments about their everyday experiences at the hands of the professionals. One of the most telling comments which parents can be heard to make over and over again regarding their relationships and dealings with professionals is 'why does everything have to be such a battle?'

Opposing Positions?

The emphasis on 'parents as partners' and current practice in the field is viewed by some as merely a form of 'window dressing' (Wolfendale, 1986). For example Potts (1983, p. 185) contrasts the 'press release' concerning the rhetoric of parents with the 'internal memo' which reads:

> Keep parents in the classroom, playroom or sitting room and off the management committee, . . . as parents do not have the specialized skills and knowledge to help their children on their own, pro-

fessional jobs need not be threatened, . . . working with parents prevents them from organizing themselves too well into a separate force and can actually extend the professional role.

She goes on to ask, in essence, whether more parental involvement means that parents are 'empowered', that is, more able to influence those people, organizations and institutions which affect their own and their children's lives, with the obvious implication that this is certainly not necessarily so.

Gliedman and Roth (1980, p. 227) note that:

> . . . traditional models of disability prevent the professional from establishing cooperative, non-oppressive relationships with the handicapped child and his parents.

Disability is predominantly perceived as abnormal, deviant, as the individual's problem and undistinguishable from him or her as a person (Sutherland, 1981; Shearer, 1981).

People with disabilities are placed in the 'sick' role, suffering from Down's Syndrome for example, and it is assumed they need expert knowledge and skills if they are to improve.

> Even though you say you value me as a person, my experiences tell me that you are unable to distinguish me from my disability . . . Your society operates as if my disability and the problems it presents are the most important and perhaps the only thing worth mentioning about me . . . The question of 'what do I as a person need?' becomes 'How do you deal with me, this problem?' Too often your thinking begins to follow this logic:
>
> This person is disabled.
> His/Her disability is a problem.
> This problem needs to be fixed.
> Special people are needed to fix it.
> (Brost *et al.*, 1984, p. 4).

The same logic underlies the assumption that the presence of a child with a disability creates a 'handicapped' family. Little if any acknowledgment is made of the role of societal responses to disability, to discrimination, deprivation and dehumanization in the creation and maintenance of handicap both for the child and the family. In these circumstances, Gliedman and Roth (1980) are suggesting that conflict is inherent in the relationships between parents, professionals and children. It is embedded in assumptions about disability itself, and relationships are necessarily oppressive. They suggest that parents overseeing and orchestrating the services provided for their children, therefore being able to pick and choose and evaluate professional performance, is a necessary pre-requisite to improving parent–professional relationships.

In defence of the concept of parent–professional partnership, and current practice, as Wolfendale (1986) points out, parents do sit on Portage management committees and school governing bodies, and 'lay citizens' are councillors and sit on education committees and so forth. Furthermore, studies report a great deal of parental satisfaction with all kinds of developments in the practice of 'parents as partners' (Dale, 1986; Cunningham, 1983; Beveridge, 1983; Lloyd, 1986), especially in the arena of pre-school home teaching schemes.

There are also reports of how 'Portage' parents have been able to challenge professionals and bureaucratic systems, and subsequently be fully involved in their child's assessment, statementing and placement (Lloyd, 1986), giving weight to Wolfendale's prediction that 'The influence of parents via and through Portage is potentially immense' (Wolfendale, 1985, p. 53). This suggests that in contrast to the implications of Potts (1983) and Gliedman and Roth (1980) above, parent–professional relationships can be positive in their results and parental involvement can and does lead to empowered parents.

However, these examples may well be the exceptions that prove the rule. A few parents may have begun to move into dimensions of partnership beyond grassroots relationships with individual teachers in the sphere of special education (Jordan, 1987). To claim that the process of parental involvement has empowered them, is on a par with suggesting that parent pressure groups, lobbying for increased provision and improved quality of service, is evidence of partnership at the level of management, policy making, planning and development. A few parents are in such positions because they have demanded them (Jordan, 1987). Arguments such as those of Gliedman and Roth (1980), and Potts (1983), draw attention to underlying assumptions about purpose in 'partnership' and perceptions of disability and therefore to the inherent inequality in parent–professional relationships.

Making Sense of 'Parents as Partners'

Lack of critical analysis of the concept of 'parents as partners' and related practices in special education, may in part be due to the relative newness of the concept. However, it is also a reflection of the lack of critical analysis in special education in general. Others have pointed to the taken-for-granted nature of special education and related this to what Tomlinson (1982) calls the traditional ideology of benevolent humanitarianism — to do good to certain children; to the dominance of a narrow psychological viewpoint and therefore excessive individualization of the 'problem' of disability and handicap; and to the pervasiveness of the medical model of disability as a deficit in the child, requiring remediation (Tomlinson, 1982; Barton and Tomlinson, 1984; Ford *et al.*, 1982; Wood and Shears, 1986). When special education is predominantly understood as a direct response to a perceived need, extensions within special education (such as parental involvement) and an increased quantity of special educational provision (such as pre-school intervention programmes) are on the whole welcomed as beneficial in a taken-for-granted manner by those involved in the field, and put across as such within the rhetoric of special needs. One of the biggest, if not the biggest, developments in parents and professionals working directly together 'in partnership' is the provision of pre-school home teaching services for children with special educational needs, sometimes called pre-school support programmes. The extension of Portage is the obvious example. Within these, special education has been specifically extended into the previously private world of child care in the home. As Russell (1986) has noted, this has predominantly meant that the mother has got to be the professional's partner, as well as the partner of her husband, and mother of her children.

The rationale for 'parents as partners' in special education is somewhat at a tangent to the rhetoric of equality since it has always been primarily concerned with maximizing the child's potential and compensating for his or her difficulties (Mittler and Mittler, 1983; Wolfendale, 1986). The medical model of disability means that the logical and moral necessity is to enlist the parents' cooperation in the professional's endeavour to enhance the child's development — that is, to provide consistency of approach between home and school, to effect more of the child's life, more of the time. For example, in 1978, at the height of calls for the development of parental involvement in special education, particularly the education of children with severe learning difficulties, Mittler (1978, p. 248) remarked that:

> No matter how successfully a child is taught in school the effort is largely wasted unless systematic steps are taken to help the child use and apply his learning in his own home and in all other real life settings in which he moves. The collaboration of parents is indispensable for this purpose.

By the early 1980s Mittler and Mittler were drawing a distinction between parental involvement and collaboration, and partnership along the lines of Pugh's (1987) model.
They added:

> A commitment to partnership rests on the assumption that children
> will develop and learn better if parents and professionals are
> working together on the basis of equality than if either is working
> in isolation (Mittler and Mittler, 1983, p. 10).

It is clear that the basic underlying premise remained unaltered from the
professionals' point of view, the justification for partnership lying with the
child's learning difficulties. It is interesting to note that in 1978 Mittler
backed his argument with a quotation from a parent who said 'we want to
be worked with, not compensated for' (Mittler, 1978, p. 249). How far such
a comment has been seriously taken on board is a question for debate.

The provision of pre-school home teaching services is similarly if not
more entrenched in the same rationale. More so, in that it is very obviously
interventionist in approach and preventive in ethos, one of the underlying
assumptions being that 'early intervention' prevents or lessens the need for
special education at some point in the future. The government's linking of
provision of Portage services to the Education Support Grant for Local
Education Authorities has reinforced this rationale and emphasized pre-
school intervention as a legitimate extension of special education.

The concept of 'parents as consumers', and therefore ideas concerning
their rights to information, records and files, involvement and participation
in decision making, are secondary to the recognized need of the professionals for parent collaboration and thus the interventionist and preventa-
tive purpose.

Cunningham (1983), for example, in his description of the Hester
Adrian Research Centre infant programme claims that in the consumer
model, which the programme has adopted:

> . . . we do not try to change the consumer (the parent) into a pro-
> fessional teacher; we do not attempt to transplant professional skills
> into the home so that professional therapies *per se* are maintained
> and extended via the parent,

since,

> To do this is to risk rejection of the intervention. Instead we offer
> parents what *we feel is the necessary information* for them to live with
> and help their infant with Down's Syndrome (Cunningham, 1983,
> p. 96, my emphasis).

The basic conception of partnership within special education has been
therefore, from the professional's point of view, not one of sharing in any
real sense other than extending the professional's sphere of influence,
helping parents to be better parents for the sake of the child. It is further-
ance of the professional's *raison d'être*. Where parents are involved in deci-

sion making this is predominantly concerning their own child rather than development of or control of services in a more general sense. In any case, part of the rhetoric of 'parents as partners' is for parents to be better informed so they make the appropriate decisions regarding provision for their child, and have a 'better grasp' of his or her special educational needs. Indeed as Wolfendale (1986, p. 12) has noted:

> we (professionals) may be put into the position of appearing to be moral arbiters precisely *because* the relationship between professional and parent-as-client was never perceived to be one in which complimentary expertise was shared.

The purpose of pre-school intervention is not generally questioned by professionals. The value of the extension of special education into the home is taken as virtually self-evident. Parents are frequently so grateful for someone visiting at home rather than having yet another appointment to attend, that they may actively encourage this taken-for-grantedness. Similarly, the concept of special educational needs being employed in relation to preschool children has received little critical analysis, and the purpose and roles of parent and teacher in home-based pre-school intervention projects have hardly been critically examined.

Those research studies which have been completed (for example, the evaluation of the Wessex Portage scheme), are based within the confines of the traditional ideology of special education. Their focus is predominantly the effectiveness of intervention in terms of outcomes for the child, that is, improved performance. Although there is a growing acknowledgement that pre-school support for children with special educational needs, and their families, should encompass more than helping parents sustain their role as the child's primary educator, (Cameron and Poidevin, 1985; Cameron, 1985) in for example, the development of listening and counselling skills on the part of the home teacher and the provision of a range of services from which parents may choose, there is as yet no alternative ideology and set of guiding principles in which these developments can be constructively grounded.

Partnership: Deskilling and Disabling?

The 'new philosophy of parentology' is a phrase coined by Dessent (1985, in Russell, 1986), who asked if parentology is the latest 'bandwaggon' in special education, with pre-school intervention particularly in mind. Pugh (1987, p. 94) reported from her study of parents' needs in the pre-school years that:

parents tended to feel confused and lacking in confidence in the face of professional expertise . . . made to feel that there must be a 'right way' to bring children up if only they could decide which expert to believe . . . They also think they should not try what they intuitively feel is right unless an 'expert' has advised it.

This new philosophy of parentology might well be labelled, in contrast, as deskilling. The growth in the recognition of the importance of home life and pre-school years for the developing child and young adult appears to have brought with it a corresponding growth in the professionals needed to service this area. The home has not been a traditional site of intervention for educationalists, yet the social pathology model of special educational needs offers the professionals the legitimate authority to implement pre-school home-based intervention, and the ideology of benevolent humanitarianism reinforces the intervention as a helpful extension of special education, professionals helping parents in partnership. Cunningham (1983, p. 97) notes:

Human experts and rabbits have much in common. Firstly, they multiply at a prolific rate. Secondly, they are both highly susceptible to infection, rabbits catch myxomatosis and experts catch expertosis. The symptoms are common to both: the head swells and the patient goes blind.

Illich (1977) and McKnight (1977) talked of the 'disabling professions' and drew attention to what they saw as the tendency of professionals (especially the 'caring' professions) to produce inertia and inability to act for themselves in their clients — in Cunningham's terms, to subject clients, in this case, parents, to doses of 'expertosis'. The significance of behaviourist teaching technology, dominant in pre-school intervention programmes and in the education of children with severe learning difficulties in particular, with its pseudo-scientific approach, and its emphasis on individualizing the problem, should not be underestimated here. Furthermore, Pugh (1987) has noted, making parents feel responsible for their children's successes, as in the Portage teaching model, also means making them feel responsible for failures. Parents may see the child's performance as a measure of their own success. Such a model also makes it easy for professional's to blame 'uncooperative', 'unmotivated' parents rather than examining their own methods and approaches.

McKnight (1977, p. 30) sees disabling effects as intrinsic to modern professional services, because of the basic assumption that 'you are the problem' and 'I, the professionalized servicer, am the answer'.

Individualizing need removes people and 'their' difficulties from a social context and out of the political arena. Furthermore, clients are increasingly understood as 'a set of manageable parts' each of which requires its own service mechanic. The multi-disciplinary team can come more than close to such a description: '... the compartmentalization of the person removes even the potential for human action' (McKnight, 1977, p. 29).

Drawing attention to concepts such as deskilling and the disabling professions could be interpreted as advancing some sort of conspiracy theory, with professionals deliberately deskilling parents in order to increase their own spheres of influence and safeguard their job security. Rather, I aim to draw attention to disabling effects as unintended consequences, which are nevertheless significant in attempting to understand the issues involved in 'parents as partners', the divide between rhetoric and practice, and professional intentions and parents' experiences.

That parents have commented so positively about pre-school home teaching services (Buckley, 1985; Dale, 1986), seeing the home teacher as a 'partner' and the process of working together as one of gradual empowerment (Lloyd, 1986; Philps and Jones, 1985), may have more to do with the personal qualities of people who take on the role of home teacher or Portage worker, and the immediacy of the situations they find themselves in with parents, than it has to do with the implementation of underlying principles and philosophies. Professionals, for example, may have no real option apart from walking out of the home, to sitting and listening to parents and taking on board their concerns. It may be that, despite the possibly disabling effects of the service system in general, the regular and sensitive home teacher, as a *visitor* in the home, is in a position to develop a relationship with a parent that, at least on the surface, has a close resemblance to the concept of partnership. My point is not that this is an illusion, but that it is partial, and may well occur despite the system the professional is grounded in and the structure she is offering to bring to the parent – child relationship, rather than because of it. If partnership develops by default in this way it leaves little scope for recognizing the important factors affecting such a relationship and how it develops.

Furthermore, to refer glibly to Portage and other popular types of parental involvement in the education of children with severe learning difficulties as 'partnership' because of the existence of these types of relationships between individual professionals and parents may be naive and short-sighted. As already indicated, such a 'partnership' occurs only at one level, in one dimension, and may well decapacitate people through creating dependent relations and reinforcing recognition of the role of the expert at other levels.

A further, related, 'unintended consequence' is that by viewing Portage and similar pre-school home teaching services, as a model of parent–professional partnership to be replicated, the focus is drawn to the provision of a standardized service and away from provision of a range of services from which people can choose, and therefore have some more direct control over as a consumer:

> . . . we (professionals) recognize some increasingly familiar cue and are likely to produce an increasingly familiar recipe for action (Cunningham, 1983, p. 97).

Redressing the Balance

There is a vast asymmetry in need between parents and professionals which relates further to asymmetry in power. 'The parent needs the professional far more than the professional needs any one parent' (Gliedman and Roth, 1980, p. 232). Services for children with special needs are still few, and parents seek out professionals rather than vice versa. The lack of choice for parents in itself puts professionals in very powerful positions, as well as reinforcing the notion of professional expertise.

Furthermore, as many parents are quick to describe when given the opportunity, and indicated by one parent's comments quoted earlier, they frequently get treated as if they are the ones who are sick, alongside their son or daughter. The fact that the child does not have a structured position as part of the partnership between parents and professionals but is rather on the receiving end of it, reinforces the role of the parent as the professional's enforcer and therefore client themselves. This is in itself disarming, disabling, and inhibiting, and leads parents to put up with services of which they may be privately heavily critical.

Seldom do professionals recognize that their expectation that parents *should* cooperate with them is a value judgement, based on taken-for-granted assumptions about what it means to be a 'good' parent. Rather, as the rationale for partnership in special education shows, professionals see parental cooperation as a means of enhancing their effectiveness and minimizing the child's learning difficulties. The expectation of parental involvement and partnership is viewed as stemming from professionals' own knowledge and expertise. It is something to be instigated by them on behalf of the child.

As Tomlinson (1982) has pointed out, special education is coercive in nature, and legally enforceable once a statement of special educational needs has been made. Despite the rhetoric of 'parents as partners', the 1981 Education Act has set up lengthy and complex bureaucratic procedures for assessment and statementing which may have reinforced this coerciveness. Certainly the Act has added to the mystification of the procedures of special education and the aura of professional expertise.

Deskilling and asymmetry of need and power are products of traditional models of disability which remain predominant, taken for granted in everyday life, and existing in an unquestioned form in dominant modes of professional practice with children with special educational needs. Some attempt to recognize the shortfalls of the pathological concept of disability in providing services to children with special needs and their families has been made by Bronfenbrenner in his advocacy of an ecological model:

> . . . approaches that are family-centred rather than child-centred, that cut across contexts rather than being confined to single settings, that have continuity over time and that utilise as the primary agents of socialisation the child's parents, other family members, adults, and other children from the neighbourhood in which he lives, school personnel, and other persons who are part of the child's enduring environment (Bronfenbrenner, 1976, in Hellier, 1986, p. 155).

However, in the context of the special education system, this takes little account of the consequences of special education — categorization, segregation, discrimination, the embarkation upon a 'special career' as a second-class citizen. As Tomlinson (1982) has pointed out, the rhetoric of special educational needs draws attention to how to meet 'recognized' needs and away from questioning why it is necessary for so many children to be categorized out of ordinary education in the first place, and thus the covert purposes and political nature of special education. It is therefore insufficient to call for a family-centred rather than child-centred approach as an antidote to the present shortfalls and the dangers of unintended consequences in the concept of parent–professional partnership in special education.

Parent–professional partnership is something of a myth in its present terms even though individual relationships may be satisfying and empowering to both parties. If teachers want to consider partnership with parents in more depth they will have to be prepared to make themselves more aware of what special education is actually offering and why, of the processes they are involved in, whether intentionally or unintentionally, and the consequences for themselves, children and parents. They will have to be prepared to alter structures to make room for parental choice, control and evaluation. They will have to be able to work within more open situations which involve sharing with and supporting other professionals, as well as parents. They will have to be prepared to critically examine their own practice themselves, and accept such from parents. They will have to be more open about what they are doing and why, to question their own motives, stances and the principles as well as the rhetoric upon which special educational provision is based.

In the context of pre-school support services teachers will have to recognize the conflict embedded in the home-based intervention model of parent professional partnership. In Portage the premise is specifically to teach parents to teach their children in a precise manner, directly extending the ideology of special children, special teaching, where the professionals control the techniques which parents 'need', thereby also furthering the model of defective parents. Yet the rhetoric is of an equal partnership, respect for complimentary skills, and 'parents as experts'. Teachers will have to recognize the conflict involved in their own positions, as employees of an education authority with set tasks, purposes and procedures, yet working with parents in their own homes, on their territory. Pugh (1987, p. 102) draws attention to the conflict the home teacher may experience:

> . . . between the need to give guidance and enforce a structure, and the wish to respond to the parents' needs . . . if the parent is to have true power, she must have more than the right to admiringly agree to the tutor's suggestions. But can the professional take a back seat if the selection of objectives seems inappropriate or even perverse?

If partnership is to become a viable and enabling process it needs to be set firmly within the debate concerning the politics of special education, with consideration given to questions of its purpose, control and consequences, as well as strategies for implementation. Whose responsibility is partnership? What are the boundaries being adopted for professional, parent and child roles? What creates these boundaries and inhibits sharing in other spheres at other levels? Whose partners are parents? Whose partners are professionals? Whose partners are children? These are some of the questions we need to urgently and seriously consider today.

Notes

1 At the outset I would like to acknowledge that developments in special education are connected to wider movements and more general issues currently popular within society, and do not occur in isolation. In this respect, the interest in and development of 'parents as partners' in the educational enterprise can be seen as occurring within the context of a more general move towards, and expansion of, community-based services and an emphasis on consumer rights. Due to the constraints of space and time, reference is not made to these wider movements in this chapter. For the same reasons the issues of race and class as factors impinging on parent–professional relations are not discussed. This note

does not excuse the omission of these wider issues but hopefully will alert the reader to the necessity to bear them in mind during the course of the chapter.

References

AKERLEY, M. (1979) 'False Gods and Angry Prophets', in *Parents Speak Out*, TURNBULL, A. and H. (Eds), Ohio, Bell and Howell.

BARTON, L. and TOMLINSON, S. (Eds) (1984) *Special Education and Social Interests*, Beckenham, Croom Helm.

BEVERIDGE, S. (1983) 'Developing Partnership: The Anson House Pre-School Project, in *Parents, Professionals and Mentally Handicapped People Approaches to Partnership*, MITTLER, P. and McCONACHIE, (Eds), Croom Helm, London.

BROST, M., JOHNSON, T., WAGNER, L. and DEPREY, R. (1984) *Getting to Know You: One approach to service assessment and planning for individuals with disabilities*. Wisconsin Council on Development Disabilities.

BUCKLEY, S. (1985) 'The Effect of Portage on the Development of Down's Syndrome Children and their Families — an Interim Report', in *Portage: The Importance of Parents*, DALY, B., ADDINGTON, J., KERFOOT, S. and SIGSTON, A. (Eds), Windsor, NFER-Nelson.

CAMERON, R.J. (1985) 'A problem-centred approach to family problems', in DALEY, B., ADDINGTON, J., KERFOOT, S. and SIGSTON, C. (Eds) *Portage: The Importance of Parents*, Windsor, NFER.

CAMERON, R.J. and LE POIDEVIN, S. (1985) 'Is there more to Portage than Education?', in *Portage: The Importance of Parents*, DALY, B. *et al.*, Windsor, NFER-Nelson.

CUNNINGHAM, C.C. (1983) 'Early Support and Intervention: The HARC Infant Project', in *Parents, Professionals and Mentally Handicapped People, Approaches to Partnership*, MITTLER, P. and McCONACHIE, H., London, Croom Helm.

DALE, N. (1986) 'Parents as Partners: What does this mean to parents of children with special needs?, in *Education and Child Psychology*, Vol. 3 No. 3, pp. 191–199.

DES (1978) *Special Educational Needs*, (Warnock Repsort), Cmnd 7212, London, HMSO.

FAMILY FOCUS (1983) 'Parents: Underrated but Undeterred?' in *Special Education, Forward Trends, Vol. 10 No. 4*, pp. 27–28.

FORD, J., MONGON, D. and WHELAN, M. (1982) *Special Education and Social Control: Invisible Disasters*, London, Routledge and Kegan Paul.

FOX, M. (1975) *They Get This Training, But They Don't Really Know How You Feel*, Horsham, National Fund for Research into Crippling Diseases.

GLIEDMAN, J. and ROTH, W. (1980) 'Parents and Professionals', in *The Practice of Special Education*, (Ed.) SWANN, W., Milton Keynes, Open University Press.

HANNAM, C. (1975) *Parents and Mentally Handicapped Children*, Harmonsworth, Penguin.

HELLIER, C. (1986) 'Meeting Parents Needs: How can Special Educators Help?', in *Education and Child Psychology*, Vol. 3 No. 3, pp. 155–162.

ILLICH, I. (1977) *Disabling Professions*, London, Marion Boyers.

JORDAN, L. (1987) 'Parents, Power and the Politics of Special Education in a

London Borough', in *Including Pupils with Disabilities*, BOOTH, T. and SWANN, W.P. (Eds), Milton Keynes, Open University Press.

LLOYD, J.M. (1986) *Jacob's Ladder*, Tunbridge Wells, Costello.

LUNT, I. and SHEPPARD, I. (Eds) (1986) 'Participating Parents: Promise and Practice', in *Educational and Child Psychology*, Vol. 3, No. 13 (Special Issue).

McCORMACK, M. (1978) *A Mentally Handicapped Child in the Family*, London, Constable.

McCONKEY, R. (1985) *Working with Parents: A Practical Guide for Teachers and Therapists*, Beckenham, Croom Helm.

McKNIGHT, J. (1977) 'Professional Service and Disabling Help', in *Handicap in a Social World*, BRECHIN, A., LIDDIARD, P. and SWAIN, J. (Eds), Milton Keynes, Open University Press.

MITTLER, P. (1978) *Choices in Partnership*, Congress Proceedings of the International League of Societies for Mental Handicap, ILSMH, pp. 243–251.

MITTLER, P. and MITTLER, H. (1983) 'Partnership with Parents: An Overview', in *Parents Professionals and Mentally Handicapped People*, MITTLER, P. and McCONACHIE, H. (Eds), Beckenham, Croom Helm.

MOSES, D. and CROLL, P. (1987) 'Parents and Partners or Problems?', in *Disability Handicap and Society*, Vol. 2 No. 1, pp. 75–84.

PHILPS, C. and JONES, C. (1985) 'Parent Role in Portage: a consumer view', in *Portage: The Importance of Parents*, DALY, B. *et al.* (Ed.), Windsor, NFER-Nelson.

POTTS, P. (1983) 'What Difference Would Integration Make to the Professionals?' in *Integrating Special Education*, BOOTH, T. and POTTS, P. (Eds), Oxford, Blackwell.

PUGH, G. (1987) 'Portage in Perspective: Parental Involvement in Pre-School Programmes', in *Extending and Developing Portage*, HEDDERLY, R. and JENNINGS, K., Windsor, NFER–Nelson.

RUSSELL, P. (1986) 'Working with Parents: A Framework for Collaboration and Partnership', in *Education and Child Psychology* Vol. 3 No. 3, pp. 29–41.

SCHULZ, J. (1979) 'The Parent Professional Conflict', in *Parents Speak Out*, TURNBULL, A. and H. (Eds), Bell and Howell pp. 29–36.

SHEARER, A. (1981) *Disability: Whose Handicap?*, Blackwell, Oxford.

SUTHERLAND, A. (1981) *Disabled We Stand*, London, Souvenir Press.

THOMAS, N. (1986) 'Children, Parents and Teachers', in HEASLIP, P. (Ed.), *The Challenge of the Future*, Bristol Polytechnic.

TOMLINSON, S. (1982) *A Sociology of Special Education*, RKP, London.

TURNBULL, A.P. and TURNBULL, H.R. (1979) *Parents Speak Out*, Ohio, Bell and Howell.

WOLFENDALE, S. (1985) 'A Review of Parental Involvement and the Place of Portage', in *Portage: The Importance of Parents*, DALY, B. *et al.* (Ed.), Windsor, NFER-Nelson.

WOLFENDALE, S. (1986) 'Routes to Partnership with Parents: Rhetoric or Reality?', in *Educational and Child Psychology* Vol. 3 No. 3, pp. 9–18.

WOOD, S. and SHEARS, B. (1986) *Teaching Children with Severe Learning Difficulties: A Radical Reappraisal*, Beckenham, Croom Helm.

WYLIE, P. (1986) 'Finding Out: A Groupwork Perspective', in *Portage: More than a Teaching Programme?*, BISHOP, M., COPLEY, M. and PORTER, J., Windsor, NFER-Nelson.

Notes on Contributors

Len Barton is a Principal Lecturer in Education at Bristol Polytechnic. He is chairperson of the *British Journal of Sociology of Education* and Editor of the International Journal, *Disability, Handicap and Society*. He is particularly interested in the politics and social aspects of disability.

Hazel Bines has taught in primary, secondary and special schools. She recently completed her doctoral research on new approaches to remedial education in secondary schools and is now a Senior Lecturer in Special Educational Needs at Oxford Polytechnic.

Marion Blythman was head of the Department of Special Educational Needs at Moray House College of Education in Edinburgh, but now is head of a larger department mainly concerned with Post Qualifying Studies in Education. Over the last three years she has also worked as an educational consultant with the City University of New York project, concerned with infants and pre-schoolers defined at risk. Her main preoccupation is with shaping-up mainstream education so that the system can deal with all our children.

Tony Booth is a lecturer in education at the Open University. He was a secondary teacher and an educational psychologist. He has written on the theory and practice of integration and is currently working on a project on power and authority relationships in education.

Bunty Davidson, is a former teacher in primary schools and head of department in a special school for severe learning difficulties, and Senior Lecturer in Education and co-ordinator of Postgraduate Certificate in Education courses at Bristol Polytechnic.

Andrea Freeman works at Edge Hill College of Higher Education after working in local authorities and Lancaster University. She is very interested in stress and coping, particularly within the education setting.

Alvin Jeffs is at present Senior Lecturer in Education at the Department of Education, Bristol Polytechnic, specializing in aspects of special educational needs. This follows 16 years teaching, during which he worked in secondary modern, comprehensive, support team and adult literacy settings. His particular areas of interest include effecting change within schools, structuring staff development and supporting parents. He is the author of a number of articles and booklets on these topics.

John Lee is a Senior Lecturer in Multi-ethnic Education at Bristol Polytechnic. He has a long-standing commitment to creating progressive primary practice within the context of the debate on equality and justice in education.

Mike Oliver is a Principal Lecturer in Special Needs at Thames Polytechnic, having previously worked as a Lecturer at the University of Kent as a Development Officer for Kent Social Services. He is the author of numerous articles on disability and the book *Social Work with Disabled People* (MacMillan, 1983), and is actively involved in the disability movement, currently serving on the Executive and Management Committee of the Spinal Injuries Association.

Rob Withers is a Director of Studies at Bishop Grosteste College, Lincoln. An experienced primary school teacher, he has a long-standing commitment to progressive practice and equality of educational opportunity. He is interested in the philosophical aspects of special education.

Sue Wood works in a pre-school support service for children with special educational needs in Essex. She has worked as a teacher in special education for seven years mainly with children with severe learning difficulties and autism. She is co-author of *Teaching Children with Severe Learning Difficulties: A Radical Re-appraisal* (Croom Helm, 1986).

Index

Abbott, R.   73
Akerley, M.   195
Alexander, R.   84, 154
Althusser, Lousd   19
American sign language   110
Anderson, R.D.   41
Argyll Commission   38
assertiveness   125, 139
assessment   44, 175–89
  Burt and Schonell tests   179
  case studies   184–8
  criteria
    and comprehension   180–2
    and learning   182–3
  ideology of   176–84
  IQ tests   177
  norm-referenced tests   181
  of social competence   125–6
  of teachers   188–9
  profiling   183–4
  progress records   178
  testing   3, 80
Assessment in Schools (Satterly)   179
Association for Spina Bifida and
  Hydrocephalus   22
Association of Blind and Partially Sighted
  Teachers and Students   26
Association of County Councils   60
Association of Disabled Professionals   25
Atkinson, P.   84, 87, 88
Attendance Allowance   22
Attfield, R.   128
Attkisson, C.   137, 141
autism   135

Badley, G.   65–6
Ball, S.J.   155
Bank-Mikkelson, N.E.   106
Barthes, R.   180
Barton, L.   1, 1–9, 4, 5, 79–95, 100, 101,
  148, 165, 198
Becher, T.   66
Beckett, M.   23
behavioural problems   19, 135
behaviourism   83, 171, 201
Bennett, A.   24
Bennett, N. *et al.*   154
Bernstein, B.   80
Berry, P.   169
Better Schools (DES)   60, 61
Beveridge Report   14
Beveridge, M.   165
Beveridge, S.   197
Bines, Hazel   145–60
Binet, A.   102, 115
black people, *see* ethnic minorities
Blaxter, M.   132
Blytham, Marion   32–57
Bogdan, R.   33, 80, 89, 90
Bolam, R.   73
Booth, Tony   4, 5, 71, 90, 99–122, 165
borough schools   34, 38
BOSS   129–31
boundary management   74
Boyd-Orr, Lord John   37
Braginsky, B.   125
Braginsky, D.   125
Brennan, M.   108
Brennan, W.K.   161, 164, 165

Brisenden, S. 6, 181
British Council of Organizations of
    Disabled People (BCODP) 25, 26
British sign language 110
Brockington, D. 164, 169
Brofenbrenner 204
Broskovsky, A. 137, 141
Brost, M. *et al.* 196
Buckley, S. 202
buildings, inaccessability 17
Bull, S. 165
Bullock Report 61
Burden, R. 99
Burgess, R. 81, 87, 88
Burt and Schonell tests 179
Burt, Cyril 80
Butt, N. 150–1, 154

Cameron, R.J. 195
Campaign for Mental Handicap 103
Campbell, R.J. 63–4
CARE 84
Care Attendant Agency 26
Carr, W. 52, 92
Cave, C. 83, 85, 146
Centre for Studies on Integration in
    Education 26
Centres for Integrated Living
    (CILS) 26–7
change 58–78
  agents *see* change agents
  designated teacher and 61–5, 75
  disturbance of status quo 69
  LEAs and 72
  national dimensions 71
  realities within schools 68–70
  research to encourage 79
  school based 70
  school dimension 72–5
  social interaction 69
change agents 65–7
  external 69–70
  institutions as 67–8
  internal 66
  outside 67–8
Chart of Initiative and
    Independence 125–6
child deficit model 48, 53

child guidance clinics 20
Children and Their Primary Schools see
    Plowden Report
Chin, R. 68
Clark, Margaret 46–7
Clark, M.M. 146
cluster concept 74
Cockburn, C. 2
Cockcroft Report 61
Cohen, A. 44
Cohen, L. 44
Cohen, S. 19
Cole, T. 120
community-care policies 100, 101
Community Service Volunteers 26
competence, social *see* social competence
competitiveness, increase in 3
comprehensive schools
  conflict of equality and excellence 44–5
  Scotland 53–4
conflict accounts 15
Conlon, J. 66, 74
consensus paradigm 14–15
Conti-Ramsden, G. 165
Cooper, B. 171
coordinators, *see* designated teachers
coping 126, 129–33
  BOSS and EMPLOYEE 129–31
  definitions of 129
  failure by teachers and parents 137
  gender differences 126
  social class and 126
  social competence 131–2
Corrie, M. *et al.* 89
Couchman, T. 125, 128
Coulby, D. 119
Craft, M. 33, 39, 42
Crewe, N. 26
Croll, P. 127, 177, 179, 181, 187, 193, 194
Crossroads Care Attendants Scheme 26
Crouch, C. 68
Cunningham, C.C. 197, 199, 201, 203
Cunningham, J. 163, 170
curriculum 161–74
  cause of learning difficulties 44, 48–9
  context 163, 165–8
  cross-curricular approach *see* whole
    school approach
  hidden 139–40

industry and   164
methods   170–2
national   3, 70, 162
no funding for changes   163
politics and   163–4
Scottish   43–4
social competence and   139–42
teacher–pupil interactions   163, 168–70

Dale, J.   15
Dale, N.   197, 202
Daniels, E.   147
Darby, A.   2
Davidson, Bunty   161–74
Davidson, R.E.   169
Davis, George   36
Davis, K.   27
day centres   15
De Sousa, E.   2
deaf people
    bilingual approach   108
    incompetence expected of   135, 137
    limited educational sights   111–12
    normalization of   105–14
        prejudice against sign
            language   107–11
        pressure to conform to majority   108,
        112–13
decarceration   100, 101
Dee,   1, 88
deferring   125
Delamont, S.   169
Denmark   167–8
Denscombe, M.   83
Denzin, N.   79
dependent status   6
Derbyshire Coalition of Disabled
    People   27
DES   59, 146
    Better Schools   60, 61
    Education 5–9   61
    national curriculum consultative
        document   3–4
Design for living programmes   44
designated teachers   58, 59
    change and   75
    developing concept of   61–2
    failure of training   70

problems and constraints   63–4
range of duties   64–5
deskilling of parents   200–3
Desloges, Pierre   110–11
Dessent, T.   4, 5, 146, 200
devaluation *see* equality of value
differential responsibilities   73–4
disability
    care further disables   23
    conflict accounts   15
    created by society   17, 21
    critique of existing services   22–3
    defined by disabled themselves   26
    financial cutbacks   22
    humanitarian approach   14, 21–2
    institutionalized disablism   20–1
    lack of independence   135
    organizations of and for disabled   25
    personal tragedy theory   16
    politics of   21–8
    professionalization of provision   23
    redefinition   24–5
    restructuring of services   26
    rigid categories of   146
    social constructist approach   16
    social control approach   14, 15–16
    social investment approach   14–15
    socially constructed   16–17
Disability Alliance   14
Disabled Peoples' International   17, 25
Disablement Income Group   14
disabling of parents   200–3
District Handicap Teams   192
Doris   47
Dudley, J.   89
Dunlop, S.   74
Durward, L.   14
Dyson, S.   181

Eastern Nebraska Community Office of
    Retardation   103
Edgerton, R.   89–90, 125
Education 5–9 (DES)   61
educational context, special education
    in   2–4
educationally sub-normal *see* ESN
Edwards, Viv   33
Elliott, J.   82

Ellis, V. 66
EMPLOYEE 129–31
Employment and Science, Department of
  see DES
equal opportunities 148–52
Equal Opportunities for All see Fish Report
equality of value 116–19
Erting, C. 92
Esland, G.M. 68–9
ESN 20
ethnic minorities 55, 118
  disproportionate ESN numbers 113, 115
  doubly disadvantage 1–2
  institutionalized racism 20–1
  native special schools 27
  pressure to conform to majority 108
ethnographic research 86–9
  within community setting 89–91
evaluation *see* assessment
Evans, J. 148
Evans, M. 161
Evans, P. 179
examination results, publication of 44
existing services
  for disabled, critique of 22–3
  for special education, critique of 23–4

failure 44
  institutionalized 4
  part played by school in creating 47
Family Focus 194
Farrell, P. 99
Ferro, N. 116
Field, Tiffany 170
Filcher, G. 5
financial cutbacks
  disability 22
  special education 23–24
Finkelstein, V. 15–16, 17, 23, 25
Finn, D. 2
Firth, H. 103
Fish, John 28
Fish Report 58, 70, 74, 118, 150
Floden, R. 82
Fontana, D. 171
Ford, J. 4, 5, 19, 198
Fox, M. 194
Franklin, B. 5
Freeman, Andrea 123–44
functionalism 14

gaelic language 42
Gains, C.W. 146
Galletley, I. 146
Galloway, D. 4, 5, 71, 165
Galton, M. *et al.* 154
GCSE examinations 164
gender differences 2, 42, 55, 118
  institutionalized sexism 20–1
Giles, C. 74
Gipps, C. *et al.* 146
Gliedman, J. 196, 197, 203
Goffman, E. 125, 137–8
Goldby, M. 146, 147
Golding, William 140
Goode, D. 92
Goodwin, C. 146, 165
Grampian Regional Council 44
Greenspan, S. 127–9
GRIDS 73
GRIST 60, 62
Gross, N. *et al.* 69
Gulliford, R. 146
Gulliver, J.R. 146, 147

Hackney, A. 169
Hall, P. 15
Hall, Stuart 1–2
Hallmark, N. 146
Hamlyn, D. 180, 182
Hammersley, M. 84, 87, 88
handicaps *see* disabilities
Hanko, G. 75
Hannan, C. 194
Hargreaves, D.H. 86, 87, 147, 151–2, 169
Harris, A. 14, 16
Hart, S. 152, 153
Hattersley, Roy 37, 45, 54–5
Havelock, R.G. 65, 66, 67
Hegarty, S. 74, 79, 120
Hellier, C. 204
Her Majesty's Inspectors of Schools *see*
  HMI
Heshusius, L. 89
Hester Adrian Research Centre 199
Hestor, S.K. 87
hidden curriculum 139–40
Hillier, H. 169
HMI 139, 164, 166
  encouragement of innovation 71
  The Progress report 32, 47–50

Hodgson, A. *et al.* 62
Holly, P. 73
Holmes, T. 132
home helps 22
Hoyle, E. 68, 70, 74
humanitarian approach 14, 18
  disability 21–2
Humes, W.M. 36, 42
Hustler, D. 92
Huxley, T.H. 35

ILEA 21, 157
  see also Fish Report
Illich, I. 201
Independent Living Schemes 26
individualism, cult of 147
INSET
  failure of SEN training 70
  funding 58, 59, 91
  hopes and reality 59–61
  qualification courses 59
  school based 59, 61
  school focussed 60, 67
  training provided by TRIST 66
  see also GRIST provisions
integration 145
  conceptions of 99–122
  countering discrimination 106–7
  creation of abnormality 105–6
  definitions of 101
  equality of value 116–19
  normalization of the deaf 105–14
  Wolfenberger's normalization 101,
    102–7, 117
  see also whole school approach
IQ tests 177

Jackson, B. 74
Jeffs, Alvin 58–78
Jensen, A.R. 177
John, M. 24
Jones, C. 193, 202
Jones, Howell 44
Jordan, L. 197

Kahn, R. 69
Katz, D. 69
Kemmis, S. 92
Kendall, A. 103
Kirk, G. 38

Kirp, D.L. 24, 25, 147, 150
Kogan, M. 72
Kugelmass, J. 33

labelling *see* stigma
Lacey, C. 81, 83
ladder of merit 33, 39, 42, 44
Lampert, M. 83
Land, H. 15
language 169–70
  difficulties in Scotland 39–41, 42
Lanr, Harlan 110, 111
Laskier, M. 147
Lavers, P. *et al.* 147
Lawn, M. 85
Lawton, Denis 84
learning support *see* support services
LEAs *see* Local Education Authorities
Lee, J. 73, 175–89
Leeming, K. *et al.* 161, 169
Leonard, Tom 40–1
Lewis, G. 147
Liberation of People With Disabilities 25
life skill course 126–7
Lin, G. 5
Lindsay, Geoff 184, 185–8
Lint, I. 191
Lloyd, J.M. 197, 202
Local Education Authorities 60
  change and 72
  duty to educate 149–50
  range of duties of designated
    teachers 64–5
Loney, M. 1
Low Attainers Projects 67
Lynas, Wendy 101, 102, 105–14

McConkey, R. 191
McCormack, A. 194
Macdonald, B. 67
McDonald, George 41–2
Macdonald, I. 125, 128
McDonald, Ramsey 41
McEnvoy, M. 163, 170
McGrath, G. 108
MacInnes, D. 1
McIntyre, D. 81
McKnight, J. 132, 201, 201–2
McLean, John 36
Maclure, S. 66

McMahon, A. 73
McNicholas, J.A. 146
McPherson 53
Madison, P. 83, 85, 146
maladjustment *see* behavioural problems
Malthus, T. 37
Manpower Services Commission 2
Marguiles, N. 66
Marland, Michael 43
Marxists 15
Masson, J. 133
mature students 165
Meacher, M. 23
Mellor, F.S. 87
mental retardation, research 80, 89–90
Mercer, J. 137
Merry 119
Miles, S. 2
Mishra, R. 14
Mittler, H. 191, 192, 193, 198–9
Mittler, P. 59, 99, 191, 192, 193, 198–9
mixed ability groups 43, 69, 155
Mongon, D. 19
Morris, A. 23
Morris, P. 129
Moseley, D. 146
Moses, D. 127, 177, 179, 181, 187, 193, 194
Multiple Sclerosis Society 25
Musgrove, F. 81

National Association of Remedial
    Education (NARE) 65, 146
National Curriculum 3, 70, 162
national priority areas 59
National Union of the Deaf 26
needs
    identification of 5
    of disabled and carers 27
    of parents and children 27
    special *see* special educational needs
negotiation 140–1
Nixon, J. 84, 91
Nordqvist, V.M. 163, 170
normalization *see* integration
normative-reeducative approach 68
Nuffield Science 67

occupational therapy 22
Oldroyd, D. 73

Oliver, M. 13–29, 102
Open University 99
    *Advanced Diploma in Special Needs in
        Education* 91
    assessment case studies 184–8
Oracle Project 169

Pack Report 44
parents 74, 115, 142, 190–207
    as consumers 193–4, 199
    asymmetry of need and power 203–5
    critical analysis 197–200
    deskilling and disabling 200–3
    dimensions of involvement 191–2
    failure to cope by 137
    inequality of relationship with
        professionals 197
    negotiation and parenting 140–1
    parental choice 3
    parents view of partnership 194–5
    Portage 193, 194–5, 197, 198, 199–200,
        202, 203, 205
    pre-school teaching at home *see* Portage
    professional view of 195–7
    unsatisfactory relationship with
        professionals 194–5
Parents Campaign for Integrated
    Education 26
parish schools 34, 38
Parker, R. 15
Patterson, H. 36, 42
Pearlin, L. 126, 129
Peddiwell, J. 142
Philps, C. 193, 202
Plowden Report 178
pluralists 15
Pocklington, K. 74
Pocklington, P. 120
Poidevin, S. 195
politics 5–7
    disability and special needs 21–8
Pollard, A. 88, 169
Portage 193, 194–5, 197, 198, 199–200,
    202, 203, 205
Portugal 166–7
Potts, P. 71, 116, 150, 165, 194, 195, 197
poverty 14, 17, 18
power-coercive strategy 68
*Principle of Normalization in Human Services,
    The* (Wolfenberger) 101, 102–7, 117

Producing and Reducing Disaffection   119
professionalization
    disability   23
    special education   24
professionals
    judgment of competence   132–3, 134,
        137
    unconscious ideologies of   103–4
    see also parents: professionalization
profiling   183–4
Pugh, G.   190, 200, 201, 205
pupil teachers   38

Quicke, J.   92

Rabinow, P.   183
racism *see* ethnic minorities
Rahe, R.   132
rational-empirical approach   68
remedial provision   146
    Scotland   45–6
    staff   49, 51
Renfrew Division (Strathclyde)   45
research   79–95
    action   84
    clinical perspective dominance   80
    encouraging change   79
    ethnographic   86–9, 89–91
    initial observations   79–81
    mental retardation   80, 89–90
    policy makers and   79–80
    qualitative   85–8
    social interactions   85, 87–9
    teacher education reform through   81–5
    teacher researchers   84, 85, 91, 168
    within community settings   89
residential homes   15
responsibilities, differential   73–4
restructuring of services
    disabled   26
    special education   27–8
Roaf, C.   150
Rogers, R.   88
Rose, N.   178
Roth, W.   196, 197, 203
Royal National Institute for the Blind   25
Russell, P.   195, 198, 200

Sarah, E.   169
Sarason   47

Satterly, D.   179
school leavers
    delinquent   139
    unfit to work   138
school leaving age   42, 43, 44
Schooler, C.   126, 129
schools
    borough   34, 38
    comprehensive, in Scotland   42–3
    parish   34, 38
    sink   4
    size and designated teacher role   63
Schools Council   63, 161
    Humanities Project   67
Schultz, J.   194
Scotland   32–57
    1975 to 1980   45–7
    academic curriculum in   43–4
    comprehensive schooling   42–3
    historical background
        post-1872   37–8
        pre-1872   34–7
    literacy prized   37
    pupil teachers   38
    selection and segregation   38–42
    use of English   34, 39–40
Scull, Andrew   100, 101
Sedgewick, Peter   100, 101
segregation
    establishments   19
    remedial education   46
    Scotland   38–42
    self-perpetuating ghettos   46–7
    social practices   15
selection
    academic from non-academic   41
    by ability   149
    Scotland   38–42
SEN coordinators *see* designated teachers
Sewell, G.   146, 147
Sexism *see* gender differences
sexual abuse   133
Shear, B.   198
Shearer, A.   16, 22, 194, 196
sheltered workshops   15
Sheppard, I.   191
Shotter, J.   87
Sigmon, S.   5
sign language   107–11
significant living without work   18

Simon, Brian   79–80
Simon, T.   102, 115
sink schools   4
Slaughter, R.   143
Smith, Adam   35, 36
Smith, K.   73
Smith, M.   66
Smout, T.C.   34, 35, 37–8, 42
social competence   123–44
   assertiveness   125, 139
   assessment measuring   125–6
   character changing attempts   128
   children not considered competent   133
   coping   126, 129–33, 131–2
   curriculum and   139–42
   disability and lack of independence   135
   incompetence expected of hearing
      impaired   135, 137
   necessary conditions   124–5
   passive role of deferring   125
   possible futures for   141–2
   professional judgments of   132–3, 134,
      137
   social awareness   127
   special needs and   133–9
   success measures   124
social context   13–29
   competing conflict account   15, 18
   humanitarian approach   14, 18
   social constructist approach   16
   social control   14, 15–16, 18–19
   social investment approach   14–15, 18
social control   14, 15–16, 18–19, 32–3, 36,
   123, 139, 141
social interactions in research   85, 87–9
social investment approach   14–15, 18
Soder, Martin   100, 101
Solity, J.   165
Solomon, J.   2
Spastics Society   25, 26
special education
   conflict approach   15, 18
   critique of existing services   23–24
   financial cutbacks   23–24
   humanitarian account   18
   individual problem   20
needs
   definitions   4–5, 19–21
   politics of   5–7
   status of teachers   84

professionalization of provision   24
redefinition   25–6
restructuring of services   27–8
schools   15
social control   18–19
social investment   18
vested interest approach   15, 18
Spender, G.   169
Spinal Injuries Association   25, 26
staff development policy   73
Standard English   38–41, 42
Stenhouse, L.   84, 171
stigma   89, 115, 137–8, 147, 166, 167
Stockport LEA   63
Stone, D.   5, 16
Strathclyde Report   46
streaming   4, 43
stress
   coping and   131–2
   individual differences and   132
Stubbs, M.   169
Sugden, M.   99
support services   146, 152–3
   collaboration with mainstream teachers
      153–7
   external   69–70
   staff   48, 50–2, 169, 170
Sutherland   196
Sutherland, A.   6, 16, 24
Swann, W.   116, 117, 165, 171, 184–5
Swedish sign language   110

Tawney, R.H.   117
Taylor, P.   81
Taylor, S.   80, 89, 90
Taylor-Gooby, P.   15
teacher education
   reform through research   81–5
   student utilitarian concerns   82, 83
teacher-pupil interactions   163, 168–70
teachers
   as researcher   84, 85, 91, 168
   assessment of   188–9
   designated *see* designated teacher
   differential responsibilities   73–4
   failure to cope by   137
   low level work, or child minding   84
   mainstream and support services   153–7
   pupil teachers   38

remedial   46
   in Scotland   49, 51
   support teachers   48, 50–2, 153–7, 169,
      170
   teamwork skills   73
teachers staff development policy   73
Teitelbaum, K.   82
temporary emotional upsets   51
testing *see* assessment
Thomas, D.   103
Thomas, G.   74, 154
Thomas, N.   191
Times Educational Supplement   3, 60, 84
Tom, A.   81, 83
Tomlinson, S.   4, 5, 29, 44, 48, 80, 100,
      101, 123, 148, 149, 150, 165, 197, 198,
      203, 204
Topliss, E.   14–15
Tough, J.   169
Townsend, P.   14
Townsend, R.   14
TRIST   66
Turnbull, A.P.   194
Turnbull, H.R.   194

Union of the Physically Impaired Against
      Segregation   15–16, 25
Ursin, H. *et al.*   129

Verma, G.   2
vested interest approach   15, 18
Vislie, L.   116
Visser, J.   153
vocational training   141
Vonnegut, Kurt   118

Walker, R.   67
Walker, S.   1
Wallace, J.   66
Waller, W.   81
Warnock, Mary   118
Warnock Report   4, 19–21, 28, 32, 58, 60,
      70, 74, 85, 145, 191

Weatherley, R.   116
Webb, A.   15
Webster, H.   138
Wedell, Klaus   85
Wells, G.   169
Wessex Portage scheme   200
wheelchairs   22
Whelan, M.   19
When the Mind Hears (Lane)   110
White, R.   124–5, 128, 164, 169
Whitty, G.   86
WHO   16, 17
whole school approach   48–50, 51, 72, 74,
      145–60
   boundary management   74
   collaborative relationship   153
   consultation on change   70
   educational rights   148–52
   implementation   152–7
   individual need   147
   social gains   151–2
   special schools and   156–7
Whyld, J.   169
Williams   53
Williams, V. *et al.*   169
Willis, P.   2
Wilson, M.   161, 165
Winterton, J.   101
Withers, Rob   175–89
Wolfenberger, Wolf   101, 102–7, 117
Wolfendale, S.   191, 193, 195, 197,
      198–9, 200
Wood, S.   190–207
Woods, P.   82, 87, 89
working-class education   33
Wragg, E.   80–1, 84
Wylie, P.   194, 195

Young, Michael   86
Youth Training Scheme   2, 139, 164

Zeichner, K.   82
Zola, I.   26